FIRST WORLD
NATIONALISMS

FIRST WORLD NATIONALISMS

Class and Ethnic Politics in Northern Ireland and Quebec

Katherine O'Sullivan See

The University of Chicago Press
Chicago and London

Katherine O'Sullivan See is associate professor, James Madison College, Michigan State University

The University of Chicago Press, Chicago 60637
The University of Chicago Press, Ltd., London
© 1986 by The University of Chicago
All rights reserved. Published 1986
Printed in the United States of America

95 94 93 92 91 90 89 88 87 86 5 4 3 2 1

Library of Congress Cataloging-in-Publication Data

See, Katherine O'Sullivan.
  First world nationalisms.

  Bibliography: p.
  Includes index.
  1. Northern Ireland—Ethnic relations. 2. Nationalism
—Northern Ireland. 3. Northern Ireland—History—
Autonomy and independence movements. 4. Québec
(Province)—Ethnic relations. 5. Nationalism—Québec
(Province) 6. Québec (Province)—History—Autonomy and
independence movements. I. Title.
DA990.U46S44 1986   305.8'009416   86-4370
ISBN 0-226-74416-7
ISBN 0-226-74417-5 (pbk.)

To My Parents

Katherine Merriam See
and Edgar Thorp See

Contents

Tables

Preface

This book is a work of historical sociology. But it is also a product of social and personal histories, and I would like to share with the reader those moments and individuals that have shaped its direction.

Few who came of age in the 1960s were immune to the impact of the American civil rights movement. It reached into and altered our lives, spawned other movements, and shaped much of our scholarship. It reminded us of the power of history, of the legacy of a past which could not be easily altered. At the same time, participation in the movements of that period generated a sense of the immediacy of our revolutionary moment and a belief in some inevitable political trajectory. Like many in my generation, I was caught in the particulars of that American moment, a time-and space-boundedness which belied historical and global experiences of social change. It was in this context that I received in 1970 a fellowship from the Thomas J. Watson Foundation which allowed me to apply my activist concerns for race relations at home to patterns of ethnic conflict abroad. The Watson year provided me with the opportunity to interview and observe ethnic activists in Northern Ireland, Israel, Kenya, and South Africa. It was this experience that taught me most viscerally the need for a historical and comparative lens through which to see ethnic conflict. I am especially grateful to the foundation and its president, Robert O. Shulze, for encouraging me to continue my explorations through graduate school in sociology, to discipline my activist instincts, without sacrificing a fundamental commitment to political change in intergroup relations. But it was graduate school in sociology at the University of Chicago that allowed me to define this project more clearly.

Graduate training is a mixed experience for those of an activist bent. If it is not a solitary experience, it is often politically and socially isolating. I owe special debts to those who taught me that the discipline of sociology need not be abstracted from political commitment. Most especially, I am grateful to my teacher, William Julius Wilson, who taught me the basic tools of the trade and their applicability to questions of social momentousness. I also owe special thanks to Ira Katznelson and Michael Burawoy, whose provocative questions sought to keep me clear-sighted. I have benefited as well from rigorous and friendly criticism as I worked on this project. I would like, especially, to thank Allen Batteau, Morris Janowitz, Joane Nagel, Susan Olzak, Terry Sullivan, and Ken Waltzer for their comments about weaknesses in conceptualization and their suggestions for reformulation. My ability to take their insights seriously and incoporate their suggestions was enhanced by a fellowship from the Rockefeller Foundation which provided a year of support at the Center for the Study of Human Rights at Columbia University for the revisions of this book. The problems in analysis remain my own.

For many years this work has been a major focus in my life, and I owe a special debt to those who have helped me maintain a sense of proportion about myself and this project. My friends Priscilla Trubin and Patricia Myles Hummer sustained me throughout. Ted and Ellen See, Sandy and Emmy See, and Eloise and Bob McGraw reminded me in their very familial ways that the sociological vision is not the only form of perception. Len Isaacs taught me that challenge and love are partners. Finally my parents, Kay and Eddie See, fostered the concerns and critical instincts which have carried me through this work—as through much else. My gratitude for their unwavering support is too deep to speak.

This work is much abstracted from its original impulse in the effort to understand what generates ethnic conflict and what makes its resolution possible. If it focuses more on what confounds hope for positive intergroup relations, it is also based on a belief that knowing what holds us back may bring us together.

1

Introduction:
Ethnic Nationalism as a
Sociological Problem

In the last several decades, ethnic separatist movements, spanning from Brittany to Zaire, have competed with international terrorism to command world attention. This proliferation of ethnic outbreaks has been challenging to social scientists. Do these movements constitute a universalization of ethnicity which has replaced the nineteenth-century model of a transnational class struggle?[1] Are they the inevitable product of industrial modernization, in which ethnic identity is a most efficacious basis for political mobilization?[2] Are ethnically based demands for self-determination a passing phase on the road to modernization, or do they represent a serious and constant threat to global peace? This book contributes to the effort to answer these questions—to explore the factors which generate ethnic separatist movements, the historical shapes such movements assume, and their consequences for social and political relations.

The book begins with a brief introduction to and assessment of the major theories of ethnic nationalism. On the basis of this critique, chapter 2 outlines an analytic framework for understanding the rise of separatist movements. This framework constitutes a theory sketch. Rather than a set of logical propositions and hypotheses which seek to predict patterns of ethnic group behavior with exactitude, my effort is to present a set of analytic categories which should sensitize readers to what to look for in understanding the dynamics of ethnic mobilization.[3] I then explore the history of ethnic relations in Northern Ireland and Quebec to examine the usefulness of the theory sketch for understanding two of the most interesting modern cases of ethnic separatism. I compare them during three distinct periods of history: early settlement and the colonial regimes; capitalist industrialization; and advanced industrialism. In each period, I examine the major patterns of ethnic mobilization, applying and refining the theory sketch accordingly.

Why Northern Ireland and Quebec? Students of ethnic relations have come to recognize that the search for general principles of intergroup behavior requires a comparative and historical approach. Examining patterns over time and space makes it possible to cull what is universal and what is particular to such behavior. And in both Ireland and Canada, the long history of contact, conflict, and accommodation between the two major ethnic groups provides a base for understanding the effects of different patterns of colonization, industrialization, and capital development on group relations. In both cases, religion (both institutionally and culturally) has been a major ethnic boundary, shaping resources and identities. But Quebec has made a successful transition to a secular state, whereas Northern Ireland has been racked by sectarian struggle. Both areas experienced a resurgence of ethnic conflict in the 1960s, including demands for an independent ethnic state formation. Yet in Northern Ireland, these conflicts produced enduring civil war; in Quebec, they were managed and absorbed into normal politics. This is particularly impressive, given the fact that language differences have posed significant problems for the modern Canadian state, whereas the material differences in culture are less significant in Ulster. A comparison should provide some clues about the variable role of religion and of language in ethnic relations and about the conditions under which ethnic demands can be answered without major social upheaval. Finally, these two cases are worth consideration because each provides us with an interesting contrast to and perspective on our own history as a nation of ethnicities.

ETHNIC NATIONALISM AS A CONCEPTUAL PROBLEM

With the exception of the term *class,* a few social scientific concepts are more slippery than the construct *ethnicity.* Unlike gender, religion, age, and other forms of ascription, ethnicity is not a bounded category. Religion may be an attribute of ethnic identity, yet one can abandon the practice of Judaism and still be a Jew. Language may be another index, yet most Polish-Americans are Anglophones. What then are the boundaries of the ethnic group?

We can conceive of ethnic groups as Richard Schermerhorn has defined them: "collectivities within a larger society, having real or putative common ancestry, memories of a shared historical past, and a cultural focus on one or more symbolic elements, defined as the epitome of their peoplehood."[4] From this perspective, it is not a set of cultural attributes per se that makes ethnicity; rather it is a *sense* of commonality and of shared history. Without that sense, a group with common cultural attributes is analogous to Marx's conception of peasants who lack class consciousness. Like a sack of potatoes, they may be in the same situation, but they are incapable of common action or a sense of collective interest. It is precisely for that reason that a historical approach is necessary; for we seek to understand how that common identity and sense of a shared past is constructed, imagined, and produced. But ethnicity is not made ex nihilo. Cultural attributes do make a difference, and a particular constellation of cultural elements (language, religion, custom, costume, etc.) will have a logic of its own. If we recognize that different cultural attributes such as language and religion are not functional equivalents, the value of a comparative approach becomes much more apparent.[5]

Why do we identify with these cultural attributes? Social scientists have taken two approaches to the creation of ethnicity: primordialist and instrumentalist. Primordialists argue that there is something fundamental and given in the nature of ethnicity which precedes and transcends its objective attributes (language, race, culture, religion, territoriality). These symbols of ethnicity encapsulate "man's need to be in contact with the point and moment of his origin and to experience a sense of affinity with those who share that origin."[6] Our fundamental need for identity and self-esteem can be met only in collectivities where we connect to others like ourselves, see ourselves in the community, and find an identity in something larger than our own individuality. But if there is a strong psychodynamic component to ethnicity, as primordialists suggest, ethnic group formation is much more than a product of individual need. As Max Weber emphasizes, ethnic membership per se does not constitute a group; "it only facilitates group formation of any kind, particularly in the political sphere. . . . It is primarily the political community, no matter how artificially organized, that inspires belief in common ethnicity."[7]

In contrast to the primordialist emphasis on psychological needs,

instrumentalists have expanded Weber's insight to claim that physical and cultural attributes constitute a resource used to organize a
collectivity of people in order to advance certain material interests.
A group constitutes itself as ethnic because it is politically useful,
not because the members feel any psychological bond. And ethnicity will be abandoned when it ceases to serve that instrumental purpose.[8] From this perspective, ethnicity is simply a social grammar
that is useful for organizing and mobilizing. Yet this ignores *why*
such a grammar is so useful. Pierre van den Berghe has trenchantly
criticized both of these perspectives, pointing out that there is a
conjunction of subjective and objective conditions in the making of
ethnicity. "There can be no ethnicity (or race) without some conception and consciousness of a distinction between 'them' and 'us';
but these subjective perceptions do not develop at random, they
crystallize around clusters of objective characteristics that become
badges of inclusion or exclusion. Nor are the characteristics seized
upon as a matter of capricious choice. Some are clearly appropriate. Others are not."[9] And, as the analysis in later chapters will
make clear, there are certain conditions under which cultural characteristics become politically salient.

The next problematic concept is that of nationalism. Nationalism
refers to the efforts of a social group to ensure and protect its own
political, social, and economic autonomy through self-government
in an independent state and to justify that movement by claiming
the group's status as a nation. There is, then, both an ideological
and a political aspect to nationalist movements. The approaches to
nationalism parallel those toward ethnicity, reflecting the sense that
such movements are either inevitable or merely instrumental. For
example, Hans Kohn, in his classic work, defines nationalism as
"a state of mind permeating the large majority of a people and
claiming to permeate all its members; it recognizes the nation state
as the ideal form of political organization and the nationality as the
source of all creative cultural energy and of economic well being.
The supreme loyalty of man is supposedly rooted in and made possible by its welfare."[10] Like primordialists, Kohn obscures the distinction between national sentiment and political action. He implies
that nationalism is automatically activated group sentiment, but as
K. H. Silvert points out, to state that something exists as a feeling
"and then hazily to add that this ideational commitment leads to

overt political action leaves out the proof of the relationship."[11] However, more instrumental definitions also have limitations. For example, Chong-Do Hah and Jeffrey Martin attempt to circumvent the problem of psychological reductionism by defining nationalism as "organizationally heightened and articulated group demands directed toward securing control of the distributive systems of society."[12] But this definition can apply equally to the efforts of a class movement to overthrow capitalist ownership and management and to a mobilization to take over a government on religious grounds. Class and nationalist struggles must be analytically distinguished, even though they may be historically connected.

What is the difference between an ethnic group and a nation? In a sense, the nation constitutes a politicized ethnic group. It is "a large group of people who feel that they form a single and exclusive community destined to be an independent state." Its key criteria are largeness in scale, group solidarity which views the group as the "terminal community," and the "assumption of a national destiny of independent statehood in the modern world."[13] Unlike the ethnic group, the nation requires a sense of territoriality. The ethnic group can retain its identity without a geo-regional locus (e.g., Afro-Americans, Gypsies); the nation cannot. And, although ethnic groups may act as political forces in various ways, they become nations only through the movement toward political independence. Hence, ethnic nationalism is the movement of an ethnic group to develop a sense of national identity and to establish political, economic, and social independence on the basis of its common cultural features. The emphasis is upon two loyalties: to ethnic identity and to political self-determination in a particular region. The focus of the movement depends upon the nature of the group and its social position. If it is already a nation-state, then the nationalist focus is on maintaining boundaries; if the group has a clear regional or ethnic identity, then the effort is to shape a sense of nationality and to secure recognition as a legitimate nation. And if it is part of an ethnically plural state, its efforts are to separate and attain independent status. Hence, for the ethnic group, nationalism has a dual purpose: the development of a solidary mobilized nation, or nationbuilding; and the establishment of an autonomous political community, or state building.[14]

Nationalism is distinct from other ethnopolitical movements.

Ethnic groups can also attempt to assimilate, abandoning a distinctive identity, or they may seek a system of political pluralism with distinctive ethnic rights and resources. What are the conditions under which nationalism is the choice? To answer that question, we must turn to the broader literature on nationalism, social movements, and ethnic relations. This is a vast and rich literature which could engulf even a scholar skilled at swimming the academic currents. To manage those channels, I will concentrate here on several seminal sociological approaches, outline their explanation for ethnic nationalism, and discuss their insights and limitations. Among the most important are modernization theories; plural society and power conflict theories; and Marxist and neo-Marxist models.

MODERNIZATION APPROACHES TO NATIONALISM

Modernization theories derive from the Durkheimian emphasis upon social differentiation as society develops from the small traditional group—family, tribe, clan (gemeinschaft)—to the interest-based community—class, party (gesellschaft). Industrialization, more complex forms of social organization, urbanization, and the development of a centralized state system all disrupt traditional community forms and allegiances. The uniformity and mobility which are characteristic of modern societies simultaneously blur and encourage a sense of ethnicity.

For economic and political development to take place, a state must encourage integration of groups and must moderate the tensions that develop as previously isolated groups come into contact with one another or become aware of one another through modern communication systems. Nationalism represents an attempt to resolve the tensions generated by this transition. It is, in this sense, an integrative force which emerges to provide security and identity under the dislocating impact of modernization. Why does it provide that security? First, nationalism connects the traditional community with the modern society by providing symbols of consensus in which the various social groups can find some sense of personal and collective identity. Second, it serves as an integrative ideology, one which provides a sense of social place and meaning for non-elites during the modernization process and hence which helps moderate social conflicts. Third, it provides a rationale for modernization, a set of symbols which functions to break down parochial attachments, to legitimate a new authority system, and to develop a rational and modern system of production.[15]

State builders within an ethnically plural society will seek to encourage assimilation of culturally distinct groups within a territory. Nationalism is one vehicle for accomplishing this goal—but the efforts are not always successful. Modernization is uneven, and integration is not automatic, especially where the forces of assimilation (a common language, schooling, mass media) do not keep pace with the forces of technological innovation, industrial employment, and urban settlement.[16] The modern centralized state, with its impersonal bureaucracy and rational principles of organization and its uniformity and overspecialization, may itself upset traditional communal balances and create a sense of anomie, a loss of identity. Ethnic revivals then can constitute a reaction against modernization—an effort to return to the true community.[17] How is an ethnic nationalist reaction to uneven modernization sparked? According to modernization theorists, a special leadership role is played by the intellectual elite within ethnic groups. In modernizing societies, this intelligentsia is likely to be alienated from traditional communal values by education and exposure to secular, universalist norms. On the other hand, they may have limited opportunities for mobility in the bureaucracies of the modern state system, if it does not expand as quickly as the educated populace. As a result, the ethnic intelligentsia is both culturally and economically displaced. These leaders may seek to resolve this displacement and their own alienation by tapping the grievances of other groups and rearticulating these in the language of ethnonationalism. Peasants, threatened by changes in the traditional economy and culture, and tradespeople, craftsworkers, and small shopkeepers, displaced by the competitive power of industry, become the following for this intellectual elite, who rephrase "individual and group grievances into something more than simply a catalogue of complaints, so that they relate to a large national whole, which has its own grievance against another whole. . . . The grievance of the nation subsumes all individual grievances. Thus, there arises the notion of a reciprocity of dependence."[18]

The historical global diffusion of the idea of national self-determination can also challenge state building along nonethnic lines.

According to Walker Connor, the endorsement and legitimation of the principle of self-determination in the last quarter-century has made ethnicity itself a legitimate basis for political organization, by holding that any group, which claims to be a people, has the right to rule itself.[19] The association of the abstract idea of popular sovereignty with principles of nationalism has spread in a kind of twentieth-century process of ideological migration, propelled by evidence of success elsewhere, by mass education, and by telecommunications. There are, then, several bases for the surge of ethnic nationalist movements in the contemporary world: one is structural—the uneven process of modernization, which generates self-conscious ethnic units through increased interethnic contact and social communication before these groups can be assimilated into a homogeneous secular national culture; the second is psychological—the "divergence of basic identity which manifests itself in the us-them syndrome";[20] the third is political—the diffusion of the concept of self-determination by a self-interested intelligentsia and the evidence of its success.

Modernization theories raise many pivotal issues: the importance of industrialization in throwing previously isolated groups into contact, the disruption of traditional institutions, which leaves modernizing groups culturally suspended, the significance of modern communication vehicles for forging collective identity and mobilizing groups, the crucial role of intellectuals, and the independent effect of ideology. But, there is, as numerous critics have pointed out, a teleological bias to modernization models—an assumption that there is a singular path to development which, if left alone, will produce group integration, concensus, and order. There is little consideration given to conflicts of material interest or to the divisiveness and dissension that result from resource competition.[21] Moreover, the concept itself is so broad and all-encompassing that it is difficult to test. Certainly, all situations of modernization do not generate ethnic reaction; and there are numerous fully modern states which have experienced separatist movements. How do we explain the emergence of ethnic separatist movements in some ethnically heterogeneous modern states (Canada) but not in others (Switzerland), or in some developing and ethnically plural societies (Nigeria, India) but not in others (Ghana, Brazil)? To remedy these defects, scholars have adopted more structural analyses which root ethnic nationalism in power relations between competing ethnic groups. Among the earliest and most influential of these efforts have been plural society and power conflict approaches.

PLURAL SOCIETY AND POWER CONFLICT APPROACHES TO NATIONALISM

The plural society model originated with the efforts of anthropologists and political scientists to counter the static bias of consensually oriented social science and to emphasize the conflictual aspects of intergroup relations. The early models emphasize the "ordered segmentation" resulting from colonization. Historically, imperial expansion and colonization have involved the domination and differential incorporation of ethnically distinct groups into the colonial state and economy and the preservation of ethnic and cultural differences through separate social institutions. In such cases, the colonial state constitutes the means for controlling indigenous populations, by limiting their economic and political resources. And nationalist movements are the effort of the subordinated group to secure control over its own political interests.[22] From this perspective, separatism is rooted in a rational power struggle rather than in cultural anomie or psychological alienation. And it is spoken in ethnic terms because explicit social segregation rather than uneven processes of assimilation has preserved cultural distinctions.

When do groups make the choice to engage in nationalist struggle? Here, power conflict theorists built on the basic premises of the early plural society model and indicated that the power resources of the subordinated ethnic group will govern the patterns of mobilization. According to William J. Wilson, an early conflict theorist, "a group's beliefs regarding its ability or inability to produce change are based on perceptions of both its own relative power resources and the magnitude of the problem to be solved."[23] The historic linkages between the groups and the present restrictiveness of the social structure will determine the actual and potential resources available to a group, determining the forms of and targets for mobilization, that is, whether it is overt revolution, furtive acts of rebellion, or secessionist movements. When groups are competing in a relatively restrictive structure, the powerless are likely to avoid direct and ultimate confrontations and to adopt a posture of apparent accommodation. When the social structure is more flexible (especially during periods of social change) and new resources are available, conflicts and tensions become more overt. In such situations, the leadership will seek new ways to secure power. Nationalist movements tend to emerge when the subordinate group lacks resources for effective competition and when there is a high degree of social segregation from the larger society. They are a kind of tactical withdrawal from direct competition and an effort to consolidate resources on behalf of the group as a whole. In such cases, minority leaders advocate the establishment of a separate and independent society, based upon common cultural institutions and identity.[24]

The strength of the plural society and power conflict models lies in their concern with the conflictual and competitive process whereby ethnic groups define and protect their own interests. This is a more dynamic approach than the modernization school, insofar as it emphasizes the shifting behavior and interests of groups as they respond to changes in their own resources. However, like the modernization theorists, these models also draw a picture of ethnic group solidarity which is historically inaccurate and theoretically misleading. They incline toward a reductionism which views ethnic group relations as a single dichotomy, thereby eclipsing the significance of intraethnic relations or conflicts of interest within ethnic groups. And, because they fail to provide an explanation for the development of particularistic economic and political interests for a segment of a dominated group, these approaches tend to portray the subordinate ethnic group as thoroughly victimized. Hence, there is little consideration of how ethnic leaders may manipulate groups to pursue activities which do not reflect the interests of the group as a whole. And here, Marxist and neo-Marxist theories are more useful.

MARXIST AND NEO-MARXIST APPROACHES TO NATIONALISM

Marxist theory begins with an emphasis upon the primary role of the system of production in shaping social aggregates and interests and in defining the political relations between groups. In primitive subsistence economies, where no surplus wealth is accumulated, groups organize into clans and tribes to protect communal territory. Political relations in these societies are defined primarily along the line of affinal ties of kinship. It is in these economies that ethnicity originates; it forms the basis for group organization and the locus around which economic competition for the control of territory develops. And it is within this political economy that the dominance of different clans or tribes, the first form of ethnic differentiation, appears. Hence, stratification and ethnicity are simultaneous historical appearances. Accordingly, orthodox Marxists tend to see ethnicity as a vestige of an archaic mode of production, a relic which becomes decreasingly significant with the development of class relations.[25] This is not to say that ethnicity dissipates with the emergence of feudal classes. Rather, it takes on the form of a protonationality.

For orthodox Marxists, protonationalism was the ideological device of feudal lords and their clerical elites in western Europe, as they sought to conquer territories beyond their own boundaries and to consolidate their rule within feudal states. Early imperialism and monarchy were justified on the basis of the common religious identity and mission of the feudal community. Thus, "the predatory interests of the feudal crusaders were concealed by the concept of liberating the holy places and waging a holy Christian war against the Islamic and Slav peoples."[26] However, this nascent expression of nationality was fully articulated only with the emergence of capitalism, as the feudal aristocracy and emerging bourgeoisie began to compete for control over the centralizing state. Feudal monarchs sought to retain power, to preserve feudal relations, and to inhibit the rise of capitalism by consolidating the peasantry along traditional and religious lines. At the same time, the new bourgeoisie sought to attract support for market interests and freedom from central control by demanding broader participation in government and by creating more secular national slogans. In short, nationalism is rooted in class struggle. As Lenin argued this view: "For the complete victory of commodity production the bourgeoisie must capture the home market, and there must be politically united territories, whose population speaks a single language. . . . Unity and unimpeded development of language are the most important conditions for genuinely free capitalism, for a free and broad grouping of the population in all its various classes, and lastly for the establishment of close connections between the market and each and every proprietor, big or little, and between seller and buyer."[27]

As capital historically concentrated in fewer hands and monopolies developed, capitalists developed mechanisms to protect their competitive advantage. One such mechanism, protective tariffs, was adopted to benefit the bourgeoisie within a particular state. Thus, capitalist states were set one against another in the struggle for economic dominance. At the same time, within these states the investment of capital in labor-saving devices displaced workers, reduced the ratio of income to capital, and led to the serious problem of underconsumption and oversupply.[28] The need for new markets for export occurs at the same time that displaced workers in capitalist societies begin to mobilize against the bourgeoisie. In response to these periodic problems of increased competition, a declining rate of profit, and class agitation, capitalist states adopt programs of nationalist imperial expansion. They invade and colonize nonindustrial regions, extracting raw materials for home industry, using the colonies as a market for export, employing colonial labor as a cheap supply, and returning some benefits to the home labor market, which begins to constitute a "labor aristocracy."[29] This entire process is justified by ideologies which proclaim the superiority of the core state's nationality and hence its inherent right to dominate. And within the core state, the ruling class will also moderate class conflict by fostering ethnic antagonisms among workers through such mechanisms as differential wage rates and segregation. In this way, worker solidarity is reduced within and between nations. Ethnic allegiances thus obscure the oppression generated by the international development of capitalism, because they are used to reinforce political boundaries, to eclipse workers' common interests, and advance the development of capital within the state.

Marxists have vacillated on the implications of this interpretation. On the one hand, they view imperialist expansion as a necessary and positive product of capitalism, insofar as it draws peripheral areas into the capitalist orbit. Only with the triumph of global capitalism can an international proletariat and true communist revolution develop. On the other hand, in specific situations, national attachments can serve as a base for opposition to capitalist domination and hence as a tool in forging class consciousness. Indeed, in colonial and neocolonial situations, nationalism is the only escape from metropolitan capitalist dominance.[30] For Marxists, nationalism is a double-edged sword. One edge, carried by the bourgeoisie, slices away at the real interests of the workers, while the other edge is honing a revolutionary proletariat within a colonized state, thus advancing the cause of socialism.[31]

Orthodox Marxism has been roundly critiqued for its schematic economism and the crudeness of its monocausal account of ethnicity, which simply cannot account for the complexity of nationalist movements. This approach, for example, cannot account for the resurgence of separatism in advanced capitalist societies or by groups that are not colonial subjects. Moreover, it fails to explain how and why appeals to *ethnicity* are so effective. However, work of recent neo-Marxist scholars seeks to remedy these problems. Among the most influential of these revisionist theories are three models of ethnic mobilization: internal colonial, uneven development, and split labor market theories. These models share the Marxist view that ethnoregional and ethnonational movements are the product of the general processes of capitalism's uneven development. They agree that the historic growth and concentration of capitalism in core states precipitated a reaction by the emergent bourgeoisie in peripheral colonized areas against metropolitan domination. Appearing first in extensively settled colonies, such as North America, where there was a shared political ethos with the metropole (and hence a demand for "equal treatment"), such movements then developed in more administrative colonies where an indigenous middle class served the metropole as bureaucrats and middlemen. Over time, the relative deprivation of the "peripheral bourgeoisie" laid the ground for populist demands for independent state formations, so as to develop the "national" economy and secure a more favorable place in the world system.[32] However, occasionally, this dynamic was interrupted by reactive ethnic mobilization: organized opposition to a secular (class or regional) movement in a peripheral region and the development of organized efforts to define political and economic interests in explicitly ethnic terms. In such cases, a secular nationalist movement against a metropole could founder into ethnoregional or ethnonationalist politics.

Among the most prominent of these interpretations by neo-Marxist scholars is the internal colonial model of ethnonationalism elegantly spelled out in the work of Michael Hechter. Following Marxist assumptions, Hechter proposed that uneven economic development and political dominance by a core state set the ground for quasi-national solidarity in a dependent periphery. In the process of development, dominant or metropolitan regions create a hierarchical and coincidentally cultural division of labor, in which high-status and occupations are reserved for the metropoles. The exploitation of resources and labor in the hinterland is reinforced by metropolitan judicial and political practices. There is, then, a clear material basis for a reactive ethnic group mobilization on the part of the subordinated ethnic region.[33] Such mobilization is more probable where a relative economic deprivation coincides with a high degree of cultural difference. And this is most characteristic of developing regions, with low levels of industrialization. Sharp ethnic differences can be more easily preserved in preindustrial societies, where the populace is less mobile and where communal associations are stronger. "Language societies, cultural festivals and dissident religious sects provide the necessary internal organization of the region that is the prerequisite for a social movement. They are the institutional base from which ethnoregionalism springs. The preservation of rituals from the past promotes a sense of community not only for people whose social structural roles make them feel marginal within society as a whole, but also for those who wish to change the allocation of societal resources. This sense of community can consequently become the basis for collective action of a political sort."[34] In short, in preindustrial agrarian societies, the higher degree of "institutional completeness," in which cultural attributes are encapsulated in social institutions, makes mobilization on the basis of ethnicity likely. As industrialization increases and contact between the core and hinterland accelerates, more secular nationalist responses are likely.[35] But as Susan Olzak has pointed out, this viewpoint really coincides with linear development theories, such as modernization and classical Marxist models. "Reduction of the cultural division of labor due to peripheral development, worker solidarity, or some other cause can hypothetically produce a decline in ethnicity."[36] This assumes that over time class or other rational forms of mobilization will supersede ethnicity, an assumption that may be belied by the resurgence of ethnicity in advanced industrial areas during the postwar period.

Unlike internal colonialism, which views the ethnic division of labor in a more undifferentiated way, uneven development theorists emphasize the crucial role of the elites in the periphery and the importance of the structure of the state in shaping ethnic relations. Most evident in the work of Tom Nairn, this perspective argues that uneven economic development may provide a core state with the resources to respond flexibly to the interests of peripheral elites, providing benefits from imperial expansion and tolerating or encouraging an ethnic labor aristocracy. Thus, in the peripheral region, there are likely to be differential reactions to the metropole, depending on class position within an ethnic group. Reactive mobilization is likely in a period of significant economic change, when traditional patrimonial relations between the elites of the center and the periphery are destabilized. The dominant classes are unable to differentially reward a fragment of the peripheral working class and sustain their paternalist relation with them.[37]

Split labor market theory is an influential variant of uneven development analyses but disputes the central proposition which roots ethnic antagonisms in *capitalist* efforts to deflect class conflict. This approach views ethnic antagonism as the product of a triangular conflict between capital, indigenous "high-priced" labor, and ethnically distinct "cheap labor." According to Edna Bonacich, the architect of this theory, capital is essentially unconcerned with ethnic difference; left to its principles of efficiency, impersonal labor market rules, and accumulation, capitalist growth would erode such distinctions. However, capitalists are not unconstrained. An indigenous labor force may already monopolize a market and seek to protect its incremental advantages through political actions: exclusionary movements, job segregation, or protectionist policies which block access to cheap labor. If it has greater political resources than its cheap competitors, high-priced labor is likely to limit capital's ability to use workers interchangeably. In short, the sector of the working class with incremental political and economic advantage is the real source of ethnoracial and discrimination and hence is most likely to make "ethnonational" claims. It is labor rather than capital that instigates reactive mobilization.[38]

These revisionist Marxist approaches are of some value in understanding the material bases for ethnic nationalist politics in capitalist societies. Unlike modernization theorists, they emphasize the exploitative aspects of development and the importance of ethnic regions as interest groups. Unlike power conflict theorists, they emphasize that there are sectors within an ethnic group who utilize cultural institutions and grievances to advance their own concerns. But the most problematic aspect of these approaches is the tendency to reduce ethnicity to a problem of economic relations. This makes it difficult to explain how the *ethnic* content of the movements develops. Only the internal colonial model focuses at all on the importance of cultural symbols, and it assumes that this will erode with industrialization and urbanization. As Stanley Ryerson has so cogently argued: "Classes embody relationships of property and work in the context of a mode of production. The nation-community embodies relationships of a different order. Hence, while it is inseparable historically from class structures and modes of production, the national community is more than just an aspect of any one of them. This is so because the nation-community embodies an identity; linguistic and cultural, that is not simply an 'effect' of class, however closely its evolution may be interwoven with the shifting patterns of class relations and struggles." A significant part of ethnic separatism is the emphasis on the cultural rights of a historic community, "the belief in the distinct even unique character of an ethnic community which entails the right and duty of the community to run its own affairs according to internal historical laws, without outside interference."[40] It follows then that we must be very careful not to transform the problem of ethnic identity into the fundamentally different although empirically connected problem of class relations but must carefully delineate their interaction.

SUMMARY

In this chapter, I have argued that ethnic boundaries have both a situational and a psychological dimension; ethnic identity is not simply chosen on the basis of rational calculus, but neither is it an automatic given. Rather, ethnic boundaries are constructed through a process of group interaction in the context of political and economic interests. The decision to mobilize on the basis of ethnicity occurs only under certain circumstances. Most scholars agree that the processes of modernization contribute significantly to the likelihood of ethnic mobilization and nationalism. However, they differ in their claims about which factors are most instrumental in moving groups in the direction of national aspirations. Traditional modernization theorists focus on the ways in which development processes trigger a return to ethnic identities because of the disjunction between development and cultural assimilation or as a response to the social dislocations of development. The remaining models emphasize the conflictual aspects of ethnic identification, claiming that ethnic mobilization is in large part determined by the ways a particular economic system supports group images and social solidarity and by "the intrusion of the political process in the form of perceived domination, competition, threats or advantage."[41]

These models also differ in the ways in which they examine the intersection of class and ethnic processes in state systems. Modernization theories simply do not consider class processes as independent contributions to ethnic conflict. Plural society and power conflict approaches do not distinguish between class and ethnic structures and hence fail to define the important role of class relations within ethnic groups. Internal colonialism also assumes a coincidence of class and ethnic interests, at least in preindustrial societies. In contrast, uneven development and split labor market analysts are wary of this approach for its failure to consider internal differences within ethnic groups. They place a particular emphasis on the significance of economic relations within *and* between ethnic groups. But there are differences between these last two models as well: uneven development theorists consider the decline of particular economic sectors and hence the relations between the capitalists of the metropole and the capitalists of the peripheral region to be crucial to the contours of ethnic conflict; it is the diminishing political and economic power of indigenous capital that precipitates reactive ethnic mobilization, when the peripheral elite can no longer provide support for a "labor aristocracy," or when their own privileged position is undermined by multinational corporations. The split labor market model focuses on labor market interests within particular firms, views the efforts to rationalize a market as the primary precipitant of reactive ethnic mobilization, and sees this mobilization as instigated largely by high-priced workers.

In the following chapter, I show how an alternative approach, the resource competition model, may synthesize the insights of each of these models but overcome their deficiencies and usefully explain historical patterns and variations in ethnic politics.

2

Toward a Theory of Ethnic Nationalism

Ethnic nationalism is premised on a rejection of the goal of political assimilation and cultural accommodation in a multiethnic state. If nationalism is not simply a reflection of primordial commonality, then why would individuals support such a rejection? In an analysis of the dimensions and implications of ethnic inequality, Stanley Lieberson argues that "the fundamental difference between ethnic and other forms of stratification lies in the fact that the former is nearly always the basis for the internal disintegration of nation-states. On both theoretical and empirical grounds, only ethnic groups are likely to generate a movement toward creating a separate nation-state."[1] This is an incisive contention, indicating the essential difference between ethnic and other forms of stratification. However, the statement can be misleading if it is read to imply that separatist movements are simply efforts by subordinate groups to eliminate the power differential. That interpretation obscures the flexibility of nationalism as a mobilizing principle and the variety of political responses which ethnic groups can make in response to systems of differentiation.[2] Ethnic nationalism is an ambiguous principle and can be adopted in numerous settings for a variety of goals. It may constitute the attempt by a superordinate ethnic group to retain political power in the face of minority demands for equality (as is the case for Afrikaner nationalists in South Africa); or it may provide a mechanism for an elite sector of an ethnic group to obtain valued jobs and property (as in the case of Quebec separatists); or it may seek a total redistribution of power within *and* between ethnic groups in a specific territory (as the Official Irish Republican Army seeks to do). Although we can begin with the assumption that nationalism is a product of and response to ethnic stratification, we must recognize that it is not a singular tactic, adopted only by a subordinate group for its ends. Our concern then is not with ethnic domination per se but with the ways in which historical patterns of domination and competition create and reproduce material boundaries between ethnic groups and generate ethnically defined interests and claims. We must then seek to identify the conditions under which those claims take the direction of separatism.

ETHNIC CONTACT AND THE ORIGINS OF ETHNIC STRATIFICATION

What are the antecedent conditions for the development of a system of ethnic stratification, given intergroup contact between two culturally distinct groups? We can begin with Donald Noel's classic threefold explanation of the sources of structured inequality: differential distribution of power, competition over scarce resources, and a sense of in-group solidarity or ethnocentrism.[3] Without an unequal distribution of power, of course, one group would not be able to dominate another. But power differences are insufficient, because groups can simply migrate away from or accommodate to one another. Therefore some degree of competition for the same scarce resources is needed. Moreover, as Donald Noel points out, "the number and significance of the scarce common goals sought determine the degree of competition, which can in turn significantly affect the probability that ethnic stratification will emerge."[4] But the factor that separates ethnic stratification from other forms of group differentiation is the element of ethnocentrism. Only through a correspondence of cultural symbols of identification and group interests will a sense of *group* position exist. "Without ethnocentrism, the groups would quickly merge and competition would not be structured along ethnic lines."[5] It is for this reason that a purely instrumentalist view is insufficient. To the extent that cultural differences are considerable, institutionalized (e.g., religion), and not easily abandoned (e.g., color, language), ethnocentrism is likely to be intensified.

This model provides a framework for understanding why groups may accommodate to one another over a sustained period of contact but become competitive during a period of development in which natural resources become more significant, so that ethnicity may become salient. However, the model needs to be developed if we are to distinguish and understand patterns of ethnic mobilization. The conditions of intergroup contact must be considered first, since variations here will shape the kinds of power resources and forms of competition. There are numerous sequences, but for our general purposes they can be reduced to several major types: colonization, annexation, forced migration, and voluntary migration.[6]

Colonization refers to the control of a specific territory by a non-indigenous group through either limited or massive settlement.[7] Colonies of limited settlement are generally designed to establish military superiority and administrative control over a particular region, either for military reasons or for the extraction of natural resources. These efforts may lead to severe conflicts with the indigenes and to military occupation and the displacement or decimation of the native population. But they are unlikely to produce a rigid system of ethnic stratification, since the primary interest is the control of territory and resources—not labor. Indeed, the administrators may intermarry with the indigenous population, adopting their language and customs. Or they may manipulate the indigenous populace, providing rewards to a social elite for serving on behalf of the metropole. In both cases, the degree of ethnocentrism of both groups is likely to shape the ways in which colonization develops. Colonies of limited settlement were characteristic of the patterns of imperial expansion of the absolutist states in western Europe. They also constituted the first stage of the capitalist colonization of Asia and Africa. They may generate reactive and local outbreaks in resistance to encroachment upon the land, but such outbreaks are unlikely to assume a nationalist guise, since the colonists do not seek to impose extensive political and institutional controls over the indigenous population.

Limited-settlement colonies with more substantial numbers of settlers aim to control territory for explicitly economic purposes. Although originally sparsely colonized, with the influx of more settlers the metropole not only uses the colonies to expropriate resources for its own economic development but can begin to market its surplus, and develop industries at low labor costs. Richard A. Schermerhorn has described this process: "Usually the land of the colony was sufficiently fertile and the climate salubrious enough to attract many farmers from the home country of the colonizers. These agriculturalists then appropriated large tracts of land for themselves, pushing original inhabitants into increasingly crowded areas. Newcomers then utilized the dispossessed for large scale labor in farming, mining or industrial enterprise at lower cost levels."[8] Although colonial settlers remain a numerical minority, they can secure significant control over the land in the colony with the protection of the metropolitan army. Such a system of colonization is much more exploitative of the indigenous population than colonies of limited settlement. And as the indigenous population is drawn into the colonial economy (as laborers on commercial farms, tenants, sharecroppers, industrial wage labor), the political infrastructure will develop to protect the interests of the colonial regime. Hence it tends toward an exclusionary administration. Indigenes may be hired as low-level functionaries, but clear status lines are drawn restricting their mobility. Ethnocentric ideologies develop to rationalize this pattern of stratification. India and South Africa in the eighteenth century constitute classic cases of limited colonial settlement. In these situations of colonization, there is a strong material basis for ethnic mobilization to overcome the exploitation of indigenous labor or to expel the colonizers.

The most extensive pattern, massive colonial settlement, is a by-product of this previous stage (either because limited settlement is not successful in securing control over territory or because the metropole seeks to solve its own labor problems by encouraging colonial emigration). As the colonists increase numerically, their situation is characterized by increased independence from the metropole. Some surplus is reinvested in the economic development of the colony, a political infrastructure is developed, and the settlers begin to see themselves as having distinctive interests and identities. In such a case, a distinct "national" identity may develop among the colonists, depending on the degree of isolation from and political subordinance to the metropole and the degree of competition with the indigenes. This was evident in the settlement of the Americas in the eighteenth century.

A variation on these patterns is the *annexation* of a contiguous territory and incorporation into the metropole, either by force or by purchase. Annexation is very likely to transform an inchoate sense of collectivity into a distinctive ethnic consciousness. Fighting over territory reinforces boundary consciousness. And centralization of command during warfare is likely to lead to the development of a political and normative infrastructure, which can use propaganda myths of origin to mobilize the population. Hence war and annexation itself may generate and accentuate ethnic consciousness.[9] In many cases, annexation results in a pattern of internal colonialism, in which residents of an annexed area are deprived of certain civil liberties or equality with the metropole, underscoring a sense of ethnic distinctiveness.

A third type of intergroup sequence is *involuntary, or forced, migration*. This often occurs in colonized areas where the indigenous population is small or cannot be subdued into labor. For example, the demand for cheap workers on agricultural plantations and in extractive industries in the colonial Americas and in the independent United States produced a system of slave transfers and indentured and contract labor. The subordination of migrants in this situation is ensured through coercive control, political exclusion, and economic dependence.

Finally, *voluntary migration* refers to the movement of numerically smaller groups to a larger society. This includes such patterns as the internal migration of groups from one area within a state to another, the admission of temporary or permanent immigrants into a host society, sojourners, and the reception of political refugees and displaced peoples. In every case but the last, such movements tend to be labor transfers, generated by the economic needs of the host area. The likelihood of stratification in any case depends on the extent of competition with indigenous workers and the power resources available to the incoming groups and hence is shaped by the political eonomy of the host country and the political solidarity and organization of the groups in contact. Insofar as the migrants are voluntary, they are more likely to be open to the culture of the host society or to adapt themselves to an occupational niche which does not compete with the positions of indigenous workers. Perhaps the exception here are sojourners, who understand themselves to be temporary migrants, with enduring connections to the homeland.[10] Insofar as the host society can incorporate migrants into its economy without labor competition, it is likely to adopt policies that encourage social integration or that tolerate and accommodate cultural difference. However, to the extent that these migrants compete with indigenes for scarce resources (land, jobs, schooling), the pressure for exclusionary policies will increase. The response of the host society will depend in this case on the distribution of power within the core state. For example, in a situation of labor migration such as the "guest workers" in Western Europe, the collective power of trade unions and the number of jobs available have together shaped the availablity of schooling, social services, and labor benefits to the sojourners.[11]

These sequences of intergroup contact can certainly overlap in time and space. The patterns of ethnic stratification in the United States, for example, have been conditioned by all of these sequences: limited settlement and the conquest and annexation of the lands of the native peoples; a more extensive settlement and colonization resulting in forced slave transfers and indentured servitude; contract labor and massive voluntary migrations with the emergence of an industrial economy; the annexation of contiguous and noncontiguous areas; and the admission of political refugees. The reception accorded each entering group was shaped by its political and economic resources upon arrival, by the degree of competition for labor and land at that particular time, and by the extent of cultural differentiation from the dominant group. Thus there cannot be a single model for the structuring of ethnic contact and the resultant patterns of stratification. Rather, one must examine three factors: (1) the political economy and development of groups prior to contact, which determine their power differentials and whether they will be in a competitive position vis-á-vis one another; (2) the socioeconomic interests of the groups at the point of contact (again a product of political development and social organization), which shape the likelihood of direct competition; and (3) cultural differences between groups, which allow for ethnocentric justifications of interests and actions.

This typology appears to have little *explanatory* value for students of ethnic mobilization. It does identify variables that can be observed and quantified—and hence can determine the likelihood of forms of stratification developing. But it does not explain how ethnic stratification produces particular political outcomes. To understand this process, we must turn to the scholarship on resource competition and the dynamics of economic and political development.

RESOURCE COMPETITION AND ETHNIC MOBILIZATION

Given contact and competition between two groups with distinct cultures and differences in power, what will the powerless group do? My basic assumption is that the members of each ethnic group will behave in ways to maximize their own perceived interest, acting in accord with some calculation of resources, organization, and likely outcome. Since individual competition would dissolve group boundaries, individuals must be persuaded to compete as inclusive groups.[12] It is worth restating and underscoring my earlier argument that ethnicity itself constitutes a potent, if intangible, resource for mobilizing and organizing individuals in pursuit of a claimed collective interest, precisely because it combines interest and affective ties. "Claims are made on the basis of ascriptive or group identity, rather than individual achievement, and this is reinforced by the nature of the political process, which emphasizes some group coherence, as a means of being effective in that arena."[13] When several cultural attributes are combined with distinctive interests, there tends to be a multiplier effect, reinforcing the appeal of ethnic politics. Nevertheless, cultural attributes are only *potential* resources; and ethnic interests are only one set of concerns for any individual. We need to look more closely at how class and state structures encourage or discourage ethnic politics.

STRATIFICATION, COMPETITION, AND ETHNIC MOBILIZATION IN PREINDUSTRIAL SETTINGS

As the foregoing analysis indicates, many forms of ethnic stratification can result from intergroup competition, depending on the resources available to each group and the degree of ethnocentrism of each group. In preindustrial settings, stratification can range from ethnoregional domination along the lines specified by internal colonial and uneven development models to a split labor market generated by differential privileges granted to colonial settlers from the metropole or to forced or contract labor on agricultural plantations. An exhaustive examination of all possible patterns is beyond my purview here; but a few general observations can be made to show how the resource competition argument can be applied in different preindustrial settings.

At first glance, we could assume that ethnic politics would be especially strong in precapitalist, sedentary farming communities. Prior to invasion or conquest, agricultural communities are often characterized by what Orlando Patterson has called "kin hegemonic" organization: patriarchal family-based leadership, intense localized networks, solidarity, religious symbols that reflect the local nucleus, and shared legends and myths of territoriality. Such communities are not necessarily egalitarian. Certain families may have amassed greater economic resources, through hoarding a surplus and through intermarriage with other hoarders. Leaders, especially religious figures, are singled out for respect and influence.[14] When colonization, annexation, or some other form of competition for land takes place, the strong localism provides the interpersonal networks, and agrarian mores and customs provide the distinctive identities and leadership necessary for ethnic mobilization.

On the other hand, we could also predict in such settings that some members of the newly subordinate group will see real advantages in aligning themselves with the dominant group: "those deprived under the old regime who are likely to regard an external presence as protective, those with high social and economic stakes who stand to lose in unsuccessful resistance or in mobilizing less favored groups," or even religious leaders who may seek to become part of the new state apparatus or to have their elite status reinforced.[15] As we shall see in greater detail in the next chapter, such collaboration with the dominant group was the case in New France, when it was annexed by the English. The colonial government secured the compliance of the agrarian French settlers by granting special political privileges to the clerical elite and their political allies. These leaders then sustained their own elite positions by arguing that resistance to and competition with the dominant English would destroy French culture and the special religious mission of the settler community "to possess the earth, to spread ideas, to cling to the soil, to raise large families, to maintain the hearths of intellectual and spiritual life."[16]

In contrast, where there is no significant class differentiation within the subordinate group, a politics of collaboration is less likely. In such cases, ethnic mobilization will be constrained more by the resources available to the subordinates and the degree of coercive control exercised by the dominant class. Numerous studies indicate that enslaved Africans in the United States rationally calculated the extent of coercive control in the hands of the planter class and adopted a politics of resistance through apparent accommodation. This included individual mechanisms of survival, such as assuming the characteristics dictated by racial stereotyping to secure advantages within the slave system. As in French Canada, the most important arena was the religious one. But this was a religion which did not counsel acceptance of a social structure. Instead, it stressed the injustice of the slaves' position and a message of salvation in the "next world" beyond the slave system. This combination of a religious and a secular vision of emancipation repudiated the ideological authority of the dominant group without jeopardizing the safety and survival of the slaves. It functioned to forge an ethnic solidarity and shared political vision and so constituted the seedbed for more overt forms of action.[17]

There was a clear difference between the religious nativism of French Canadians and the messianic vision of Afro-American slaves. Both embraced a holistic vision of religious mission and identity. But, in the former case, it was the effort of an ethnic elite to justify its own interests through what Ralph Linton has called "rational nativism," which seeks to maintain an old order and to justify that desire by an appeal to cultural symbols.[18] In the latter case, it was a reflection of the powerlessness of an oppressed class which recognized the futility of direct challenge. To summarize, an understanding of the patterns of ethnic politics in preindustrial societies requires that we consider the ways in which the elite of a dominant ethnic group will utilize its political and economic resources to constrain the possible options for action. Special attention should be paid to the extent to which the traditional leaders in the subordinate group are drawn into the state.

Regardless of the particular structuring of class and ethnicity, however, research indicates that ethnic mobilization in preindustrial societies tends to be shortlived, sporadic, and localized. Without extensive communication and networks developed between communities, the members of a colonized region or dominated group are likely to experience their exploitation and to calculate their resources in a highly localized way.[19] We should look more carefully at how capitalist development and industrialization are likely to alter preindustrial stratification systems and generate new political resources.

DEVELOPMENT, COMPETITION, AND ETHNIC MOBILIZATION

As we have seen in chapter 1, scholars are in some dispute about the effects of development on ethnic relations. Most agree that political and economic development is not an even, uniform process—ethnic regions may persist, sustaining traditional communities and reinforcing a geoethnic division of resources or an ethnically split labor market. Industrialists may manipulate ethnic antagonisms through discrimination and job segregation. The resource competition model shares with some neo-Marxist theories the assumption that capitalist development may make ethnicity more, rather than less, significant—but it does not predict that this is a product simply of continued *economic* segregation or stratification. Rather, it argues that the processes of development are likely to increase competition between ethnic groups in a number of areas. According to Joane Nagel and Susan Olzak, who have synthesized the recent resource competition literature, there are five interlocking processes of development which facilitate ethnic mobilization: urbanization, increased scales of organization, expansion of the secondary and tertiary sectors of the economy, political expansion, and the establishment of supranational organizations.[20]

Urbanization, industrialization, and the concomitant expansion of secondary and tertiary economic sectors produce new interests and new resources, enhancing both the likelihood of ethnic competition and the ability of groups to act on their interests. For example, as labor markets become relatively more fluid, the level of direct contact between previously separated groups may increase and generate intergroup job competition. "Employers may try to lower wages or break up labor organizing efforts by opening formerly segregated job markets . . . or organized ethnic groups themselves can attempt to corner job or commodity markets for purposes of economic advancement."[21] Moreover, challenges to ethnic stratification are more likely in a developing urban economy. Ethnic associational networking is more easily accomplished in urban areas than in agrarian settings. Groups may be residentially segregated (either by choice or discrimination). Ethnic leaders can utilize developing neighborhood and urban networks to mobilize the populace and to persuade others that solidary mobilization is in their collective interest. A concentrated population also provides a base for the expansion of ethnic institutions and the genesis of new organizations. This institutional diversification can create more autonomy from traditional leaders who may have accommodated to ethnic stratification. Consequently, the possibility is enhanced not only for ethnic mobilization but for new forms and ideologies of ethnic politics.[22]

Similarly, the introduction of supranational organizations alters the traditional distribution of power resources and bases for competition. Multinational corporations, for example, can provide the elites of the dominant group with new resources (e.g., managerial positions in the corporate outposts), but they can also erode the power of those elites by displacing traditional ethnic industries, undermining local capital and its control over the labor market, and increasing the likelihood of ethnic competition.[23] But not all bases for mobilization are economic. In contrast to the neo-Marxist models, resource competition theorists emphasize the varying kinds of interests produced by development processes.

Expansion of the state sector through introduction of welfare systems and increased state-private planning introduces new arenas for ethnic competition, as individuals seek positions within a growing administrative bureaucracy. State intervention in the economy (for industrial and development planning, resource acquisition, wage labor and price regulation) and in the social sector (schooling, housing, social services) makes access to and acquisition of state power more crucial.[24] State development can also underscore the connection between cultural differences and individual interests. For example, where language or religious differences exist, the difficulties of securing power or competing in a larger heterogeneous political body are intensified by the numerous potential arenas of conflict: schools, courts, legislature, and industry.[25] Like industrialization and capitalist growth, this expansion of state activity can erode the hegemony of traditional ethnic elites, increasing the possibilities for new leadership within a subordinate ethnic group.

Finally, state actions and ideologies can provide substantial resources for competing groups and can shape the direction of political mobilization. The dissemination of principles of self-determination, of distributive justice, and of the right of oppressed or colonized nations to self-governance serves to encourage ethnic demands. And when states institutionalize this recognition, they may "demarcate and activate ethnic boundaries. Civil rights laws, constitutional guarantees of regional or ethnic equality and rights of redress through legal and judicial channels all target and define given populations, perhaps emphasizing an ethnic boundary over some other potential boundary."[26]

To place the argument on a more theoretical level, we can expect ethnic mobilization to occur under a range of circumstances:

1. Where a hierarchical ethnic division of resources exists within a state system (either regionally or through a cultural division of labor);
2. Where shifts in labor market composition and job opportunity generate greater intergroup competition;
3. Where urbanization increases intergroup contact and competition for control of residential territory;
4. Where bureaucratization and centralization of the state erode the competitive advantages of classes within the dominant ethnic group and the leadership of the traditional elite within the subordinate group;
5. Where ethnic institutions in urban neighborhoods provide a base for networks, organization, and mobilization;
6. Where principles of ethnic group rights and self-determination have been broadly disseminated and appeals can be made linking these to traditional group values.

This model allows us to examine varying bases for ethnic politics and to appreciate the numerous forms which such politics may assume—but it does not explain the conditions under which that mobilization is likely to result in separatism. To which members of competing groups is separatism likely to appeal? And how is that appeal then made more generally? Why should individuals invest in a separatist movement?

THE PROMISE OF ETHNIC NATIONALISM

Certainly, the appeal of separatist ideologies depends significantly on the governmental structure. Liberal assimilationist governments which grant equal rights to individuals are less conducive to nationalist claims than corporate pluralist states in which ethnicity is formally recognized as an aspect of citizenship. However, government action or inaction contributes just as much as government structure to the appeal of separatism. Discrimination and/or failure to take ethnic grievances seriously will tend to produce a more solidary nationalist politics. "An approach which envisages the participation of the community in shaping its own local destinies will tend to head off the separatist appeal and support autonomist or communalist" or federalist options.[27]

Individuals must be persuaded, even in the face of government discrimination or inaction, that nationalism will bring them advantages. The material benefits of nationalism seem evident. Ethnically sovereign statehood can mean exclusive access to nationalized jobs, the transfer of control over goods (from natural resources to social services), and regulatory authority (taxation, budgets, trade relations). But not all material benefits will be distributed evenly. For example, in newly independent regions of economically developed societies, particular opportunities may be opened to an educated managerial class which can take over the reins of the state bureaucracy and industry. Industrial wage laborers and small entrepreneurs, on the other hand, may be no better off under the new regime and may be asked to suffer financial sacrifices. Are the collective aspects of nationalism, that is, the psychic benefits (ethnic pride, equal international status, a sense of self-determination), sufficient to persuade all members of the group to support such a movement and to compensate for possible material loss?[28] There is no single answer to this question; it depends in part on the available rival political ideologies.

Ethnic intellectuals play an important role in persuading individuals to invest in ethnic separatism rather than in assimilation, to view themselves as nations first rather than classes or members of a political interest group. There is no single intellectual class with identifiable interests that span all time and space. Intellectuals can include traditional religious leaders, educated citizens, and free-floating social commentators. Nonetheless, special attention can be paid to changes in the situation and status of those who are the purveyors of ideas within the ethnic group. The blocked occupational mobility and status aspirations of Western-educated intellectuals in the Third World has been well documented as a major source of anticolonial nationalist ideology. Similarly, a cultural division of labor in an expanding bureaucratic state may thwart the aspirations of minority ethnic intellectuals and provide them with a base for nationalist mobilization.[29]

Regardless of their own discontents, the intelligentsia must fashion a rationale for mobilization which can subsume the grievances of particular segments of the ethnic group into an appeal to the whole. Nationalism does this. Premised on the principle of self-determination, nationalism promises a realization of human aspirations for freedom and for community.[30] However, the persuasiveness of the separatist strategy depends on the preeminent ideas about self-determination in the particular historical period and community and the extent to which the intelligentsia incorporates these into its own nationalist vision. In a society in which religious leaders exercise great authority, the principles of liberation are likely to orient the population toward spiritual, rather than material, goods—and hence historicist ideas about class struggle will be eschewed. But spiritual emancipation can be wedded to nationalist ideology. For example, until World War II, the strength of ecclesiastical authority in French Canada ensured that the Enlightenment vision of popular sovereignty through an individual adherence to a social contract and later Marxist ideas of class struggle would be rejected in favor of an ideology of the national spiritual mission of the Quebecois. Only when the secularization and bureaucratization of the welfare state eroded clerical power and influence did intellectuals successfully replace this romantic nativism with a more secular version of self-determination.

SUMMARY

At the core of ethnic solidarity is the synergism between interest and affect, between the drive to meet material aspirations and the desire for identity within community. Distinguishable cultural markers can evoke a sense of similarity and commonality and simultaneously legitimate efforts to restrict access to valued social resources by excluding "them" from "our community." I have sought to sketch out in this chapter general conditions under which intergroup contact will trigger competition and ethnic politics. I have argued that the likelihood of ethnic mobilization is conditioned by the historical sequences of intergroup contact and consequent patterns of stratification between ethnic groups. Ethnic mobilization is most probable where there is an unequal division of resources in a state system along ethnic lines (either a cultural division of labor or regional stratification). However, the form such mobilization can take depends primarily on the interaction between class and ethnic stratification. This interaction is at the core of ethnic politics because it will condition the extent to which ethnic identity becomes institutionalized in the state and the economy and hence will shape subsequent reactions to development. In preindustrial societies, ethnic mobilization against a system of dominance depends upon the ways in which traditional leaders are incorporated into the ethnic and class elites and upon the degree of coercive powers in the hands of those elites. If mobilization does take place, it is likely to be local and sporadic. However, the processes of development greatly enhance the likelihood of ethnic mobilization insofar as they enhance competition between groups, alter traditional ethnic and class structures, and provide new resources for effective politicking. The likelihood that this mobilization will become a separatist movement depends on the ability of those interested in nationalist control of resources to wed the traditional symbols of group solidarity to widely shared principles of distributive justice and self-determination and to the interests of particular classes within the ethnic group.

In the next three chapters, I will seek to refine this sketch by tracing in detail how the recursive relations between class, state, and ethnic structures and processes of development are evident in the histories of Northern Ireland and Quebec.

3

Colonialism and the Origins of Ethnic Conflict

The colonization of Ireland and Canada was part of the strengthening and expansion of the great states of western Europe from the sixteenth through the eighteenth centuries. However, the colonizations began at different points, for distinct reasons, and followed dissimilar patterns. The colonization of Ireland was undertaken for two reasons: the need to consolidate Protestant power during the Reformation and the strategic importance of Ireland for the protection of England's boundaries and economic interests. The brutal conquest and subsequent subjugation of the indigenous populace resulted in two forms of colonization: limited settlement in the south and west, where the native population was denied any political rights and where control over the land was in the hands of administrators acting on behalf of absentee English landlords; and substantial settlement in the north by Scottish Presbyterians, who were granted some control over the land and some political rights. In Canada, French colonization occurred in the seventeenth century to provide the Crown with an outpost for trade in the New World. Settlement in seventeenth-century New England, on the other hand, was motivated by the need to solve problems of labor surplus and social conflict in the metropole, as well as to provide a base for trade. These different interests also resulted in distinctive patterns of colonization. New France was characterized by limited settlement, largely fur traders, merchants, and clerics, who were all oriented toward the enrichment of the metropole and motivated to avoid conflict with the indigenes. New England, however, experienced much more extensive settlement, competition for land, and conflict with the native populace. Its colonists acquired significant political power and some control over the reinvestment of their economic surplus.

In both Ireland and Canada, these differing forms of colonization produced a power disparity between the major groups. The subsequent development of ethnic stratification derived in large part from the differing relations of the colonists with the metropolitan state and the resulting inequalities in economic and political resources. Hence before comparing these two cases it is really necessary to examine them individually in order to appreciate the significance of different sources and patterns of colonization. I will begin in each case with a consideration of the political economy before intergroup contact in order to understand the extent of power differentials, grounds for ethnocentrism, and bases for competition. I will then examine the patterns of colonization, the resultant ethnic stratification, and the ways in which these shaped the solidarity and political actions of the subordinate ethnic groups. As I pointed out in chapter 2, sectors of a colonized populace may be incorporated into the colonial elite, as administrators or as commercial middlemen. To the extent that these collaborators share in the benefits of colonization and cultivate linkages with the metropole, they may secure some concessions for the indigenous population, but they will be unlikely to challenge the system itself. This was the case in Canada, where the Catholic church served as the protector of the French language and cultural traditions and, at the same time, helped maintain the economic subordinance of the French settlers by discouraging economic and class competition. Such colonial patrimonialism was also the case for the Scottish Presbyterians in the north of Ireland, who secured particular religious and economic rights exclusive to the Ulster settlers. There are, then, two lines of analysis in this chapter: the conflicts *between* ethnic groups, generated by the patterns of colonization; and the divergence of interests *within* ethnic groups, shaping political resources, goals, and efficacy.

CONQUEST, COLONIZATION, AND THE ORIGINS OF ETHNIC STRATIFICATION IN IRELAND

At the time of the Anglo-Norman invasion of Ireland in 1169, Ireland was not a single political entity but was divided into a number of autonomous kingdoms, organized on the basis of pastoral communalism and seminomadic patterns of seasonal migration between pastures. Land was held in common and clan chiefs governed by the sufferance of the people. The major social ties between kingdoms were language and religion.[1] The seminomadic economy, tribal political organization, and decentralized church system of Ireland contrasted with the sedentary agriculture characteristic of the Anglo-Normans, the concentration of feudal power in the centralizing state, and the close links with the Roman Catholic church. Indeed, Ireland's social structure was perceived by Europeans as primitive. The Anglo-Norman invasion was strongly supported by Pope Adrian in language which reflected their ethnocentrism. He argued that Henry II's conquest provided an opportunity to "enlarge the bounds of the Church, to teach the truth of Christian faith to the ignorant and rude, and to extirpate the roots of vice from the field of the Lord."[2] However, Henry lacked sufficient resources to colonize the island. The effort was effective only within the Pale, a narrow strip of land which included Dublin and its environs, on the southeastern edge of Ireland. Within the Pale and in the metropole, the Irish were viewed as savages, whose religion was at best a pagan adaptation of Christianity and whose tribal organization appeared primitive to the strong feudal state. Those few invaders who ventured outside the Pale were gradually absorbed by the Irish, adopting their language and customs.

Although the Irish remained under titular English jurisdiction throughout the Middle Ages, it was not until the reigns of Henry VIII and Elizabeth I that the monarchy sought to strengthen its power over these nominal subjects.[3] Serious colonization and the effective imposition of English dominance began with the nationalization of the Church of England and the efforts to prevent an alliance between the 89 percent Catholic island and the Continental powers. In 1541 an act of Parliment declared Henry VIII King of Ireland and made the Irish chiefs vassals and subject to English law. To reinforce his political control, Henry granted plantations to English landholders and levied high settlement rates on Catholic tenants. It was not until the Elizabethan era, however, that significant efforts to secure control over all of Ireland were undertaken. From 1565 onward, the Crown organized and encouraged individual colonization schemes to replace Irish peasants with English planters. Private troops were engaged to suppress any resistance to the plantations; those tribal leaders who rebelled were executed or enslaved; communities were massacred or forced into special res-

35

ervations. And as Nicolas Canny has pointed out, the colonization was justified by ethnocentric claims about the savage and unchristian Irish, who "live like beasts, voide of lawe and all good order . . . more uncivill, more uncleanly, more barbarous and more brutish in their customs and demeanures, than in any other part of the world that is known."[4]

By 1590 Ulster was the only one of Ireland's four provinces that was entirely free from English domination. There, under the leadership of Hugh O'Neill, the Irish fiercely resisted English plantation. In 1595 the O'Neill clan defeated twenty thousand troops dispatched to quell the Ulsterites. This victory swept the entire island into resistance, and the Spanish promised to send arms in support of the Irish. But Ireland was outmanned and outarmed, and in 1603 O'Neill was defeated. The "flight of the earls" (the preeminent O'Neill clan, which had led the resistance against English dominance) from Ulster to the Continent in 1607 marked the complete conquest of the island.

The struggle between the Irish and the English for control of this territory exhibited the necessary conditions for a system of ethnic stratification: significant cultural differences had underscored English ethnocentric attitudes from the earliest contact; but religion was made even more salient given the political struggle of the Protestant monarchy with Catholic Spain, Portugal, and Rome. The prospect of an alliance between Ireland and Catholic Continental powers increased the value of control over Irish land. No longer would policies of accommodation or assimilation suffice. Ireland was to be subjugated; and the Crown had sufficient resources to effect that subjugation. But it was the new colonization schemes which established the pattern of ethnic stratification. In 1607 James I passed a series of settlement acts, designed to guarantee Crown dominance and to increase plantation revenues. Large tracts of land were confiscated and granted exclusively to Crown-appointed Englishmen, called undertakers, who brought over English and lowland Scots peasants to populate the estates. The scheme worked only in the easily protected coastal areas of the northeast province of Ulster in the counties of Down and Antrim, where 150,000 Scots and 20,000 English migrated.[5] In that area, the Irish were relegated to a series of small reservations and were restricted to these on penalty of death.[6]

To those Scots who settled in Ulster, the land was not unfamiliar. Sea passages across the North Channel were not infrequent, and the cultural correspondence between the two areas was extensive; rural housing patterns and most patterns of folk customs and festivals were similar.[7] However, the Scots and Irish did differ in two important respects. In contrast to the Gaelic-speaking Irish Catholics, the new immigrants were generally English speaking and Protestant. Such differences alone may not have produced any conflict; but the settlers also constituted a classic frontier society, surrounded by a native populace which had been displaced from its land and which challenged their property. They depended on the metropole for protection from periodic Catholic raids, and in turn they served the Crown as a foothold for capital growth and as a bastion of Protestant support. It was in this context that ethnicity acquired its significance and that patrimonial relations between the colonial settlers and the metropole developed.

The Scots immigrants also brought to Ulster experience with commodity farming and skills at linen manufacture.[8] Military protection combined with a system of land tenure (long fixed leases, no rent increase on improved land—later known as the "Ulster Custom") attracted immigrant to Ireland and provided the new settlers with a stable basis for the growth of cottage industry. With such political protection and the natural advantages of the region (a harbor area, waterpower, the rich Lagan Valley with corridors easily reaching other parts of the northeast), a marketing infrastructure quickly grew in Ulster. By the 1650s the economy in the north of Ireland was characterized by the general spread of low-level capital among the settlers.

If the colonization schemes brought economic benefits to the settlers in Ulster, the effects on the indigenous populace were devastating. Legislation did permit the undertakers to take Irish tenants on reserved areas of their estates, generally those of poorer quality, in towns bordering the upland areas, which were marginal for farming. By 1659 English and Scots settlers constituted 37 percent of the households in the province of Ulster, but the densities ranged from 11 percent in Upland County Monaghan to 45 percent in lowland Antrim.[9] Forced to surrender all but the worst-quality land in the north, the Catholics remained near the settlers, "a standing challenge to the property of the new settlers and to their religion."[10] In the south, where plantation was resisted by Anglo-Irish landholders, the natives were restricted to the land on sufferance leases. Development of this land was constantly undermined by shifts in metropolitan policies caused by the changing English market demands for specialized agricultural produce. The system of land tenure was characterized by a complex system of middlemen, of interests within interests, and subtenancies. This infused capital into England and weakened the development of the economy in the south. With no rights to resist exorbitant rents or arbitrary eviction, it was futile for native peasants to attempt land improvements.

The mere fact of ethnic stratification does not tell the full story of clashing interests and politics between settlers and natives. I have already pointed out that the Protestant settlers, especially in the north, constituted a frontier society, surrounded by a large dispossessed Catholic population. At several junctures in the seventeenth century, the tensions between these populations exploded, triggered by the parliamentary struggles in England. An analysis of these instances of ethnic mobilization is important, because it is instructive about the emergence of the earliest expression of Protestant politics of "loyalism" and the political process by which an ethnically split labor market was produced.

When Charles I attempted to impose a new Anglican liturgy on the Church of Scotland, Presbyterians throughout the British Isles expressed revulsion at what they considered his "papish innovations" and mobilized in resistance. This schism between settler and Crown was an opportunity for the Irish, and in 1641 northern Catholics attacked the Presbyterian settlements. The settlers found themselves in a contradictory position: they opposed Charles's religious reforms, but they needed his protection. In a covenant signed by Presbyterians throughout Ulster, the settlers proposed a conditional loyalty "to preserve and defend the King's person and authority in the preservation and defense of the true religion and liberties of the kingdom."[11] This agreement instituted the conditions for loyalism among the Presbyterian settlers: loyalty to the king was predicated on de facto protection of Presbyterian religious liberty and property. Charles's belated signature thrust Presbyterian settlers into firm support of Cromwell and his challenge to the throne. The few remaining Catholic landholders supported the Crown, hoping that Charles would protect their land claims. The Anglican landholders wavered between the two, distrustful of Cromwell's Puritanism but cognizant of his growing power. The Catholic peasantry saw the struggle as an opportunity to secure their lands. The Civil War was

marked by virulent fighting in Ulster between Catholics and Protestants. The fighting was finally quelled when Cromwell invaded
Ireland, massacred the rebels, confiscated 8 million of Ireland's
12.5 million arable acres, and distributed these to his army and
loyal supporters. When this was added to the land already owned
by settlers and absentee landlords, Catholics possessed only 14 percent of the land base (only 5 percent in Ulster).[12]

The death of Cromwell and subsequent dynastic struggle precipitated another major ethnic war in Ireland. Under James II land was
restored to those Catholic gentry who were prepared to support the
king and his army. To Presbyterians, James' overtures to Catholics
signaled his lack of fidelity to a Protestant Crown. Ulster Protestants rose up behind William of Orange; and when James fled to
Ireland, the Presbyterian Apprentice Boys locked him out of the
city of Derry, resolving "to stand on our guard and defend our
walls and not to admit any papish whatsoever to quarter among us,
so we have fairly and succinctly determined to preserve in our duty
and loyalty to our sovereign Lord the King, without the least um-
brage of inviting seditious opposition."[13] This was not simply a
laager mentality. In the populist consciousness of the Ulster frontier, religious and economic interests were coterminous. Catholics
were seen as de facto disloyal subjects, by virtue of their religion.
Therefore any economic liberties ceded to them were evidence of a
fissure between God and Crown and a violation of the covenant of
loyalism. With the victory of William at the Battle of the Boyne in
1690, such violations were finally prevented. A system of ethnic
stratification was firmly cemented in Ireland.

Under William, the Anglo-Protestant Ascendancy consolidated
its position by eliminating all traditional laws and enacting the
Penal Codes, a series of laws which relegated Irish Catholics to the
social margins. The harshness of these laws, which excluded Catholics from sitting in Parliament, holding government office, possessing arms, operating schools, acquiring land, and even from
owning a horse worth over five pounds, induced Catholic gentry
to emigrate, and only a handful of tradesmen, professionals, and
landowners remained. Those who still held land did so only under
the protection of Anglicans. To secure the island to English control
and ensure that the Irish lacked any institutional basis for resistance, the Penal Codes attacked the corporate Catholic church as
well. The bishops were banished; no Mass could be performed un-

less the priest took an oath of allegiance to the king and Church of England.[14] Enforcement of the Penal Codes combined with the land tenure system to reinforce the uneven economic development and ethnic stratification of colonial Ireland.

ETHNIC STRATIFICATION AND MOBILIZATION IN IRELAND IN THE EIGHTEENTH CENTURY

In the south of Ireland the land system was characterized by absentee ownership and a complex hierarchy of middlemen. The result of this structure was an infusion of rents into England, increasing from eight hundred thousand pounds in 1670 to two million pounds in 1720. And unlike the patrimonial relations between landlords and renters in the settlements of the north, there was no sense of mutual obligation in the rest of Ireland. Richard Kee characterizes the social relations of production in southern Ireland: "The Irish peasant lived on sufferance, paying the highest possible rent that could be extracted from him. He had neither rights against exorbitant rents nor against arbitrary eviction, whether paying rent or not, nor rights to any improvements he might carry out. In fact, to carry out improvements at all was undesirable because to do so only raised the value of the land and thus the rent."[15] The most burdensome aspects of the land tenure system were the dependency of the tenants on British regulation of grain prices and their inability to protect investments in the land. The dominance of the metropolitan legislature over land use ensured that protectionist measures (heavy tariffs, restrictions on export and trade, embargoes on produce) were consistently adopted in the interests of English landholders, with particularly disastrous effects on the peasantry.[16] A poor harvest or a fall in grain prices left tenants with insufficient income to pay the rent and also care for their families.

Peasant outbursts were frequent during the eighteenth century. Local tenant associations had developed throughout Ireland as loci for recreation (cockfights, dances, wakes, markets) and for ritualized forms of peasant justice. Feuds between individual peasants were often worked out through these quasi-political, quasi-recreational associations. Gradually these evolved into more formal, secret societies for reacting to landlord and government exactions. In the south of Ireland, agrarian outbursts were almost exclusively nonsectarian, since there was little direct competition with Dissenters and since the landlords were the major and immediate source of grievance. Although the outbursts can be correlated with particular policies (e.g., requirements that peasants repair the roads without pay, imposition of a new tax), they were local and sporadic, focusing on individual landlords and constituting what have been called "primitive rebellions," rather than political movements.[17]

The combination of the land system, political exclusion, and poverty in the south inhibited the growth of an internal market and an urban middle class there. In contrast, because of the Ulster Custom and favorable ethnic position, in rural Ulster cottage and textile industries, a brewing industry, and relatively successful small-scale agriculture developed. And in Belfast and Derry, a small mercantile class emerged to manage trade and commerce. But all of Ireland was a colony. That the Crown did not see a particular affinity for or obligation to the economic interests of the settlers was evident in the protectionist measures that were adopted from plantation forward in the interests of metropolitan landholders and merchants. In 1665 export of dairy products to England was banned; in 1680 a regulation was passed requiring that Irish trade take place on English ships; in 1699 Irish woolens were excluded from English markets; and after 1720 all brewers were required to purchase hops in England.[18] Both rural peasants and the urban commercial class felt the negative impact of such regulations. Moreover, after William's death, Dissenters were no longer exempt from the Penal Codes. Sacramental tests kept Presbyterians out of state administrative posts and hence restricted their voice on commercial matters.

Throughout the seventeenth century, the government of Ireland was a paper tiger, unable and often unwilling to mediate conflicts of interest of Anglo-Irish landlords and English mercantilists. In fact, between 1586 and 1692, the Parliament had sat in Dublin for a total of only fifteen years. In 1719 the dependency of the Irish government was underscored when the English Parliament passed a Declaratory Act, guaranteeing English control over all Irish legislation. Ulster was particularly vulnerable to imperial protectionist measures, since it relied on England for its markets in agricultural produce and in linens, wool, and other domestic manufacturing products. The small urban mercantile class suffered deeply from differential taxation and protectionist measures. And thousands emigrated to America, where by the mid–eighteenth century, they formed a sixth of the population.[19] Those who remained in Ulster, like those who emigrated, were to form the core of the colonial nationalist struggles of the late eighteenth century. Increasingly they were willing to ally themselves with the small Catholic middle class. The situation was strikingly different however for rural farmers and craftworkers. Having established an ethnically split labor market through the Ulster Custom, neither the Crown nor the settler bourgeoisie could easily undo it. The forms which ethnic conflict took and the outcomes of these conflicts in the mid and late eighteenth century illustrate this well.

The success of landed metropolitan interests in imposing high trade restrictions on Irish agricultural commodities did not go unfelt in rural Ulster. Beginning in the 1740s Anglo-Irish landlords throughout Ireland were forced to reduce the acreage for planting and to shift to grazing. The inevitable and awful effect was massive displacement of tenants and escalating competition for land. In Ulster landowners relinquished their traditional religious patronage and began to replace Protestant tenants with Catholics who were willing to pay the higher rents and to farm on smaller plots. This abandonment of an "understood" covenant embittered the Presbyterian tenant farmers, for whom "the combination of domestic industry and small scale agriculture had been the sheet rock and their most valuable economic asset."[20] Secret paramilitary groups, such as the Peep O'Day Boys, the Oakboys, and the Hearts of Steel, sprang up in Ulster, attacking both landlords and Catholics and demanding a return to the covenent of Protestant loyalism. The Hearts of Steel sought perpetual leases of land at the present values, with Catholics excluded from renting; in County Armagh, the Peep O'Day Boys banded together to prevent Catholics from bidding for Protestant farms and expressed their fury at landlords who would turn out good Presbyterian tenants for "Papists who will pay any rent."[21] They succeeded in driving an estimated seven hundred Catholic families out of the Armagh area in 1795. Not all agrarian outbursts were sectarian. In Antrim and Down, Protestant tenants used secret societies to pressure for the abolition of tithes, county cess taxes, and other state impositions. The sectarian structure of these parapolitical groups provided a fertile turf for the growth of ethnic antagonism. Eventually, it far exceeded the competition between Catholic and Dissenting peasants and workers.[22]

A second source of competition and ethnic mobilization occurred in the weaving industries. Because of the extensive cottage industries which Scots settlers had the resources to develop, weaving was until the late 1770s an almost exclusively Protestant industry. The craftworkers organized associations similar to the rural peasant groups and gradually developed the Orange Society as their locus for recreation and trade concerns. If the ethnic exclusivity of the craft was largely the result of economic history, to "the weavers of Armagh [it] constituted a recognition by manufacturers of the traditional obligations to loyalties which many landlords had recognized before."[23] Consequently, when the introduction of power spinning in 1780 increased the opportunities for employing weavers and many manufacturers began to hire Catholics in their shops, the Orange journeymen went into action. Claiming a violation of the Ulster Custom, Presbyterian weavers responded to potential displacement by smashing the looms of Catholic families and attacking the mill owners and manufacturers who employed them.[24] Following a battle with Catholic tenant farmers in 1795, the craft and tenant associations consolidated in the Orange Society to secure their privileged position in the countryside.

Both on the land and in the craft shops in the late eighteenth century, ethnic conflict was rooted in the efforts of local capital to abandon the split labor market encouraged by the metropolitan colonizers. Protestant labor insisted on setting limits to the dominance of the landed elite; in so doing, they secured privilege within a system of ethnically defined patrimonial class relations. However, they were also victims of this patrimonialism, for their world view ensured the improbability of a secular class politics or a nationalist independence movement.

By the end of the eighteenth century, Ireland was more than an ethnically stratified tripartite society of Anglo-Irish and English landlords, Presbyterian settlers, and Irish peasants. A class and ethnic structure had developed in which each group had distinct relations to the metropole and to one another. Despite the dominance of Anglo-Irish and absentee English landlords over the peasants, this class was itself subject to the control of metropolitan interests. Large numbers of these landlords, however, capitulated to the metropole so long as they secured military support against peasant uprisings and for the collection of rents. Uneven regional development and an ethnically split labor market meant that Presbyterians experienced a degree of internal class differentiation as well as ethnic privilege. In contrast to rural Irish Catholics, Ulster Presbyterians could demand and shape the patrimonial relations with their landlords. As a result peasant and labor discontents ran in localized and sectarian channels. Ulster's commercial middle class, in contrast to Protestant peasants, had no patrimonial relation with the Crown and no history of collaboration. "This middle class was republican in politics, sympathised warmly with the rebellious American colonies and objected to the corrupt rule of the Irish landlords through the Irish parliament."[25]

During the American War of Independence, Britain was pressured to face this panoply of conflicting interests. While agrarian outbreaks escalated, the soldiers usually garrisoned in Ireland were dispatched to America. After France declared war on Britain, Irish landlords and the middle class established a militia, the Irish Volunteers, ostensibly to protect the coast from a French invasion. By 1781 this force numbered eighty thousand, providing considerable potential force to Irish politics. The following year, the Volunteers, under the leadership of Henry Grattan, organized a parliament and passed a declaration claiming Ireland as an independent country under a joint British Crown. To counter these efforts, the Crown made a series of concessions, repealing aspects of the Penal Codes which had disenfranchised Catholic landholders, expanding leasing rights, and rescinding some trade restrictions. But these efforts conciliated only the landholders. The removal of trade restrictions actually worked to the disadvantage of the peasantry, since the market in cattle encouraged landowners to shift from tillage and thus increased eviction rates. And the successes mobilized Ulster Protestants to extend their demands. In 1791 under the leadership of Theobald Wolfe Tone, they formed the United Irishmen to organize a republican independence movement.

Informed by the egalitarianism of French revolutionaries, the United Irishmen extended the demands to include the political rights of the subject masses and to oppose any vestiges of sectarianism. They forged an alliance with France, engaged military support, and sought to mobilize in the countryside. Appealing to the rural populace to support the movement, recalling the Gaelic past, stressing the grievances of the peasants, and challenging the legitimacy of English control, the United Irishmen sought to develop a secular nationalism. Despite the rational basis of their appeal, the United Irishmen were unable to sustain rural support. For one thing the leadership was largely urban and bourgeois, with few ties and limited contact with the countryside. They concentrated on issues that were the closest and most urgent for them (trade restrictions, parliamentary reforms) and gave short shrift to those pressing the peasantry. More important, they simply failed to recognize the nature and degree of sectarianism in rural Ireland. The nonsectarian claims of the nationalists were immediately suspect to rural Presbyterians, for whom religion was a symbol of economic position and social identity. The extent of the United Irishmen's myopia about sectarianism was evident when they incorporated the Catholic Defenders into the organization. This organization had formed in response to the Peep O'Day Boys and had expanded beyond Ulster on the principle that Catholics required constant defense against Protestant harassment. They often secured support for the United Irishmen by generating fears and rumors of Orange terrorism in the north. The effort to develop a united Irish nationalism foundered on the failure of Belfast's liberal Protestants to appreciate the nature and resilience of sectarian feelings in the country. In contrast, the colonialists recognized and manipulated these tensions.

Analyses of correspondence and political debates in this period indicate a general fear among imperialists of any union between Catholics and Dissenters. The claim of the Anglican Archbishop of Armagh about revisions in the Penal Codes was typical: "The worst of this is that it stands to unite Protestant and Papist and whenever that happens, goodbye to the English interest in Ireland forever."[26] The warning seemed justified when 30 (mostly urban) ministers and licentiates of Ulster's 183 Presbyterian congregations publicly supported the nationalists.[27] In response, Anglican men of power and influence joined the Orange Society and turned it to their imperial purposes: support for the metropolitan government. Loyalist associations were organized by the gentry; and Protestant Orangemen were armed and warned that they would lose their religious liberties and economic privileges were Ireland to separate from the Crown.[28]

The United Irishmen rebellion of 1798 was short and bloody, effectively undone by the limited resources of the rebels, meager support from France, poor coordination between Belfast and the south, and bad weather conditions which forced the withdrawal of the French military fleets. Its suppression effectively eliminated nonsectarian nationalism, for the imperialists had learned a strong lesson: whenever England was threatened by the possibility of a united Ireland, the state should "play the Orange hand" and exacerbate ethnic antagonisms.

COLONIZATION AND ETHNIC NATIONALISM IN IRELAND

This review of the social structure of colonial Ireland and resulting patterns of ethnic politics elucidates well the premises of the resource mobilization model sketched in the last chapter. As we have seen, the conditions for a system of ethnic stratification—ethnocentrism, competition for scarce resources, and differential access to power—were met during the extensive conquest and colonization of Ireland. Cultural differences between the English and Irish were substantial and were viewed by the colonizers as evidence of their superiority to the indigenes. Although such differences were less numerous between the Irish and the Scots, the political significance of religion at the time of migration made it more potent as a marker. Preservation of religious liberty was the symbol of colonization. For all groups, Irish land rather than labor was the valued and scarce resource: as a military outpost for the Crown and a source of rents, produce, and cattle for English landowners; as a base for grazing and farming for the natives; as a place for farming and cottage industry for the Scots immigrants. And there is little doubt of the greater power resources of the English Crown: larger armies, superior war technology, and a centralized command structure. The Scots, however, lacked any independent power base and depended on the Crown for protection and support. For this reason, the system of ethnic stratification was much more than the sheer dominance of a colonial power over a conquered territory. Rather, it was characterized by a patrimonial relation between the Scots immigrants and the metropole, deeply competitive relations between the settlers and the native populace, and enduring antagonism on the part of the indigenes toward their foreign and local landholders. And as Scots defined their class relations with landlords and with the Crown, they did so on the basis of privilege: their shared Protestant liberty required economic reciprocity. Hence, religion had a strong class component which cannot be easily separated from its ideological role.

The effects of Irish colonization on the class structure also reflect the basic assumptions of uneven development approaches. Granted some political and economic privileges, Scots immigrants were able to amass sufficient capital to develop a more differentiated class structure than the Irish populace. As a result, each class had different responses to and concerns about metropolitan dominance. Our review does not, however, support claims of uneven development theorists that the metropole sought to continually reproduce a Scots Protestant labor aristocracy in order to prevent anticolonial politics and a solidarity of Irish and Scots. Such solidarity was never evident in colonial Ireland. Rather, as split labor market and resource competition models suggest, the sustained privileges of Protestant workers were concessions, secured only through significant pressure when landlords or the Crown ignored what the Scots settlers insisted were their customary ethnic rights. The efforts of the king to abandon Protestant occupational rights during the Restoration precipitated the first wave of ethnic violence; later efforts of landlords to displace Protestant tenants and of manufacturers to hire Catholic workers precipitated the second. In short, ethnic conflicts were precipitated by political and economic changes that threatened to alter the existing distribution of resources—providing Catholics with increased ability to mobilize and threatening Protestants with a loss of privilege.

As expected for preindustrial societies, these politics were never "national" either in scope or in ideology. Although ethnic associations did provide the solidarity, numbers, and organization for political action, those associations were highly local operations, and ethnic outbreaks therefore tended to be shortlived and limited to particular counties. Until the United Irishmen, there were no internal efforts at coordinating politics throughout the island. As important, the settlers never expressed demands in terms of rights as members of the Empire, as Scotsmen, or as Ulsterites—but as Orangemen, Oakboys, and Protestants. Similarly, the major Catholic association, the Defenders, did not develop an ideology of the Irish nation—but rather of the need to protect the Catholic peasant. Most of those involved in the struggles of 1798 had little ideological or organizational perception of a *national* movement. The outbreaks that occurred were relatively autonomous from one another. And there is little evidence that the ideology of republicanism had penetrated the rural areas of Ireland, or that Orangemen expressed a deep attachment to the British Crown. Rather, the sectarian conflicts and the economic interests of the Defenders and the Orangemen were utilized by both the nationalist leaders and the state to secure their support in the struggle between the Irish middle class and Britain. Without extensive communication networks and institutional links among the rural counties, principles of national self-determination seemed vague and unrelated to local concerns.

COLONIZATION, CONQUEST, AND THE ORIGINS OF ETHNIC STRATIFICATION IN CANADA

Although Canada presents a benign picture in contrast to the dramatic colonization of Ireland, this country also lives in the shadow of a history riddled with ethnic conflict and competition.

As a European colony, Canada was originally explored and colonized by the French, whereas British energies were concentrated farther south in the New England and Middle Atlantic regions. Because of internal religious conflicts and efforts at political consolidation in Europe and its primary focus on the West Indies, the French Crown did not invest many resources in the early development of this colony, leaving it largely to the attention of missionaries and private fur traders. The development of an entrepreneurial class that might compete with metropolitan France was strongly discouraged; and the export trade was carried on largely by employers of merchants resident in France. The state also excluded lawyers from the colony and permitted only Crown appointees to hold any administrative posts.[29] The English, in contrast, adopted a more vigorous plan of colonization, seeking to create a permanent community of Englishmen overseas, which would absorb the massive metropolitan labor surplus, produce crops that could not be raised in the metropole, and serve as a base for mercantilist expansion.[30]

This different emphasis had significant consequences for the patterns of settlement and economic development in the New World. Although explored by Cartier in 1534, by 1636 only 200 Frenchmen resided in all of Canada; and between 1608, when Quebec was officially claimed for France, and 1663, when the government assumed direct control of the colony, settlers totaled only 1,200. By 1690 the immigrant populace had increased to 10,000.[31] After a century of colonial rule, only about 170,000 acres were under cultivation.[32] In contrast, Boston alone received 12,000 immigrants in the years 1630–1642. By 1759 the English-speaking colonies had a population of 1,600,000 settlers, whereas New France had only 55,000.[33]

The social structure and administration of New France mirrored but did not duplicate that of the metropole.[34] Authority rested with royal ministers, land was distributed to settlers according to the feudal seigneurial system, and the clergy played a significant political role (with their own lobby in France).[35] The settlements, though sparse, were highly organized and were concentrated along the Saint Lawrence River. Jean Charles Falardeau has described the settlement pattern that permitted residents to farm large tracts while avoiding isolation: "Each settler built his house at the extreme end of the farm facing the river, not far from that of his neighbor, with the result that an uninterrupted string of houses known as 'la cote' stretched gradually along the St. Lawrence and the rivers. . . . When all the land along the rivers was occupied, another row or rang of houses was built one mile from the coast and parallel to it; later a second rang or row a mile further and so on. . . . The seigneury was a vast rectangle, stripped with equidistant rangs. The parish itself, a wide territorial framework, could hardly succeed at first in concentrating the population spread out along the ribbon like never ending roads."[36]

In theory, feudalism was transplanted in the New World, its exercise in the seigneury was quite lax. Tenants paid few taxes and exercised freedom of tenure so long as minimal rents and services were provided. The resident seigneurs were a heterogeneous collection of merchants, clergy, soldiers, and peasants, hardly conducive to a solidary hierarchy. In many cases the Crown appointed a capitaine de la milice from among the settlers, thereby further reducing the seigneurs' formal power. Furthermore, the extremely uniform pattern and social isolation of the *rangs* produced an ethos of mutual assistance and social reciprocity.[37]

During the entire period of French rule, not a single part of the rural territory was organized into a town. Thus the parish, a wide diffuse area, began to serve the functions of political administration. In the rangs and among the traders, the Catholic church played an important integrative role and became the major social institution and primary force in the formation of a French Canadian identity. The lack of a common law and an assembly or municipal council and the nonresident status of most of the seigneurs ensured that the influence of the curé upon social and political life was paramount. Falardeau summarizes the significance of the cleric in the colony: "Without any legal responsibility, and subject to the orders of the administrators and governors, the habitant of New France hardly had the opportunity to take part in village life, of which the only known forms were spontaneous or neighborly co-operation. He was more a docile parishioner than an active citizen. The uncontested leader of the parish was the priest, whose role as spiritual minister and moral arbiter of his flock, developed into that of natural protector, advisor, and in fact pastor, in the literal sense of the word."[38] And after 1659, when Monsignor de Laval was appointed bishop of Quebec, the Canadian church adopted the tradition of ultramontism, a doctrine which viewed the state as subordinate to the church (in contrast to the gallican doctrine, which did not recognize the absolute supremacy of the Pope over the church in France) and the church as predominant in all social affairs.

The social structure of New France thus stood in dramatic contrast to that of New England: it was characterized by the absence of a foundation for the growth of a colonial settler bourgeoisie or of large commercial enterprise, by the lack of a representative system of government or strong towns and villages, by a dearth of civic consciousness, and by the strong institutional ascendancy of the Catholic clergy. The introduction of the English into Canada implied more than the meeting of two distinct language groups. However, despite the dramatic ethnic differences, the English conquest of Canada in 1759 at the end of the Seven Years' War was relatively tranquil. In fact it was an annexation to which France acceded readily, given its own fiscal problems. The French Canadians were abandoned by the metropole, left with the equivalent of eight million dollars in inflated paper money.[39]

Although the annexation and transition between governments were relatively smooth, they were to have a lasting impact on the subsequent ethnic social structure. For one thing, all but five hundred of the colonial French elite of landowners, merchants, and seigneurs returned to the metropole; those who remained had limited capital and no credit market for the purchase of canoes or provisions or to pay crews. By 1790 only four of the thirty-seven merchants resident in Quebec were French Canadian. Thus, the exodus of the French political and commercial bourgeoisie signaled not only the collapse of the French colonial venture but also the marginal economy of the French Canadian settlers. The economy of the French proceeded along the single line of agriculture.[40] Also, given their rural isolation, the replacement of French commercial entrepreneurs by the English and the dominance of the English in trade and manufacture had no immediately apparent repercussions on the lives of the habitants. In 1759 the French population was 75 percent rural; by 1825 this proportion had increased to 85 percent.[41]

Because Quebec was left to the habitants, the Catholic church became by default the undisputed central institution of French Canadians. At the time of the conquest, most of the higher clergy returned to France. From 1760 to 1766, Quebec was without a bishop. In 1765 the French Catholic population of 70,000 included only 138 priests—but those priests played a crucial role. "As the only formal organization left after the collapse of the French regime . . . and because of the lack of local government, the parish priest was not only the religious head of a parish, but also the agent in each rural community of the Catholic hierarchy's political power."[42] Initially, the British were not ready to concede power to the clergy. Despite clerical opposition, the Crown established a policy in 1763 which required all French Canadians to swear fealty to the British Crown, excluded them from positions in the colonial administration, and gave no recognition to the Catholic church. However, the constant appeals by American rebels to the habitants and the threat of a Continental war signaled to the British government the expediency of forging explicit political linkages with the French Canadian clergy. In 1774, with the passage of the Quebec Act, the British metropole essentially made the Catholic church a cornerstone of the colonial state. The act conceded to the church the right to tax the peasantry and control schools; it restored the French civil law and protected the language rights of the habitants. In short, it established an "aristocratic compact" which linked state and church and signaled to the habitants that "the survival of the Catholic Church in Canada and the survival of French Canada were similar goals [and that] anything which endangered the strength of the Church endangered the survival of French Canada."[43] It was wise move; the following year, the American invasion of Canada was resisted by the French settlers.

The most significant effect of the conquest was its impact on the economic development of Canada. England was at this time the most prominent bourgeois state in the expanding world economy: its Crown was responsive to the interests of mercantilists, its economy was heavily dominated by foreign trade, and it sought to expand its operations in the Americas. Imperial policies encouraged extended mercantile partnerships in which a number of partners and merchants in the colonies and metropole shared capital to export manufactured goods from Britain and import raw or semimanufactured goods from the colonies. Although an English-speaking minority had been resident in the Atlantic provinces for many years, the American War of Independence brought waves of British Loyalists to Canada from the colonies, increasing the imperially connected commercial class. Land grants were given to Loyalists in return for their services during the war, and about half of the forty thousand United Empire Loyalists settled in Quebec. Its cultural homogeneity was permanently altered. In addition to individual Loyalists, many of the mercantile firms that had been located in the American colonies moved their colonial offices to Montreal and Quebec City.[44] This class was markedly different from the habitants in its culture, political traditions, and economic interests.

Distinguished not only by language and religion, the British settlers also had a long tradition of representative government, some independence of church and state, and commercial activities. To them, the Quebec Act not only protected the cultural autonomy of the French, it also deprived the English minority of traditional rights such as trial by jury, habeas corpus, mercantile law, and participation in government. At the insistence of the British Loyalists, a Constitution Act was passed in 1791. It divided the colony into two provinces, Upper Canada (with an Anglophone majority; it became Ontario Province) and Lower Canada (a Francophone majority; Quebec Province), each with a governor general, an elected Legislative Assembly, and an appointed Legislative Council (with possible hereditary memberships). It limited the franchise to those with an income of twelve pounds per year in the countryside and to those who paid ten pounds in property taxes or whose property brought five pounds in rent per annum in the city. Although a minority, the English settlers in Lower Canada anticipated that this restricted franchise, together with the growth of the English populace, would give them sufficient support to control an elected assembly. This was an accurate assessment, despite the limited immigration from England. Between 1793 and 1833, only six of thirty-one representatives to the Legislative Council in Lower Canada were Francophones. The representative legislature, with a Francophone majority, did not have ministerial authority and was completely subject to the governor.[45]

Although the French did not participate equally in colonial governance, a small educated class quickly perceived the potential of political participation. This elite, the sons of habitants schooled in Catholic seminaries, were not equipped to compete with English capital. Politics became their only competitive resource and they quickly learned to use it effectively. Though few in number, the French Canadian politicians of the early nineteenth century secured strong support among the habitants. Lord Durham described the special character of this class: "The most educated people of each village belong in society to the same families and have the same level of birth as the illiterate habitants. . . . The most perfect equality always characterizes their relations; the man who is superior by virtue of his education is not separated from the exceptionally ignorant peasant, who rubs shoulders with him, by any barrier of custom or pride of interest. He thus combines the influence acquired by knowledge with social equality; he then exercises on the people a power not possessed, I believe, by any educated class in any part of the world."[46] One historian has pointed out that a petition to Governor Dalhousie in Lower Canada in 1827 contained eighty-seven thousand signatures, seventy-eight thousand of which were names indicated only by a cross.[47] Equality of heritage created a bond between the habitant and the new professional; the illiteracy of the vast majority of the population made it a bond of influence. This new professional class frequently clashed with the church hierarchy on issues before the assembly. Indeed, the church hierarchy had uniformly opposed the Constitution Act, claiming that "it was badly adapted to the spirit of the [French] Canadians and has no other effect than to make the ruled insolent to the rulers."[48]

The class structure of French Canada was not well differentiated: the vast majority of the populace were subsistence farmers and low-level artisans. The small elite—the church hierarchy and the middle-class professionals—vied for their support. In contrast, the class structure of English Canada was much more diverse, and hence the relations between the English and French were not simply those of a dominant and subordinate system of ethnic stratification. On the one hand, those English settlers who monopolized the colonial administration, the important fur trade, the lumber industry, and ancillary businesses constituted a political force on behalf of metropolitan interests. On the other hand, the growing middle class and the working-class artisans, day laborers, and small farmers did not feel the same connection to imperial concerns. The Anglo-Scots party, founded to represent imperially connected merchant interests, sought Anglicization of the colony and opposed the lower-class participation which the representative assembly fostered. They argued: "This province is far too French for a British colony. It is absolutely necessary that we exert all our efforts by every available means, to oppose the French and the augmentation of their influence. . . . It seems to me truly absurd, that the interests of an important colony, as well as those of a considerable part of the commercial class of the British Empire should be placed in the hands of six unimportant shopkeepers, a blacksmith, a carpenter and fifteen ignorant peasants."[49] At the same time, some townships with a majority of English speakers returned French-speaking representatives to the assembly. And the shifting class composition of the English population after the Napoleonic Wars was to generate a more complex class and ethnic constellation of interests in Lower Canada.

After the Napoleonic Wars, when the rural economies of Ireland and England were systematically altered by the industrialization of traditional industry and the capitalist rationalization of agriculture, thousands of peasants and rural laborers emigrated to the Americas. Beginning in 1815, the Crown offered free passage, land tracts, and provisions to potential settlers. Within a decade, arable land in Lower Canada that was not monopolized by the Crown had become scarce, particularly in the region around Montreal. As a result most immigrants did not settle in this area but migrated west to Upper Canada of south to the United States. So, despite the massive migration, Lower Canada remained predominantly French Canadian (except for Montreal and Quebec City).[50] To prevent this concentrated French presence, London opposed the creation of new farms for habitants in the Crown lands. At the same time, a recession in shipbuilding and the lumber industry accelerated unemployment among the French.[51] The new professional class, cut off from opportunities in the colonial administration, began to channel opposition to metropolitan dominance. Not all French Canadians joined the opposition. The church hierarchy and seigneurs were stalwart defenders of the colonial governance. Nor was the opposition entirely French Canadian. By the 1830s emigrants from the British Isles had settled into wage labor jobs in Quebec City and Montreal (in 1831 Anglophones made up 51 percent of day laborers in Quebec and 53 percent in Montreal, up from 10 percent and 25 percent respectively in 1795).[52] With the establishment of the British American Land Company in 1833, few of the immigrants could afford the growing price of land in the townships. Many of these immigrants, especially the Irish, with their long history of antagonism toward the Crown, constituted one source of alliance.

Led by Louis Joseph Papineau, a small group of politicians formed the Parti Patriote to challenge the power of the Crown and English commercial dominance of Lower Canada. They sought political separation of the two provinces and independence from the Crown. They challenged, as well, the ability of the church hierarchy to represent the long-term interests of French Canadians in their own economic development. They argued that the church had simply accommodated to the Crown and that it was a protector of vested political interests. A parallel movement developed among the English middle class in Upper Canada. Classic settler nationalists, they sought to establish a more democratic system of representation, to challenge the oligarchy who dominated the government, and to free Canada from Crown control over administration of land. Their political reformism and considerable influence in the rangs ensured that the Patriotes would garner significant support among the habitants. Among the French, only the church hierarchy, seigneurs, and a small urban middle class tied into English commercial interests (known collectively as the *chouayens*) mobilized, unsuccessfully, to oppose them.[53] The Parti Patriote dominated the representative assembly and conflicted regularly with the administration. When a struggle over subsidies erupted in 1837 and the governor general requested metropolitan authority to ignore the legislature, the Patriotes began to organize peasants and urban workers and to mobilize against the Crown. Despite this solid support, the brief uprising of the Patriotes in 1837 was easily quelled after eight days of sporadic fighting. The Lower Canadian legislature was abolished, and the Crown dispatched Lord Durham to Canada to reformulate imperial policy.

The Durham Report, which attempted to analyze the origins of the rebellions, paid scant attention to the disturbances in Upper

Canada and argued instead that the political problems of Canada were the result of "two nations warring in the bosom of a single state. . . . I entertain no doubt of the national character which must be given to Lower Canada; it must be that of the British Empire; it must be that of the great race which must in the lapse of no long period of time be predominant over the whole North American continent. . . . It must henceforth be the first and steady purpose of the British government to establish an English population with English laws and language in this province, and to trust its government to none but a decidedly English legislature."[54] Durham recommended that the two provinces be united politically and that a policy of assimilation be adopted. Without such a policy, he claimed, the French would remain economically underdeveloped: "If they attempt to better their condition by extending themselves over the neighboring country, they will be more and more mingled with the English population. If they prefer remaining stationary, the greater part of them must be laborers in the employ of English capitalists. In either case, it would appear that in some measure, the vast majority of French Canadians are doomed to occupy an inferior position and to be dependent upon the English for employment."[55]

The Crown adopted Durham's suggestions in the Union Act of 1840. This act abolished the legislative differentiation between the provinces, created a single assembly, and distributed the seats in a way to ensure that the Anglophone population held a majority; it forbade the use of French in the legislative assembly. The Union Act was not simply an effort at assimilation. As Alfred Dubuc has pointed out, it also reflected the economic development policy of metropolitan England, which viewed a more united colony as essential to facilitating integrated internal markets and providing a better investment climate for capital outlays.[56] The act provoked strong opposition among French Canadians. The conservatives, especially the clerical hierarchy, profited from and utilized this opposition.

The church hierarchy argued that the French Canadians constituted a noble ethnic group whose language and faith and traditions and customs must be preserved. However, that group need not compete with the English population; its mission was to "preserve the legacy of their forefathers in order to pass it on to their descendents intact"—a legacy of farm and faith.[57] In return for its support during the Patriote Rebellion, the colonial administration rewarded the church by recognizing French as the language of state government and providing some financial compensation for losses habitants had suffered during the fighting. In this way, a patrimonial relation was reinforced: the church supported the colonial regime in exchange for protection of French Canadian cultural integrity and clerical dominance over the populace.

However, the church may not have succeeded in convincing the habitants of the legitimacy of its position had not the former rebels also acceded—in some part—to the union. In fact, the modifications in the union which recognized the French language generated opportunities for the professional class to participate in administration. Former Patriotes were gradually drawn into the governing elite. Thus, the church "in conjunction with the professional and conservative elite eliminated the radicals and elaborated what became the predominant ideology of French Canadian society for more than a century."[58] From 1839 until World War I, the response to the question posed by Lord Durham was framed in the slogan of the church hierarchy *la survivance* and in the correlative for guaranteeing French survival, *la revanche des berceaux,* "the revenge of the cradle."

STRATIFICATION AND ETHNIC MOBILIZATION IN COLONIAL CANADA: A COMPARISON WITH IRELAND

The patterns of intergroup contact in colonial Canada did not generate a system of ethnic stratification as they did in Ireland. Some of the conditions which foster ethnic dominance were clearly evident. The degree of ethnic differentiation was considerable: religion, language, custom, and folkways distinguished the two "charter groups" from one another. These differences were encapsulated in political and social institutions, especially the structure of government and the relations between church and state. The power differences between the two groups were substantial, as a result of the pattern of colonization. New France constituted a colony of limited settlement, managed by colonial administrators on behalf of the metropole. The limited economic investment in Canada by France and the lack of civic participation ensured that the settlers would lack the political and economic resources to compete effectively with the English. However, in spite of the considerable cultural and power differences between these two charter groups, there was little motivation for developing a structure of dominance during the era of conquest and colonization. In large part, this was due to the external threat of the American rebels, which induced the Crown to moderate its efforts to Anglicize the habitants and to create a purely English colonial government. It was also due to the existence of a frontier, which provided an outlet for the pressures on the land and labor supply in Lower Canada.

If a *system* of ethnic stratification was not established by the colonization and English conquest of Canada, the foundations for uneven development and a cultural division of labor were laid. Commercial development was centered in English institutions and enterprises with strong connections to the metropole and hence was monopolized by Anglophones. The majority of the French settlers remained in the primary agricultural sector, with a small number moving into professional positions and petty bourgeois shops and trade. Neither sector was in competition with English capital (in the primary sector or in trade). And the church, which monopolized the educational system in Lower Canada, ensured that the French would not compete with the English by emphasizing the special mission and occupational niche of the French Canadian. In contrast to Ireland, then, it was neither ethnic oppression by the metropole nor the efforts of English settlers to protect differential advantage that generated an ethnically split labor market in Canada. Rather, it was the legacy of differential patterns of colonization, which had produced the economic underdevelopment of French Canada, and the political strength of the Catholic church, which reinforced this separation.

Our consideration of these two cases underscores my point in the last chapter that any theory which hopes to account for ethnic mobilization must consider the ways in which the minority elite is incorporated into the dominant society and the extent to which traditional institutions participate in and support the state system. In Ireland the subordinate elite was effectively eliminated—many middle-class Catholics emigrated and many of those remaining were economically dispossessed. The church was suppressed, so that the clergy were unable to act as political agents. In Quebec, on the other hand, the minority elite was clearly co-opted through Britain's support of the French Canadian Catholic hierarchy.

A comparison of colonial Ireland and Canada underscores the

significance of political structure in patterning ethnic relations. The political concessions to the French, which incorporated them into the institutions of the colonial state, provided an arena for the articulation of group interests *within* the political system. Both the professional class and the Catholic hierarchy were integrated into the colonial state and provided access to an arena for securing their interests. Thus, unlike rural Ireland, where systematic exclusion and subordination produced a politics of resistance, political conflicts were managed within the state apparatus and made ''normal.'' As a result, despite significant differences in economic and political power between the two charter groups, ethnic mobilization in colonial Canada was limited. There were no major ethnic outbursts, no substantial struggles between the two settler groups. This is not to argue that the French did not occasionally chafe at their relative deprivation. Especially among the professional class, concerns about the political advantages of Anglophones increased during the early nineteenth century. But the ethnic conflicts were limited largely to constitutional questions, which were debated and played out in the chambers of the legislative assembly. The most significant conflict of the colonial period, the Patriote Rebellion, constituted a classic bourgeois nationalist struggle, successfully appealing across ethnic lines. Ethnic appeals were largely the domain of the church hierarchy, reflecting its efforts to sustain authority over the habitant populace. In its patrimonial relation with the metropole at the time of the Quebec Act and in the revisions of the Union Act, the church secured some protection of French customs and language and thus its own influential role in the French Canadian community. But, as we shall see in the next chapter, this patrimonial relationship also fostered the economic underdevelopment of that community.

4

Capital Development, Industrialization, and Ethnic Mobilization

Colonialism prepared the ground for the unequal resources and economic development of the major ethnic groups in both Ireland and Canada. However, colonial soil need not produce enduring ethnic differentiation, inequality, and conflict. In this chapter, we turn to an examination of how patterns of capitalist development and industrialization reshaped class and ethnicity in these two societies and produced new patterns of ethnic politics.

According to the modernization theorists (see chapter 1), ethnic and regional solidarity is eroded by capitalist economic and political development. In industrializing societies, traditional status relations are replaced with impersonal, contractual ones. Universal criteria (efficiency, productivity, skill) rather than traditional ascriptive identity become the bases for allocating resources and rewards. Since the rational character of industry favors organizations based on secular interest, traditional ethnic institutions are weakened, and class becomes more salient than ethnicity in determining social and political relations.[1] When industrialization and other processes of social integration are not evenly distributed, however, ethnic solidarity may persist, provoking ethnic politics as one reaction to the social dislocations of industrialization. Other theorists whom we examined argue that capitalist industrialization does not break down traditional social orders but incorporates aspects of these and hence is likely to foster an ethnic division of labor. Capitalists need not adopt uniformly rational policies in which workers are judged on the basis of skill and efficiency alone. They can tolerate a level of irrational hiring practices and still secure sufficient profit for reinvestment, development, and capital accumulation.[2] Indeed, capital may intentionally conform to an existing cultural and regional division of labor, create an ethnically distinct labor aristocracy, and sustain a patrimonial relation with the privileged workers, in order to fragment the working class, as uneven development theorists claim. Or workers who have accumulated a superior labor position as a result of the traditional class and ethnic structure may mobilize to protect their superior positions, forcing industry to capitulate to demands contrary to its own rational interests, as split labor market theory contends. Or more generally, capitalist industrialization may increase intergroup contact and competition for jobs, housing, and control over urban institutions. Within any of these situations, the likelihood of ethnic conflict depends, in large part, on patterns of political development. For example, the direction of capital investment and industrial growth depends upon the political power of competing ethnic groups and regions to attract and control industry. The structure of the state will determine—to a large degree—the resources available to competing ethnic groups and the likelihood that intergroup competition will be channeled into ethnic or class politics. In this chapter, I will reconsider the relative merits of these various interpretations through an examination of ethnic and class stratification and patterns of political mobilization during the period of industrialization. In Ireland, I will focus on the period between the Union in 1801 and the Partition in 1922. In Canada, I will consider the period between the Union in 1840 and the Duplessis regime in the 1940s.

Uneven Development and Internal Colonialism under the Union of Great Britain and Ireland

The political union of Ireland and Britain in 1801, the direct outcome of the rebellions of 1798, made Ireland an "internal colony," and the economic consequences were devastating for much of the country. Ireland's separate (and Protestant) Parliament was abolished. During the next century, the economy of Ireland was inextricably welded to the development of English capital, as a market for British manufactured goods, a source of labor for industrial development, and a supplier of food for the English market. With the Act of Union, the Irish Parliament was abolished, and policy-making power was limited to Westminster, where Irish representation was minimal. As a result, even the few protective tariffs that had existed were eliminated. Free trade meant Irish subordination, since most Irish industry could not withstand British competition. Without a state apparatus to construct trade barriers, Ireland was forced into a peripheral economic position, domestic industry was underdeveloped, and the economy became even more agricultural and rural. For example, when England lost its American market for cotton during the War of 1812, it dumped its surplus on Ireland, where employment in the cotton industries fell from 40,000 in 1801 to 5,000 in 1822. Woolen manufacture declined from 91 factories employing 4,918 in 1800 to 12 factories employing 600 in 1841. Similar declines in weaving, combing, and blanket manufacture meant that by 1825 most of southern Ireland's industry was driven out of business.[3] Between 1821 and 1841 the number of industrial workers declined from 1.7 to 1.6 million, while the number of agricultural workers increased from 2.8 to 3.5 million.[4] Land policies shifted regularly in accord with English market needs. In the first half of the nineteenth century, imperial policies encouraged subdivisions in the land, rack-renting, and a shift from stock farming to tillage (generating unproductive use of land, rural unemployment, and peasant discontent). In the latter half of the century, a shift in policies to favor livestock forced landlords to consolidate their holdings and displaced huge numbers of peasants from the land.[5]

An utterly different situation evolved in the north, where industries flourished. There, as we saw in the last chapter, successful cottage industries and maintenance of tenant rights had facilitated the growth of a capital base. The farm-based cottage industries organized on a factory basis; iron shipbuilding and subsidiary spin-offs grew up in Belfast's harbor area. These firms served the expanding trade of the British Empire and supplied an essential part of her naval power.[6] Moreover, this was the only area that was able to resist the introduction of ranching—in Ulster, oats and flax remained the cash crops.[7]

Inevitably, these regional differences entailed variations in social relations, political infrastructures, and reactions to imperial dominance. In the south and west, politics were rooted in rural and commercial issues, particularly land reform and the franchise. In the north, rural concerns were gradually subordinated to the needs of the urban centers, and politics became focused on industrial issues. Since the south could not provide a market for Ulster's expanding industrial trade, Belfast's bourgeoisie were increasingly drawn into

British markets and credit structures and wedded to imperial policies. In short, regional differences in the mode of production constituted a powerful obstacle to national unity. But uneven development alone does not sufficiently explain the bases for or structure of ethnic politics. Not all Catholics suffered or Protestants benefited equally from the fruits of imperialism. To understand the nature of ethnic interests during this period, we need to examine carefully the economic and social changes and the role of ethnic organizations in political mobilization. For analytic purposes, I will examine the north and south separately, but I will also seek to delineate the ways in which the political economy and social relations in one region affected those of the other.

For the south and west of Ireland, the most obvious problem under the Union was economic underdevelopment, fostered by the land system, the decline of industry, and the absence of many alternatives to farming. Until the middle of the nineteenth century, land was held in large part by absentee owners, who let their tracts be managed and sublet by others, increasing the rents and imposing serious burdens on the tenants. The dilemmas generated by this system were exacerbated by the severe pressures on land use, which resulted from political dependency and demographic change. In response to British demands for cattle, for example, grain acreage decreased from 5.4 million acres in 1827 to 5.2 million in 1857. At the same time the population increased from 6.8 to 8.2 million. Population increases combined with a decline in crop holdings ensured that the demand for land far exceeded the supply and inevitably led to rack-renting.[8] Within this context, the peasants lived a precarious existence. Few ate bread, salt, or butter; most subsisted on potatoes alone. Exclusive dependence on the potato meant severe hardship during potato blights, and blights were not uncommon: famine occurred throughout Ireland in 1817, 1822, and from 1845 to 1848.

The Great Famine was the centerpiece of nineteenth-century Irish history and revealed the full horror of imperial dominance of the land and state system. Throughout the famine, foodstuffs were exported to England and little was done to regulate the export of grain and cattle or to relieve the starving Irish.[9] Some relief measures were passed, but they were regulated within the context of landlord and mercantile interests. Thus, because the Poor Relief Acts stipulated that grain could not be distributed if it competed with private companies, a shipload of American grain was placed in storage in 1845 so as not to disturb the trade.[10] When the government established a system of public works, landlords objected so vehemently that the policy was abandoned. The Poor Relief Acts only exacerbated the dilemma of the Irish peasant. They forbade employment or food to any who retained more than one-fourth of an acre of land. Hence, many tenants were forced to either starve on their land or abandon their tiny holdings. The major land law passed in this period, the Encumbered Estates Act of 1849, favored landholders, permitting them to sell their land through the courts and retain the residue of the purchase price, once debts were paid.[11] Until 1870, not a single act was passed at Westminster in favor of the Irish tenantry.

With repeal of the Corn Laws, the price of grain declined, forcing many landlords to consolidate their land and shift from crops to grazing. In the years 1847–1852, eighty-four thousand tenant farmers were evicted and the number of small holdings fell steadily. By 1871 over half of all farms were thirty acres or larger, whereas prior to the famine this proportion had been only 18.5 percent (see table 1). Land consolidation was accompanied by a decrease in cultivated crops, an increase in livestock, and a decline in the ability of the land to support the population.[12] Inevitably, because the land system could not support the population, vast numbers emigrated— nearly four million between 1841 and 1880.[13]

It follows from this sketch that the Union brought few benefits to the mass of peasants in southern Ireland; it inhibited capital de-

Table 1 Agricultural Holdings in Ireland over One Acre (In Percentages)

Year	Total Holdings	1–5 Acres	6–15 Acres	16–30 Acres	Over 30 Acres
1841	691,114	44.9	36.6	11.5	7.0
1851	608,866	15.5	33.6	24.8	26.1
1861	610,045	15.0	32.4	24.8	27.8
1871	592,590	13.7	31.5	25.5	29.3
1881	577,739	12.7	31.1	25.8	39.4
1891	572,640	12.3	30.3	25.9	31.5
1901	590,175	12.2	29.9	26.0	31.9

Source: Department of Agriculture, *Agricultural Statistics of Ireland, with Detailed Report for the Year 1901* (London: Her Majesty's Stationery Office, 1902), pt. 1, p. 15.

velopment and reinforced the inequities of the land tenure system there. This is not to argue that the Union was the only source of Ireland's economic underdevelopment. The country was poorly equipped for competition in the nineteenth-century industrializing world economy. Coal and iron resources were limited; no decent transportation infrastructure existed; and British industry was already mechanized and could probably have survived any protectionist measures of an independent Ireland. Nor would independence necessarily have produced a change in the land system. Irish landholders held mortgages in banks whose focus on London's money market meant that a nominally independent Ireland would have remained bound to the English economy. Nonetheless, because the Irish had no significant voice at Westminster, British policy consistently worked to the country's disadvantage.[14]

As the solitary locus of relatively equitable landlord-tenant relations and of industrial and technological development, Ulster was the only area in Ireland which prospered under the Union. Linen, shipbuilding, and shirt-making industries survived, in part because the successful cottage industries and the maintenance of tenant rights had permitted the growth of a capital base, and in part because the industries did not compete with any English trade. By 1850 there were linen mills throughout the province, and Belfast had become the focal point for rail, road, and water transportation.[15] Because the regional growth of Ulster was accompanied by industrial decline in the south, the rest of Ireland could provide neither a market for Ulster goods nor a source of credit for development. The business and professional class which had played such a significant role in the insurrection of 1798 now shifted its allegiance toward Britain; and Belfast, which had been the center of dissent before the Union, grew deaf to calls for economic nationalization. And logically so, for "it was the demand of the British market which kept the Belfast linen mills busy; after the mid century, it was to service the expanding trade of the Victorian empire that Belfast's shipbuilding industry came to world prominence. The expansion of ancillary metal industries, indeed the health of the entire economy of the region, depended on access to the British market itself and a share in the expanding overseas markets of the Empire."[16]

Ulster's prosperity was concentrated in the eastern section of the province—around Belfast and its hinterlands in the counties of Antrim and Down. Industrialization was concentrated largely in this section. In the rural north, the Ulster Custom protected Protestant tenants from the worst effects of imperial agricultural policies; but the famine and the gradual consolidation of lands produced a decline in the number of small farms in Ulster, a proletarianization of the countryside, and a migration to the cities. The most significant land consolidation and population losses occurred in the western areas, where the Catholic population was largest. Displaced from the land, these Gaelic-speaking farmers migrated to Belfast, the only area where jobs were available. There, the Catholic population increased from 16 percent of the 25,000 inhabitants in 1808 to one-third of the population of 121,000 in 1861.[17]

In short, the Union aligned the economic fortune of the urban north with those of Scotland and England, at the same time that it accelerated the underdevelopment of the south. But it also produced a proletarianization of the countryside and increased migration and ethnic contact in the urban north. In the next section, I will trace the effects of this regional differentiation and industrialization on class and ethnic relations.

CLASS AND ETHNIC MOBILIZATION UNDER THE UNION OF GREAT BRITAIN AND IRELAND

As noted, the Act of Union abolished the Irish Parliament and incorporated Ireland into the British parliamentary system. Initially the Protestant bourgeoisie and landlords had opposed this effort. One Orange lodge in Dublin resolved, "We declare, as Orangemen, as Freeholders, as Irishmen, in all the several relations in which we are placed, that we consider the extinction of our separate legislature as the immedite extinction of the Irish nation."[18] The remaining Catholic middle class experienced this concern doubly, since they were still excluded from state and municipal affairs and offices (though enfranchised since 1793). Hence, for wealthier Catholics as well as for Protestants, the burning issue was their inability to protect and advance their interests under the aegis of the state. This coincidence of class interests did not go unrecognized. In 1813 the Presbyterian Synod of Ulster called for the abolition of political distinctions on the basis of religious profession and described the system of tithe paying to the established church as "unjust in itself, oppressive to conscience, hostile to civil and religious liberty and subversive to true religion."[19] It would be a gross oversimplification then to argue that sectarian politics were automatically embraced by the Protestant or Catholic populace. Rather, they were the outcome of a number of different but interacting factors. First, when middle-class Catholic leaders sought to mobilize peasants against the exclusion of Catholics from public office, they downplayed class and emphasized ethnic concerns. A second factor was the growing economic differentiation between north and south, which created regionally defined political interests and hence made the coincidence of ethnic and class concerns seem "natural." Third, imperialists in the British government sought to divide the country whenever united opposition seemed imminent. Sir Robert Peel, chief secretary for Ireland and later prime minister of England, expresssed this policy in 1814, when he said, "I hope they may always be disunited. The great art is to keep them so, and yet at peace . . . or rather not at war with each other."[20] Finally, a schism within the Presbyterian church, combined with the impact of industrialization, reinforced sectarian sentiments among Protestants in Ulster. In the following section, I will examine how these factors together shifted the competitive situation and resources of Catholics and Protestants and undermined the likelihood of secular politics.

Although Catholics were enfranchised in 1793 on the same basis as Protestants, the Union did not end exclusion from state and municipal offices. Hence, under the Union, the burning political issue for the Irish Catholic middle class was political emancipation, inclusion in the colonial state. However, this class was very small and lacked any organizational base. Under the leadership of Daniel O'Connell, a Catholic lawyer from Dublin with parliamentary ambitions, the middle class began to forge an alliance with the peasants. O'Connell's goal was to transform the mass discontent generated by the land system into a movement that would force Westminster to make concessions to the middle class. In 1823 he founded the Catholic Association to pressure for emancipation. The membership of sixty-two was composed entirely of the elite (it included thirty-one lawyers, eleven merchants, ten landowners, three editors, four gentlemen, and one friar); and the group's activities focused on the inclusion of Catholics in the political rights of the Union—not on the expansion of political rights to include the laboring classes.[21] O'Connell's organizational skills were consum-

mate—he used the church as a grass roots organizational base, securing its support by admitting the clergy for free as ex officio
members and downplaying land claims. He was able not only to
secure clerical support but also to persuade priests to collect pen-
nies from peasants after Sunday Mass. By the end of 1823, the
association was amassing £1,000 a week and numbered over
250,000 members. Two years later, its coffers were filled at the
rate of £2,000 a week.

O'Connell's success and his reputation as the "great liberator"
are problematic. He never advanced the basic political and economic interests of the masses who supported him. He was not himself a nationalist; he had opposed the United Irishmen and supported the English monarchy, and although he spoke Gaelic fluently
(still the tongue of four million peasants), he insisted that all public
meetings be held in English.[22] O'Connell consistently opposed labor organizations and legislation and embraced the British connection. How, then, can a resource competition model explain his unprecedented success in mobilizing the peasantry? In part it was due
to personal charisma. O'Connell was a spellbinding speaker, who
could attract thousands of listeners to his "monster meetings." In
part it was due to a millennial streak in the oral folklore which
prophesied the coming of a great liberator.[23] But, for the most part,
O'Connell's success must be attributed to the support of the Catholic church, which facilitated organization at the grass roots level.
The emancipation movement successfully mobilized the Catholic
peasants in the first national movement; but it also explicitly institutionalized an association of Catholicism with mass Irish mobilization. Hence the mainstream of Irish nationalism was set; its current was Catholic and pragmatic.[24] British imperialists used this
association to channel the class discontent of the proletarianized
Protestant populace into sectarian politics. Their vehicle was evangelical Presbyterianism.

Early in the nineteenth century, Ulster's emerging industrial
bourgeoisie had shifted its allegiance to Britain, since their economic fortunes were intertwined with British economic growth and
policies. This allegiance had no sectarian overtones. Following the
Calvinist spirit of rational pursuit of duty as sacred service, this
class eschewed sectarianism and supported the goals of the Catholic
emancipation movement. This was also a period of the gradual proletarianization of Ulster, with increasing seasonal migration and a

decline in independent rural culture. The rationalist intellectualism and religious tolerance of liberal Presbyterians had little appeal to the Protestant proletariat, with its long history of sectarianism. In the 1820s, a schism within the church developed, and a fundamentalist branch, led by the fiery Henry Cooke, appealed to the wage-laboring population. The evangelicals denounced the intellectuals for their rationalism, pronounced the Bible as literal truth, proclaimed the Pope to be the Antichrist, and appealed to Anglicans and Orangemen to build a union against Catholics. In a convincing analysis of the Presbyterian schism and the development of religious enthusiasm during this period, Peter Gibbon concludes that "the urbanizing Protestant population appreciated the call for greater expression of popular feeling, the provision of an exciting religion and of enthusiastic leaders who could break down the barriers separating them from organized religion. Such leaders gave a sense of identity and strength and the population became responsive to 'enthusiastic' leadership in all fields, prone to form personalistic attachments to 'enthusiastic' leaders and men of the people."[25] Enthusiastics emphasized the elective status of Presbyterians and the coincidence of Protestantism and religious liberty. Catholic resistance to saving grace (opposition to Bible reading in public schools or street preachers or payment of tithes) was seen as evidence of opposition to religious liberty. But the Protestant crusade was not simply a proletarian movement. It was spearheaded by Anglican Tories who sought to re-create their patrimonial relation with the rural Protestants and to prevent any alliances among Irish tenants.

It is true that the Ulster Custom protected Protestant tenants from the worst effects of imperial agricultural policies; but from the outset of the Union, recurring famine, gradual consolidation of lands, the decline in the number of small farms in Ulster, increasing land competition, and the gradual proletarianization of the countryside were undermining the foundations of ethnic patrimonialism. Moreover, the Catholic emancipation movement and developing land reform movements confronted Anglican landlords with the possibilty of continuous unrest, particulary as the economic base of their cliental relations with the rural Presbyterians began to erode. To ward off the possibility of land war and to restore their patrimonial relation to Protestant tenants, the landlords turned to support the evangelistic, anti-Catholic crusade. In 1834 the Church of Ireland aligned itself with the conservative Presbyterians under

Cooke's leadership. Anglican leaders organized Orange lodges in the countryside and recruited enthusiastic Presbyterian ministers into their ranks. Each member of the higher gentry, who formed the Grand Lodge of the Orange Order, was required to join a "private," local lodge so as to "mingle with their humbler brethren."[26] Secret meetings in local lodges emphasized the shared symbols of Protestant history. When Westminster banned secret societies as provocative in 1835, the Tory gentry allowed meetings to be held on their estates. "This aspect of Orangeism was particularly attractive to the 'lower orders,' who were pleased with the idea of sharing the same sphere with so many of those moving in the higher spheres of society."[27] It was not simply status honor that Orange lodges provided; they also served as a base for recruiting and arming Protestant rural laborers to collect tithes and rents from the Catholics.[28] In this way, Orangeism became the symbol of Protestant dominance and an institutional encapsulation of the traditional patrimonial relationship between Protestant gentry and peasants. This pattern of Orange reciprocity may best explain the absence of rural Protestant participation in the Tenant League developed after the Great Famine or in the land wars of the late nineteenth century.

In this context of increasing religious antagonism in the north, the famine occurred and deprivations caused by the land system came into sharper focus. More than twenty local tenants organizations sprang up during this three-year period, and an effort was made to develop a tenants league which would force a recognition of the peasants' plight. Its appeal was nonsectarian and the leadership sought to create a national movement; but limited resources, the extreme deprivation caused by the famine, and the opposition of the Catholic church hierarchy to political mobilization limited its growth. Massive emigration was the predominant political reaction. However, in the postfamine period, a new nationalist movement did develop, pledged to an independent republican Ireland. Named after an ancient Gaelic warrior and his legion, Sinn Fein recruited among agricultural labor and urban workers in the south. The Fenian movement had little immediate impact. Led by urban intellectuals, it secured most of its support from Irish émigrés in the United States. Although the society claimed eighty-five thousand members, an uprising in 1867 was not widely supported and was easily suppressed. But however futile the uprising, the legacy of Sinn Fein was strong. It was opposed by the church, yet secured some peasant support, indicating a gradual secularization of rural politics. It reintroduced efforts at armed insurrection, a radical move from the constitutional politics which had prevailed after the Union; it relied on political and financial support of Irish Americans, thereby expanding the resources of the Irish nationalist supporters; and it resurrected the mode of organization through secret societies. Even after the Fenians were publicly abolished, a secret network persisted in the Irish Republican Brotherhood.[29] Because it was fairly localized (in the southwest), the Fenian uprising and organization had little effect on ethnic relations. However, it did have an important effect on Irish nationalism, shaping its ideology. As Conor Cruise O'Brien has noted, "the mass of people remained loyal to the Church and supported the constitutional nationalists. But they also admired the Fenians for their courage, their tenacity and their unconsummated continuity of Irish Catholic feeling. . . . The bishops with their relatively novel doctrine of loyalty to the British Crown (and therefore the Protestant succession) were on slippery ground, emotionally speaking."[30]

During the first half of the century, the major locus of ethnic violence and antagonism was in the Ulster countryside. In nearly every case, conflicts were precipitated by provocative processions and parades, sponsored by the Orange Order, and by Catholic counterresponses. During the second half of the century, however, the major situs of conflict shifted, as eastern Ulster industrialized and as the famine forced migration from the agricultural areas to Belfast.

In response to industrialization and to the famine, Catholic and Protestant labor began to migrate from the agricultural west to the coastal north. The population of Belfast increased dramatically and with it the proportion of Catholics. In 1784 Catholics represented only 8 percent of the city's populace; at the time of the Union, this had doubled to 16 percent, and by 1861 they constituted 33.9 percent of the residents (see table 2).

According to contemporary sources, those Catholics who migrated to Belfast during the Union were largely unskilled workers from rural areas where the Irish language was still strong. Owen Edwards describes this migration: "The great famine depopulated the mountainous west of Ireland where the Irish language was strongest and where school-taught English had the least impact. Seasonal migration may have played its part in introducing some

Chapter Four

Table 2 Roman Catholic Population of Belfast

Date	Population Total	Percentage Roman Catholic
1659	692	38.0
1757	9,266	6.0
1776	4,267 (families)	8.0
1784	13,650	8.0
1801	25,000	16.0
1834	61,600	32.0
1861	121,602	33.9
1871	174,412	31.9
1881	208,122	28.8
1891	255,950	26.3
1901	349,180	24.3
1911	386,947	24.1
1926	415,151	23.0
1937	438,086	23.8
1951	443,671	25.9
1961	416,094	25.5

Source: Adapted from Ian Budge and Cornelius O'Leary, *Belfast: Approach to Crisis; A Study of Belfast Politics, 1613–1970* (New York: Macmillan Co., 1973), 28 and 30. Reprinted by permission of Macmillan, London and Basingstoke.

slight familiarity with English, but it still seems reasonable to suggest that communication was possibly the most awkward barrier creating a division in the Belfast working class at the outset. . . . This in turn made the western immigrants more dependent on each other, more ready to turn to natural leaders amongst their ranks."[31] The migrants clustered together in traditionally Irish sections of the city, carving out segregated enclaves; and by 1850 Belfast was a totally segregated city.[32]

Prior to this massive famine migration, trade associations had developed in Belfast to regulate jobs in the industrializing crafts. Frequently based in Orange lodges, these were marked by an intricate system of recruitment—a combination of nepotism, localistic politics, and patronage. By the time of the famine-induced population influx, the system was quite strong; and craft exclusiveness was easily transformed into ethnic exclusivity. However, given the interests of capital, the supply of low-wage labor during the famine period, and the nonsectarianism of Belfast's liberal Presbyterians, job security was uncertain. Whenever industrialists adopted nonsectarian policies, Protestant skilled laborers mobilized through the Orange lodges, disrupted production, intimidated the new employees, initiated riots on the shop floor, and insisted on job segregation and hiring discrimination. Their success was significant. Catholics were excluded from the skilled and semiskilled jobs in shipyards, engineering, and linen mills and were restricted largely to menial jobs on the docks.[33] This period provides clear evidence of the role of high-wage labor in sustaining an ethnically split labor market. However, to view ethnic antagonism as precipitated only by the protectionist efforts of a high-wage labor force would be to oversimplify the structure of the Protestant labor force. The data on ethnic conflicts in nineteenth-century Belfast indicate that different sectors of the Protestant labor force engaged in loyalist ethnic politics for different reasons.

The skilled Protestant workers in the shipbuilding, ironworks, and engineering firms easily perceived the correlation between success of British imperialism and fluctuations in their industrial jobs. Having secured a monopoly position for itself, this high-wage sector served readily as a political linkage between the industrial bourgeoisie and unskilled labor. Studies of this period indicate that high-wage labor constituted a leadership cadre among Protestant workers that was strongly opposed to Home Rule, active in Orange lodges, and, in the Ulster Protestant Association, working to protect their ethnic compatriots from unemployment.[34] Unskilled Protestant workers, especially recent immigrants from rural areas, experienced few of these economic advantages and recognized shared interethnic class interests in temporary situations (e.g., the dock strike of 1907). For this group, ethnic conflicts during the Union can be traced more to challenges to the ethnic boundaries, forged by residential segregation and reinforced by the Orange lodges and by the significant cultural differences between Catholic and Protestant unskilled labor. This sector, many of whom had been seasonal migrants, had a long history of ethnic exclusivity. For them, loyalty to the British connection was based more on personalistic bonds than on economic competition. As Peter Gibbon states: ''In living out the situation posed by the existence of the 'enemy at the gates,' and the inevitability of repeated clashes with him, the agent added a moral unequivocality to his ethnic unequivocality. Fidelity was the primary element of loyalty. The true blue Sandy Row Orangeman's blueness (i.e. 'loyalist') ethnicity was true because he lived out its truth in faithfulness as a whole. Further, since the threat posed by the enemy at the gates was a military one in some sense (invasion, annihilation), the subjects of fidelity and reliability lived their roles as martial ones."[35]

A careful analysis of the sectarian riots in this period supports the perspective that labor market competition alone cannot explain ethnic mobilization. Almost without exception, the major conflicts in nineteenth-century Belfast were provoked by parliamentary elections (which raised the spectre of Home—and Catholic—Rule) and by marches intended to celebrate and symbolize Protestant dominance. As table 3 shows, riots were most frequently precipitated by provocative marches organized by evangelistic ministers or Orange lodges to celebrate the Protestant Ascendancy on ritual dates, or in reaction to nationalist activity. Nor is there any connection between the riots and industrial economic discontent. In 1857 severe unemployment occurred in the linen industry, but the riots preceded this recession. 1864 was a prosperous year, with high employment and high wages in every industry; 1872 was a normal year; and although agricultural depression occurred in 1886, the shipyards and docks where the leaders of the riot were employed were kept extremely busy. Moreover, none of these riots were preceded by efforts on the part of industry to replace Protestant workers with Catholics or to use Catholics as strikebreakers.[36]

Table 3   Religious Riots in Belfast

Date	Precipitating Event	Duration
12 July 1813	Orange procession	1 evening
12 July 1832	parliamentary election	1 day
12 July 1835	Orange meeting	1 day
8 July 1841	parliamentary election	2 days
12 July 1843	Protestant procession	5–7 days
12 July 1854	parliamentary election	5–7 days
12 July 1857	Orange procession	56 days (sporadic)
8 Aug. 1864	unveiling of O'Connell statue in Dublin	18 days
15–22 Aug. 1872	Nationalist procession	9 days
15–19 Aug. 1880	Catholic procession	4 days
13 July 1884	Orange procession	1 day
3 June–25 Oct. 1886	defeat of Home Rule	4 months
7–8 June 1898	Nationalist procession	2 days
11–14 Aug. 1907	undetermined	4 days
13–14 June 1909	Orange procession	2 days

Source: Budge and O'Leary, *Belfast* (see table 2 above), 89. Reprinted by permission of Macmillan, London and Basingstoke.

In short, there were varying motivations for sectarian politics in Ulster: a patrimonial alliance between agricultural landed interests and the rural proletariat in the countryside, protection of a split labor market and imperial advantages for a small sector of the Protestant labor force, and protection of residential turf combined with the "honors of the status group" for the urban proletariat. The urban proletariat were responsive to a leadership cadre of Protestant workers, the high-wage sector, who provided a political linkage between the secular Protestant bourgeoisie and the ethnic working class. During the industrial depression of the 1870s, when a serious movement for Home Rule gathered momentum in the south, this unwieldy ethnic alliance congealed and shaped the direction of Irish nationalism.

Because Britain refused to protect Ireland against foreign competition, the depression, together with three years of unusually bad harvests, had a severe impact on the island. Between 1876 and 1885 livestock prices fell by one-third, and agricultural output and commodities followed suit.[37] Although farmers went without any profit, landlords refused to lower rents to reflect market demands. In this context, a semirevolutionary organization, the Land League, was established in western Mayo, one of Ireland's most destitute counties. Under the leadership of Michael Davitt, the Land League adopted a strategy of local rent strikes and boycotts, to prevent evictions and rent increases. Unlike earlier movements, it made no sectarian appeals and focused only on land reform. No compromises were made at the expense of peasants—and all peasants were included in its efforts. The rent strikes were so effective that they polarized Ireland along clear class lines and gave further impetus to and a base for nationalist politics.

The effects of the depression were also severe for the commercial middle classes; as exports fell, rents went uncollected and commerce declined. As the spokesperson of this group, Charles Parnell used the extremism of the Land League to procure concessions from the metropole and mounted a Home Rule movement. With Land Leaguers as their radical wedge, the bourgeoisie centered in Dublin sought to secure financial and political support for Irish capital and changes in the land tenure system. Westminster responded with dual strategies, reflecting the metropolitan struggle between Liberals and Tories. Liberals sought to "kill Home Rule through kindness," adopting a series of land acts to reduce rents and legalize dual tenant-landlord ownership. Tories sought to foment resistance to Home Rule in the north.[38] The former strategy was unsuccessful. Despite the massive transfer of land in the latter decades of the nineteenth century, the land acts did not alter the decline of the agricultural sector. Instead, their chief legacy was to politicize Irish peasants. As owners of land, they were now brought into the Home Rule struggle, which had been previously the arena of the middle class. The new class of peasant proprietors became the mainstay of the nationalist movement.[39] And they were, at least, sympathetic to the small republican movement and the ideology of Sinn Fein.[40]

If land reform thrust the south into nationalist politics, it also underscored the effects of uneven development and the importance of the imperial connection to the northern economy. Belfast and Londonderry had no internal economic competition; but under Home Rule, not only would Ulster compete with the south, but it would also subsidize its competition. There was little doubt about the political allegiance of the Protestant bourgeoisie.

The loyalties of the masses of the workers were not guaranteed, however, especially since the industrial depression affected them most profoundly. Using the strategies of the Land League, republicans James Connolly and Jim Larkin initiated a series of strikes in Belfast to secure protection of labor—regardless of religious affiliation. And in particular strikes, Protestants and Catholics came together in support.[41] But, the strikes were brief and functional—never igniting the collective solidarity that characterized ethnic politics. Beyond the workplace, no other institutions supported labor solidarity. Segregated by neighborhood, attending separate churches and schools, urban Catholics and Protestants had little base for a shared communal consciousness. The labor unions were hardly solidary. The Ancient Order of the Hibernians, a Catholic labor organization, provided a powerful vehicle for worker cohesion within certain industries but an obstacle to national class politics. The Labour party in Britain excluded the Irish from its national administration, isolated Irish socialists, and refused to support the dock strike of 1907. In contrast, Belfast employers founded the Ulster Protestant Association to protect Protestant workers from unemployment and to divide the laboring class.

As the Home Rule movement gained strength in the south, the

industrial bourgeoisie warned Ulster's Protestant laborers that Home Rule would be economically disastrous, producing further unemployment and preventing social reform. Appeals by Tory leaders called on Orangemen in city and country to prove whether "all those ceremonies and forms which are practiced in Orange lodges are really living symbols or only meaningless ceremonies."[42] In 1912 at the height of Home Rule agitation, seventy British leaders came to Belfast to encourage active resistance to Home Rule. Warnings abounded that Home Rule would dismantle factories, eliminate the shipbuilding industry, destoy working-class reforms such as the eight-hour day, and lead to papist tyranny. The story of dominant class efforts to "play the Orange hand" has been told frequently.[43] To recruit working-class opposition, the Ulster Unionist Club Council was formed; its central executive consisted of six industrial capitalists, two landowners, a clergyman, a solicitor, and a "private gentleman." But its appeal was to Protestant labor in the city and rural areas. Local Orange lodges were used for recruiting support for unionism and later for training members of the illegal Ulster Volunteer Force. At the Ulster Unionist Convention in 1912, 473,000 of Ulster's 500,000 adult male Protestants subscribed to a "solemn league and convenant" to "defeat Home Rule by any means necessary."[44] A modern, loyalist convenant was crafted, calling on the tradition of Protestant reciprocity and fraternity to fight "Catholic tyranny." Following through on this pledge, Ulsterites fought vociferously against the Home Rule Bill. With the backing of the Conservatives, they established an Ulster Volunteer Force to resist any change in unionism.[45]

In summary, under the Union, the nature and source of Protestant ethnic solidarity and loyalty to the Crown was class differentiated. For the conservative Anglican landlords, this political stance constituted a defense against land reform agitation; for rural workers, it was a way to protect their coveted Ulster Custom and to accommodate to the proletarianization of the countryside. For the industrial bourgeoisie, loyalism derived from the knowledge that capital growth would be stunted were Ulster to be separated from British credit markets. And among the urban working class, it implied both a fidelity to the local community and a protection of the ethnic division of labor. These different economic interests were mediated through the agency of the Orange Order and vocalized in the language of religious fraternity. Protestant economic interests ensured that nationalism would be a virtually all-Catholic movement.

The militancy of the Ulster Unionists left Home Rulers, who had relied solely on parliamentary techniques, at a clear disadvantage. Although the Irish nationalists and Liberal party together constituted a parliamentary majority for Home Rule by 1912, the strident opposition of Ulster Protestants made it clear that eastern Ulster would not tolerate this. And the Liberals therefore argued for exclusion of Ulster from the Home Rule schemes.[46] In 1913 the Irish National Volunteers were established to counter the Ulster Volunteer Force threat. They represented an uneasy coalition of constitutional Home Rulers, republicans, and nationalists. It was in this polarized context that World War I broke out, and Britain's attention was diverted from the political struggles in Ireland. In the face of the war, Westminster sought a respite—by agreeing to Home Rule in principle but tabling its implementation. This delay fragmented the fragile nationalist coalition. The Irish National Volunteers joined the fight against Germany. Those who remained in Ireland were under the influence of the Republicans. Believing that England's difficulty was Ireland's opportunity, the Irish Republican Brotherhood and Sinn Fein formulated plans for an uprising, and sought to mobilize the population in a nationalist rebellion on Easter, 1916. The rebellion was small, ill-conceived, and not popularly supported; but it panicked the British administration in Dublin, which imposed martial law, executed fifteen of the leaders, and thereby secured much greater support for independence than had existed before the rebellion.

Ethnic Nationalism under the Union of Great Britain and Ireland

Nationalism in nineteenth-century Ireland was largely the product of regional economic differences, reflecting the different modes of production and resulting from different patterns of colonization and relations to the imperial state. In addition, the ethnic division of labor in the north disorganized working-class alliances and reinforced ethnic conflict. The recursive relation between ethnic and economic interests makes it impossible to argue that one set of loyalties categorically shaped the other. The evidence on the *rural* mobilization against land reform in the first half of the century provides significant support for claims that the capitalist elites of Ulster and England sought to reward Protestant labor for their loyalty; and that the patrimonial relations between capital and labor played a major role in fostering a sectarian politics during the Home Rule movement. The evidence also supports the resource competition claim that reactive ethnic politics are most likely when the resources of a formerly dominant group are threatened by economic changes. For this period, the existence of *prior* ethnic organizations together with an increased sense of competition for land may best explain how easily Anglican landlords accomplished their goals. The evidence about *urban* ethnic conflict again supports the claims of resource competition theorists. And although in some general sense an effort to protect labor advantages motivated Protestant working-class politics, especially as Catholics migrated to Belfast, this was only partially precipitated by the introduction of cheaper labor into the same labor market. It was also enhanced by warnings from capital that secular labor politics and Home Rule would erode ethnic segregation in industry and the economic advantages of Ulster over the rest of Ireland. However, this review also indicates that ethnic politics cannot be reduced to economic competition. Fidelity to local community, territorial competition, and a sense of a prior right to political resources sparked urban Protestant mobilization against Catholics. And the ethnically exclusive trade unions, the spatial segregation of neighborhoods, and the Orange Order all provided an institutional infrastructure for ethnic mobilization.

During this period of capital development, competition for jobs and land in the north, the salience of the Orange lodge as a source of sociability, status, and solidarity, and the influence of a populist evangelical crusade in the face of a declining rural culture made working-class Protestants especially vulnerable to calls for ethnic exclusivity. These factors, combined with the effects of uneven capital growth and industrialization increased the likelihood that any resistance to imperial dominance would be predominantly Catholic. But that nationalism was not accidently ethnic. Throughout the epoch, no movement demanded independence or Home Rule on ethnic grounds. There was no contention that Ireland was the exclusive domain of one religious group or that Protestant Ulsterites represented a different, non-Irish population. Nor did Ulster Protestants see themselves as Scots or as British. A content analysis of the political literature and public statements in the period 1819–1913 indicates that Ulster apologists embraced a view that Unionists were loyal Irish who shared the same nationality as the "disloyal Irish."[47] At the same time, a cultural nationalism developed in the south which tended to depict the struggle for Home Rule as a clash between two civilizations and to romanticize the Fenian uprisings. Padraig Pearse, for example, argued that the Gaels were the Irish Irish, thereby excluding Ulsterites from his national conception and ignoring the fact that by midcentury only 23 percent of the populace spoke any Gaelic.

If the nationalist movement was a virtually Catholic movement, it was also a fragile one. By the turn of the century, the uneasy coalition of constitutional Home Rulers (the United Irish League) and Republicans (Irish Republican Brotherhood) reflected the varying agrarian, commercial, and labor interests among those Catholics.[48] Were it not for the violent response of the British government to the ineffectual Easter Rising in 1916, this coalition might have been dismantled. But the execution of the leaders stunned those who had devoted themselves for decades to constitutional politics—leaving Britain's only support among the Protestants of Ulster. In the face of a massive outcry, Britain announced that Home Rule would be implemented immediately.

Over a century after the Union, Britain finally capitulated to the Irish, and the process of decolonization began. But Ireland had been irrevocably changed, and the creation of a single state under Home Rule was to prove impossible. A long guerilla war broke out as Protestants sought to maintain the Union, constitutionalists sought Home Rule, and radical Republicans refused the limitations of Home Rule within the British Empire. The extent of popular support for the Republican position was revealed in the 1918 elections, in which Sinn Fein won seventy-three seats, and the previously dominant parliamentary Home Rulers won only six.[49] Unionists, for their part, captured twenty-two of Ulster's thirty-seven constituencies. In 1919 full-scale hostilities broke out between the armed Republicans and the British forces. The troubles lasted until May of 1921. The final treaty resulted in the 1922 partition of Ireland, which sustained the Union between Ulster and Britain and granted the south independent status.[50] As we shall see in the next chapter, neither independence nor partition was to solve the ethnic conflicts and national struggles of Ireland.

CONFEDERATION, STATE DEVELOPMENT, AND ETHNIC DIFFERENTIATION IN CANADA FROM 1840 TO 1900

In contrast to Ireland, the Union of Canada, established after the Patriote Rebellion, lasted only twenty-five years. Its assimilationist policies were not really successful, and within several years the legislative council included French Canadians and the use of the French language. As John Jackson has put it, by 1867 the "French and English had experienced little more than a century of contact within a single colonial enterprise. The interaction between the two, though retaining a dominant subordinate relationship, resulted in a continuing recognition and legitimation of one party by the other. The subordinate party was never completely absorbed. French and English Canada faced each other in 1867 as distinctly recognizable nationalities, tied together by class coalitions."[51] The alliance between clergy and English Canadian bourgeoisie, like the earlier alliance between French clergy and seigneur and British colonial administrators, permitted British imperialism to flourish in North America. However, the need to consolidate the colony, enlarge its internal market, and create an infrastructure for capital investment and economic development became more and more apparent by the middle of the nineteenth century, especially as the imperial policies of free trade created real problems for the exporting economy of Canada and as competition with the United States increased. To develop the centralized state apparatus necessary for economic growth, Westminster passed the British North America Act in 1867. It established a Canadian Confederation, uniting four provinces (Ontario, Quebec, New Brunswick, and Nova Scotia) under a single federal government. The keystone in the confederation was a national policy of economic development which made the fixed capital of the provinces the property of the central government and which granted to the federal level the power to legislate all aspects of economic development (canals, railways, telegraphs, banking, trade, currency, credit) and control over revenues. Bilingualism was expressly protected only in the courts and legislatures of Quebec and the federal government. Otherwise, social services, education, civil rights (and by extension language rights), and nat-

ural resources were under provincial control. The French population was split in its support of confederation. One faction, the
Rouges, argued that the system of government was not really federalist but a "scheme of annihilation aimed for our destruction";
the conservative Bleu faction argued that only confederation would
prevent the absorption of Canada by the United States and the inevitable dissipation of French Canada.[52] But, more important,
French and English Canadians tended to differ in their interpretations of the *meaning* of confederation. For many of the English, it
constituted a compact between provinces, with Quebec now a government among equals. For most of the French, it constituted a
compact between the French and English nations, with cultural
identity as the essential unit.[53]

There is little doubt that confederation did not respect the principle that the English and French constituted equal nations in Canada. Under the British North America Act, French Canadians were
not guaranteed equal language rights; whereas in Quebec—the only
province with a majority of French speakers—the language rights
of the English were protected. Ontario courts and legislatures were
unilingually English; Catholic (and mostly French) schools were
held to be outside the public sector and hence received no tax support. The legislature of New Brunswick adopted an assimilationist
policy of exclusively English instruction in schooling and of double
taxation of Catholic schools. Although Manitoba adopted educational and language freedoms when it joined the confederation, by
1890 when the English constituted a majority, it rescinded these
provisions and made the courts and legislature unilingually English;
Catholic schools received no public support. In the 1890s Alberta
and Saskatchewan adopted similar policies.[54] Thus, federalism ensured the collective survival of the Francophones but effectively
restricted them to the province of Quebec, where they held an electoral majority (and where the linguistic rights of the English minority were protected). The clear message to French Canadians was
that their ethnic integrity would be protected only within the province of Quebec. Outside that province, bilingualism was not preserved.[55] However, under the act of Confederation *religious*—not
language—rights were maintained, insofar as these were part of the
legal tradition of the provinces. Hence, Catholic and Protestant
schools in Quebec were granted state support; where no such laws
had existed—as in New Brunswick—there was no protection. This

legal support for religious schools bolstered the role of the Catholic church in the Francophone community—and reinforced the conjunction between faith and language. Preservation of Catholic schools became essential to the survival of French language and letters in Canada. This protection may also have contributed to the enduring economic marginality of the French Canadian.

After confederation, Montreal developed into the heart of financial and industrial power in both Quebec and Canada and became the administrative center of national economic development. The transportation companies, the largest banks, and the headquarters of mining and industry were located there. This power and wealth were concentrated almost exclusively in English Canadian hands. In part this was the legacy of the patterns of colonization examined in the last chapter. Until the 1920s the majority of French Canadians were concentrated in rural Quebec, whereas the English minority predominated in the cities. It was also due in part to the educational system in Quebec. The separate religious schools prepared students differently for participation in a market economy.[56] Through its control of the system of education, the church shaped the skills and avenues of mobility of the French Quebecois. Habitant sons who sought to enter the professions and political life were sent to bishops' seminaries. Cut off from France and dominated by the ultramontane church hierarchy, these schools tended toward religious orthodoxy and emphasized classics and philosophy rather than education in business, commerce, engineering, or science. As a result, French Canadians tended to enter law and politics, and the English middle class experienced little competition in the business firms of the expanding capitalist economy. By educating the French for noncompetitive positions, the church also retained her own influence.[57] Local politicians, trained by the clergy, connected the villages with supravillage institutions, such as the provincial legislative assembly. Also, the ultramontane tradition ensured significant obedience to the dictates of the clergy. Herbert Guindon has summarized the church's political influence during the late nineteenth century: "Political issues were defined by the urban bourgeoisie and its internationally minded small elite, disseminated by the local bourgeoisie through the help of their partisan regional newspapers, and settled by the quite illiterate population, who were sometimes told what to do straight from the pulpit, in the name of God and salvation, by the parish priest, under the goading of an

83

aggressive bishop.''[58] Lest this seem a caricature, the legitimacy of ecclesiastical influence was propounded by the church. A collective pastoral letter to the Quebec Episcopate in 1879 expressed the ultramontane belief: "Not only is the Church independent of civil society—she is superior to it by reason of her extent and of her goal. It is not the Church which is comprised in the State; it is the State which is comprised in the Church.''[59] Clerical interference in politics was legitimated: "If the bishops whose authority issues from God himself are the natural judges of all questions which touch upon the Christian faith and morals, it they are the acknowledged heads of a perfect society, it follows that it is in their province when circumstances so demand, not merely to express generally their views and wishes in regard to religious matters, but also to indicate to the faithful or to approve the best means of attaining the spiritual ends in view.''[60] Through its dominance of education, the church maintained its own power but reproduced the noncompetitive position of the Francophones vis-à-vis the English. It rationalized the secondary status by adopting an ideology which stressed the religious agrarian mission of the French and by claiming that they were born to handle ideas, not money.[61]

If economic inequality and linguistic conflicts were exacerbated under confederation, not all French Canadians embraced the church hierarchy's isolationist nationalism and ultramontane dominance, especially as the economic base of rural self-sufficiency declined. Liberals, in particular, argued for more secular training in schools and for stronger state support for provincial economic development. The pattern of Quebec voting in federal elections indicates that they attracted a following. Although the clerically supported Conservatives captured the majority of votes and seats from 1867 to 1887, Quebec was truly a two-party state. Under the leadership of Wilfred Laurier in 1896, the Liberal party directly challenged the traditional hegemony of the church, espousing an end to clerical control of schooling. Although uniformly denounced by the bishops, the Liberals amassed forty-nine of Quebec's sixty-five seats. The church's power was further broken in the by-election of 1897, won by a Liberal candidate, Guite, who refused to capitulate to the church on education issues, arguing: "I am a Catholic and in all questions of faith and morals, I am ready to accept without restriction the decisions of the Church. In all political questions, I claim the freedom of every British subject.''[62] It appeared then, at the turn of the century, that politics within Quebec could be secularized and that Canada would develop a pluralist polity in which struggles over linguistic rights would be settled within the provinces and that issues of national conflict would be reduced to problems of provincial-federal relations, rather than ethnic identity. However, the secularization and ''de-ethnicization'' of Canadian politics were short-circuited by federal immigration policies and by the effects of industrialization and imperial policy on Quebec's economy.

INDUSTRIALIZATION, ETHNIC STRATIFICATION, AND ETHNIC MOBILIZATION IN CANADA FROM 1900 TO 1940

At the turn of the century, French Canadians faced severe economic disequilibrium, as good unsettled land in Quebec diminished. In a province with a substantially high birthrate, the farms could not support the expanding population. Many farmers sought to purchase existing farms or provide education to guarantee some secure employment outlets for their children. Both required capital and pulled the rural habitants away from their subsistence economy and into the expanding capitalist market. ''The placement of children now became increasingly dependent upon the fluctuating market from which the farmer got his money,'' as habitants attempted to develop crop surpluses and to sell produce to cities.[63] Also, Quebec farmers were not well situated; Quebec City lacked a rail link to central Canada and so was unable to capture the national market or compete with farms in Ontario. The inability of the Quebec agrarian economy to support the populace was evident in the demographic shifts at the turn of the century. Everett Hughes has calculated that when the birth rates of Quebec are taken into account, rural loss between 1871 and 1931 was never less than 50 percent.[64] In the period 1900–1911 Quebec experienced a net loss of 240,000 due to emigration.[65] But the French did not emigrate alone. Beginning in the last decade of the nineteenth century, Canada's population exploded, as the federal government encouraged immigration and agriculture as the keys to national development in the west. ''Preferential status was given to immigrants with the greatest linguistic, cultural and social affinities with the Canadian anglophone community.''[66] Between July of 1900 and April of 1909, 1,244,597 immigrants arrived in Canada—a one-third population increase in a decade. Of these immigrants, only 1 percent were

85

French speaking, whereas 40.3 percent arrived from the United Kingdom and 31.6 percent from the United States.[67] Most of the immigrants moved to the western territories, resulting in the establishment of Alberta and Saskatchewan as provinces in 1905. The French population was sensitive to the clear cultural ramifications of these migration patterns, given their experiences under confederation. Henri Bourassa, who was emerging as the most articulate spokesman of French Canadian interests, expressed these fears: "Our national unity would be less endangered if there were in the Northwest more French and Catholic Canadians and even separate schools and fewer of the thousands of strangers who have contributed nothing to the building of the country, who had made no sacrifice to the cause of national unity."[68] Although Bourassa's anti-immigration stance was clearly nativistic, it also reflects the French Canadian dilemma. The number of English-speaking immigrants ensured that French electoral power would be restricted to a single province and that language rights would be correspondingly curtailed. These fears had already been realized in New Brunswick, Saskatchewan, and Alberta. And in 1915 the Ontario legislature passed a regulation requiring the use of English as the language of instruction in all provincial schools. The few bilingual schools were placed under inspection of the state, and the study of French was confined to an hour a day. The school question underscored the dilemma of the French emigrants from Quebec and raised the question of Canada's commitment to a dual society. In response to Regulation 17, French teachers in Ontario went out on strike, and supportive collections were taken up throughout Quebec. Almost every Catholic bishop signed a petition denouncing the regulation, and a boycott of Ontario manufacturers was initiated. Bourassa's response to the regulation illustrates the predilection of the most prominent French Canadian leader of this period: "After a hundred and fifty years of good and loyal service to a Crown that we have learned to respect, we deserve better than to be considered like Savages of the old reservations and to be told: 'Remain in Quebec. Continue to stagnate in ignorance; you are at home there; but elsewhere you must become English.' No. We have the right to be French in language; we have the right to be Catholic in faith; we have the right to be free by the constitution. We are Canadians above all; and we have the right to enjoy rights throughout the whole expanse of the Confederation."[69] As French loyalties intensified, so did English hostility. The *Toronto Star* warned that the French were trying to drive the English out of Ontario, that the language conflict represented "a conspiracy devised by French priests to absorb her soil, violate her laws and undermine her independence."[70] The severity of the ethnic cleavage was evident in 1915, when French Canadian settlers in northern Ontario were forced to sign an oath to obey Regulation 17 or forfeit their land and the money paid for it.

The language conflict was compounded by the effects of World War I on Quebec. Throughout the war, Canadian industry expanded, maintaining high wages and profit. In Quebec on the other hand, unemployment increased. The sense of relative deprivation was exacerbated when French Canadian recruits into the armed forced were forced into Anglophone units, where few served as officers. When conscription was made obligatory in 1917, Quebec mobilized against the draft. Conscription laws included seminary and theological students, thereby antagonizing the church hierarchy. Throughout the province, anticonscription meetings were held with clerical support. In Montreal the home of the owner of the English newspaper was bombed; in Quebec City riots broke out which were quelled by Canadian troops, dispatched from Toronto; the coalition Union government effectively excluded Quebec representation, and talk in the province turned to secession (where the legislature debated a secession proposal for three weeks). The conscription crisis had such a dramatic impact on Quebec feelings about the Conservative party, which had introduced the bill, that between 1917 and 1945, with the exception of one election, the Conservatives did not win a single Francophone seat in Quebec (see table 4).

French Canadian isolationism derived in part from the traditional nativist ideology adopted at the time of the conquest. But it was supported by the assimilationist provincial policies and federal refusal to acknowledge the linguistic rights of Francophones in the national armed forces. French was clearly protected only within the province of Quebec. Outside that area, where the Francophone minority had no political resources to advance their linquistic interests, the binationality of Canada was a fiction. It was in this context that the impact of industrialization was felt in Quebec and that a separatist movement emerged, seeking the establishment of an independent French Catholic state.

Table 4 Quebec Voting in Federal Elections

Year	Seats Won			Percentage of Votes		
	Conservative	Liberal	Other	Conservative	Liberal	Other
1867	45	20	—	—	—	—
1872	38	27	—	—	—	—
1874	32	33	—	—	—	—
1878	45	20	—	56.4	40.1	3.4
1882	52	13	—	59.3	40.7	—
1887	36	29	—	50.6	49.1	0.3
1891	29	34	2	52.0	45.4	2.5
1896	16	49	—	45.8	53.5	0.7
1900	8	57	—	43.5	56.3	0.2
1904	11	54	—	43.4	56.4	0.2
1908	11	54	—	40.8	57.3	1.9
1911	27	38	—	49.2	50.7	0.1
1917	3	62	—	25.1	72.7	2.2
1921	0	65	—	18.4	70.2	11.4
1925	4	59	2	33.7	59.4	6.9
1926	4	60	1	34.3	62.3	3.4
1930	24	40	1	44.7	53.2	2.2
1935	5	55	5	28.2	54.5	17.4
1940	1	61	3	19.8	63.3	16.9
1945	2	53	10	8.4	50.8	40.8
1949	2	68	3	24.6	60.4	15.0
1953	4	66	5	29.4	61.0	9.6
1957	9	62	4	31.1	57.6	11.3
1958	50	25	0	49.6	45.7	4.7
1962	14	35	26	29.6	39.1	31.3
1963	8	47	20	19.5	45.6	33.6
1965	8	56	11	21.0	46.0	33.0

Source: Cohen, *Quebec Votes,* 15, 19, 24, 30, 42, 54, 62, 65, 76, 85, 93, 100.

From the turn of the century, American and Canadian capital moved into Quebec, attracted by the rich natural resources and large supply of wage labor in the region. Paper and pulp industries were established at Trois Rivières, shoe factories in Quebec City, lumber industries in Montreal, and mining and forestry in Abitibi, Lac St. Jean, and the Gaspé. The most characteristic feature of industrial development in Quebec was its stark contrast to the industrializing areas of the United States and Anglo-Canada, where labor included a huge proportion of immigrant workers. In Quebec, on the other hand, a different pattern developed, what Everett

Hughes called the "inner expansion" of capital. Management was foreign to the region; labor was indigenous and ethnically homogeneous.[71] All social classes were affected by the ethnic expansion of capitalism: Workers lost their independent rural culture, small merchants and businessmen faced tough competition from large English enterprises, and professionals' prestige was undermined by the new class of industrial managers. One can scarcely overstate the extent of English industrial dominance. In a study of the town of Drummondsville, Hughes calculated that every major industry was owned and controlled by English Canadians; only two of eleven large firms had French Canadian management. However, the lower echelons of labor were entirely occupied by Francophones. This was precisely the situation throughout Quebec in the iron, steel, and textile industries. Research on the distribution of labor in Montreal indicates that the French were uniformly located on the lower rungs of the industrial hierarchy—long after industry had been firmly established (see table 5).[72] Of the business firms in Montreal in 1931, only 48.4 percent were controlled by the English, but an analysis of the relative financial strength of all the Montreal firms indicates that 86.6 percent of capital was in English hands. Half of the investment capital was in the hands of a small number of large English corporations.[73] The firms owned by the French were secondary industries (largely boot and shoe factories), small furniture companies, and printing concerns. With the centralization of industry, these too gradually passed to English control.[74] Ethnic group representation in occupational classes replicated this pattern, with the French disproportionately located in primary and unskilled labor and agriculture. In contrast, the Anglophones dominated the professions and administrative ranks.[75]

Table 5 Occupational Distribution of Ethnic Groups in Industry in Montreal in 1931

Occupational Sector	English	French
Managers	73.8	22.6
Sales staff	62.4	34.3
Skilled workers	25.3	69.4
Semiskilled workers	19.4	74.6

Source: Everett Hughes, "French and English in the Industrial Structure of Montreal," in *The Sociological Eye,* 244.

The dominance of the English over Canadian industry was further extended by the settling of the western provinces and the expansion of trade relations with the United States and Britain. English became the language of commerce; and "as commerce and industry became more important and were regulated more and more by national policy and federal control, the need to master the English language and subscribe to English ways of business became evident."[76] It was characteristic of industrial firms in Quebec to insist that orders for the managerial staff be given in English.[77]

Nevertheless, it is important to emphasize that Anglo dominance was not simply the result of central government support of English capital. Among French Canadians, the emphasis of the political elite, especially the church, on the integral connection between traditional values and ethnic survival helped shape a nonentrepreneurial value orientation. Those who entered the professions tended to practice singly or in small firms and to develop highly personalistic ties to the community. In a study of Francophone businessmen, Norman Taylor reported their strong resistance to acquiring capital from nonfamilial sources, their reluctance to delegate responsibility, and their particularistic family orientation in business. Taylor explained that one reason for the limited growth of business had been the traditionalist orientation of the population: "Family orientation meant also that the size of the firm is related to the size, composition, inclinations and aptitudes of the family. A small family with few males, for example, is less likely to expand its business, since the persons it considers best qualified to control business operations are few in number. So long as growth can be achieved within the framework of family relationships, it is at least thinkable, but growth that entails diffusion of responsibility beyond the kinship group is another matter."[78]

Moreover, Quebec encouraged the investment of foreign capital with few dissenting voices. However, industrial expansion after World War I was so dramatic that the impact of Anglo-controlled industry upon Quebec's social structure and traditional values could not be ignored. It was clear that the French were no longer masters in their own homes. This situation produced a reaction, not against industry itself, but against the industrial overseers, "les Anglais." Among the commercial and political elite, strong opposition was expressed to English and American control of Quebec's resources. Beaudry Laman, the leading French Canadian banker, represented this perspective, when he declared in 1928 that "the most serious menace is not the penetration of money capital, but of the moral and intellectual capital of men better qualified than we to profit from our natural resources."[79]

Simultaneous with the threat industrialism posed to the French Canadian rural self-sufficiency and ethnic integrity was the threat which it posed to the power of the Catholic church. As Camille Legendre has noted, the secular values of the industrial system fundamentally challenged the authority of the parish priest, especially in urban areas, where the parish no longer functioned as the core of the community. "For the Church, industrialization carried dangerous secular values. The emphasis on materialism and on well being in this world instead of on spiritual values, as well as an economy of self-sufficiency, based on competition and continual search for profit and higher salaries instead of ethical considerations, was diametrically opposed to the system of values of this Catholic society."[80]

Competition from cheap French Canadian labor mobilized United States trade union organizers, who sought to organize in Quebec and limit the likelihood of runaway shops. The Catholic church hierarchy sought to inhibit the growth of unions in industrial Quebec, opposing their materialistic and frequently socialist outlook. Local political elites opposed unions because industrialists did not interfere with the local distribution of power, whereas union organizers challenged the entire hierarchical system. French Canadian politicians would frequently appeal to ethnic solidarity "to curb the political threat presented by the labor movement. . . . The French Canadian worker was slow to turn against his traditional leaders and to lose his hierarchical view of society. He was willing to pay the price of being distinctively French and Catholic in an industrial system dominated by the Anglo-American Protestant world which encircled Quebec."[81] But the need for labor union organization could not be ignored—as international organizers began to mobilize in industrial firms. To control the growth of the unions, the church in 1905 organized La Confédération des Travailleurs Catholiques du Canada, an organization that included 60 percent of the union members in the province. The membership was limited to Catholics and the union was characterized by its anti-internationalist, anti-communist, anti-Protestant, and anti-American stance. Milner and Milner have outlined the social structure of the confédération, depicting the extent of clerical hegemony: "Each local was run by an aumônier, a priest or chaplain whose duty it was to educate its members . . . to their Catholic duties in their role as trade unionists. . . . The aumôniers interpreted worker legislation, describing the advantages and disadvantages. . . . The only economic demand viewed as legitimate for the worker was simply that of a wage sufficient to support his family. Legal strikes were permitted only when all else failed; sympathy strikes were immoral and thus prohibited. . . . The idea of the owner as a man with a different role to play in the social order was propounded. The idea of class conflict was violently repudiated."[82] The enduring power of the clergy and their close alignment with the dominant political elites ensured that trade unionism in Quebec would be a weak and conciliatory movement. It should also be pointed out that both the Communist party and the Cooperative Commonwealth Federation showed little sensitivity to the dilemmas of French Canadians or to their particular ethnic tradition. Even progressive Francophones who opposed the reactionary aspects of Quebec nationalism were not entrusted with leadership positions or taken seriously by the internationals.[83] The extensive power of the clergy was reinforced by the credit union movement. In 1932, with clerical support, the province passed a law to support the growth of indigenous credit unions, "caisses populaires." All credit union investments would be made within Quebec, as loans to municipalities or parish schools, a modernization of the habitant tradition of neighborly assistance. To join the local caisse, one had to swear, "I am a French Canadian and a practicing Catholic."[84] In short, mobilization on economic issues occurred within the confines of traditional authority relations, hence retarding the growth of class consciousness among French Canadians and underscoring the primacy of ethnic solidarity.

Throughout the 1930s, organizations developed in response to the effects of Anglo-dominated industry, initiated and supported by the church and middle class. A group of university students formed Les Jeunes Patriotes, a right-wing nationalist movement which demanded provincial control over industry and a proportionate share of federal jobs for Francophones; they blamed their subordinate status on "Jewish liberalism."[85] The Jesuits formed L'Ecole Sociale Populaire and proposed the establishment of a hierarchical Catholic corporate state, Laurentia, in which industrial conflict would be avoided through state and church control of wages. A leading spokesman for this nationalist movement was Abbé Groulx, who published a magazine L'action française, which stressed the need to speak French in business and legal affairs and published lists of Francophone merchants to enable people to "buy French." It was in the pages of this magazine that the doctrine "la revanche des berceaux," encouraging a high French Canadian birthrate, was promulgated and the myth of the golden age of the habitants was formulated. Primacy was placed upon race as the essential element of Quebec's history. A typical statement by Groulx exemplifies the doctrines of this ethnic nationalism: "The nearly complete possession of the soil by a determined race, the profound imprint that this race was given it by its original manners and institutions, the special status reserved for it by all the political constitutions since 1701, have made of Quebec a French state that must be recognized in theory as well as in fact. It is this truth which must be replaced on high, in order that it may govern the economic order amongst us."[86] These ethnic nationalist tendencies came to political coherence in 1935 with the formation of a new political party, the Union Nationale, led by Maurice Duplessis.

From the onset of the depression, French Canadian workers faced severe economic problems. In 1932 unemployment reached a peak of 30 percent; over 100,000 Francophones were on relief in Montreal. Attacking the Liberals as an arm of the Anglo business establishment and hence responsible for the disproportionate French Canadian unemployment rates, the Union Nationale aligned with the old Conservatives, advocated low credit rates, French Canadian control over resources, and political and social reforms within French Canadian traditions. Opposed to monopoly capital as imperialist, the Union Nationale embraced an agrarian cooperative movement that drew from the tradition of mutual aid among the habitants. It supported efforts to nationalize hydroelectricity and to establish state corporations to protect small companies. It easily attracted the support of the church, won forty-two provincial seats in the 1935 election, and in 1936 captured the provincial assembly. The Duplessis regime drew from the doctrines of L'action française to espouse right-wing nationalism, the values of the ultramontane habitant tradition, and virulent anticommunism. A 1937 Padlock

Law, for example, permitted the state to close any premise selling "Communist literature or being used for Communist purposes."[87] Within a year thousands of papers, reviews, circulars, and pamphlets had been seized. And the school system had been closed "to all but Catholic doctrine and its socio-political corollary, right wing corporatism."[88] Opposition to these activities was attributed to Anglophone agitators, especially Communists and Jews. Thus by the beginning of World War II, the government of Quebec was deeply isolationist, showing sympathetic tendencies toward fascist syndicalism and ready to express immediate opposition toward what was seen as Britain's imperial war. And once again, a debate over the military draft precipitated ethnic antagonisms.

Canadian Prime Minister King was initially able to garner French Canadian support of his war policies through a deliberately ambiguous stance. He emphatically maintained that Canada would supply only economic aid to Britain and would not initiate conscription for overseas action. Believing in King, most Quebecois rejected the antifederalist, antiwar, autonomist platform of Duplessis. Francophone cabinet ministers argued such isolationism invited conscription; the church hierarchy called for victory Masses and contributions to the war effort; the Duplessis platform was soundly defeated in the 1939 provincial elections.[89] But conscription was another issue. In 1940 the Francophone mayor of Montreal advised citizens not to register for the draft. When a plebescite was proferred in 1942, Quebec opposed the conscription by 72 percent, whereas the other provinces supported it by 80 percent. In 1943 public opinion surveys indicated that 90 percent of French Canadians opposed conscription, and 78 percent of the English favored it.[90] Once again, Canadian unity was shattered along ethnic lines on the issue of service in the armed forces. An isolationist French Canadian party, the Bloc Populaire, called for the nationalization of Quebec's resources and the formation of a state within a state, as in Ireland. Although it secured the support of 37 percent of the voters in the provincial elections of 1943, it signaled that French Canadian nationalist sentiment was significant. But, unlike in Ireland, such sentiment could be absorbed into the regular political process. When MacKenzie King retired as prime minister in 1949, he was succeeded by Louis Laurent, a Quebecois Francophone, with a record sixty-eight Quebec seats supporting his Liberal party. In short, the structure of confederation itself provided a framework for accommodating to and deflecting the ethnic consciousness of French Canadians, while at the same time ensuring Anglo-Canadian dominance.[91]

ETHNIC NATIONALISM IN QUEBEC DURING THE PERIOD OF INDUSTRIALIZATION

The subordinate economic position of French Canadians and their political responses can be explained as the result of several factors acting in a recursive fashion. The residual effects of colonization retarded the development of an indigenous capital base, so that when industry began to develop in French Canada, it was controlled by aliens. The social structure of the province, itself a product of colonization, mitigated against the accmumlation of competitive economic resources (capital, a market orientation) on the part of Francophones. For one thing, the school system de-emphasized entrepreneurial skills. Catholic colleges concentrated on the humanities and on the production of priests and physicians. Of those who graduated from Quebec's classical colleges between 1939 and 1950, 37 percent entered the priesthood, 24 percent became physicians, and 10 percent became engineers. Only 6 percent went into law, 5 percent into business, and 4 percent into the applied sciences.[92] In its efforts to retain social dominance and its endorsement of traditional values, the Catholic church contributed to the limitation of competitive resources among the Francophones. Its nationalist ideology of ethnocentric isolation, agrarianism, and provincialism discouraged economic competition. It secured the support of the industrial elite and foreign capital, thereby undergirding its own power and limiting the likelihood of interest-based class politics.

In the period of industrialization, then, the development of class politics was seriously constrained by the power and paternalist dominance of the traditional elites within French Quebec. Weber argues that class hierarchies "would be threatened at [their] very root if mere economic acquisition and naked economic power, still bearing the stigma of its extra-status origin, could bestow upon any who has won them, the same or even greater honor as the vested interests claim for themselves."[93] This was precisely the case in French Canada, where the Francophones lacked the resources to compete in the market, but where the dominant English could be dismissed for their vulgar secular statuses. And this disjunction between status and class consciousness ensured that the subordinate economic position of French Canada would endure. Fundamental changes required an assault upon both the traditional and the modern industrial hierarchies.

It would be a mistake to focus only on class structure as an explanation of the patterns of ethnic mobilization in industrializing Quebec. Equally important was a political system which intentionally facilitated the English monopolization of power in the state, by failing to protect or even to recognize French language and educational rights. The assimilationist policies of the provinces encroached increasingly on the French Canadian population, forcing adaptation of the English outside the province of Quebec. By midcentury, the French population was decreasingly bilingual. According to 1951 census figures, 20 percent of French Canadians in Manitoba, 31.5 percent in Saskatchewan, and 54.5 percent in British Columbia could no longer speak French. Thus, as Jean Falardeau described these absorbing tendencies: "English speaking Canadians can move from one province to another without leaving 'chez lui'. . . . The French Canadian, on the other hand, who leaves Quebec to travel or live in another province, feels himself becoming a foreigner. For this reason, perhaps confused, but very strongly, he believes that his language, his culture, perhaps his religion are in danger there. The province of Quebec is thus not just one of the ten Canadian provinces. It is not at all interchangeable. It has been and it remains *the* French province in Canada."[94] In this sense, linguistic rights represent a kind of nonnegotiable demand; to the extent to which they are restricted to a single territory, the likelihood of ethnic mobilization within that territory escalates. But the direction of that mobilization is intricately connected to the political power and economic situation of the language group. In the case of Quebec, the special protective role played by the Catholic church and traditional political elite ensured that those politics would be isolationist and accommodationist. However, as we shall see in the next chapter, state and capital development in the postwar period were to alter the class structure of Quebec, undermining the base of traditional power and generating new arenas of conflict between Anglophones and Francophones in Canada. These changes facilitated new forms of ethnic mobilization that were no longer religious, no longer isolationist, and no longer accommodationist but strongly nationalist.

A Comparison of Ireland and Canada during the Period of Industrialization

In this chapter, I have delineated the structures and processes that sustained ethnic stratification throughout the early stages of industrialization. This review has been descriptive but should help refine the analytic framework set out in chapter 2. There, I argued that industrialization and capital development are likely to increase ethnic competition under a number of circumstances: when capitalist firms seek to break up formerly segregated labor markets, where a split labor market exists in which ethnic workers seek to monopolize a particular place for themselves, or when industrialists seek to prevent class alliances by differentially rewarding a particular sector of the labor market. I also argued that the development of more centralized state systems is likely to underscore the relation between ethnic attributes and individual interests, as numerous areas of potential conflict are introduced: schooling, legislature, and economic development policy. Finally, I argued that ethnic conflict is likely to escalate in urban areas, where competition for territory and control over political institutions is more direct, and where alternatives to traditional leadership, ideologies, and mechanisms of social control can develop. The historical review in this chapter supports this argument but also invites some elaboration. In this conclusion I shall demonstrate, in a summary form, how the argument can be applied and refined.

In both Ireland and Canada, the means and organization of production set limits on the extent to which ethnicity was the major basis for mobilization. In each case, there was a coincidence between ethnic boundaries and regional development and control of industry. This was the product in Ireland of the deliberate underdevelopment of the predominantly Catholic south and of the patrimonial alliance between the Protestant working class and the imperialists in the north. Because British and Ulster Protestants controlled both industry and commercial agriculture, the political interests and conflicts associated with these two forms of production fell along ethnic lines. Within industry itself, a split labor market developed, facilitating conflicts within the working class over access to jobs. However, it was not only workers who acted to foster ethnic antagonism. The landed and capitalist leadership encouraged regional and industrial conflicts by appeals to sectarianism, further undermining the possibility of an interethnic national or working-class movement. In short, industrialization increased ethnic conflicts because it was territorially specific and because within that territory class actions within the dominant Protestant populace could maximize their own interests only by exclusion of or discrimination against Catholic wage labor. The competition and conflict were no more frequent or more fierce in the urban areas than they were in rural Ulster. By the mid–nineteenth century the institutional links between the countryside and the city were strong; and seasonal migration ensured that they would be sustained.

In Quebec industry was also controlled by the dominant ethnic group. But, here again, the situation was less clear-cut than in Ireland. Capitalists did not seek to create or to sustain an ethnic division of labor or the regional underdevelopment of Quebec. Indeed, until World War II, Montreal was the commercial and financial center of the country. In this case, the traditionalist French Catholic elite discouraged the development of economic resources among the Quebec Francophone population. Industrialization and proletarianization of the French population introduced labor organizers who challenged the traditional political elite. Because capitalists did not interfere with their political power, the Francophone leadership aligned itself with industry as it had with British colonial rulers after the conquest. And in the face of industrial conflict, the hierarchy sought to reinforce traditional values and orientations by channeling economic discontent along ethnic lines. They did not challenge English capital overtly; instead they appealed to the values of an agrarian Catholic populace and an idyllic habitant community. Their ability to secure support attests to the enduring power of traditional structures in an industrializing world—but also to the importance of social links between the city and the rural areas. Quebec remained a predominantly rural society through World War II.

In both Ireland and Canada, state development generated greater ethnic competition—but the basis and direction of that competition can be understood only through an analysis of the *structure* of the state system. In both cases, a structural pluralist system constrained the political resources of the subordinate ethnic group; but it did so in fundamentally different ways. In Ireland, the Union and the disfranchisement of both the Catholic middle class and the peasantry produced an affinity of ethnopolitical interests across class lines. Thus, in the early years of the Union, the middle class had to harness the economic discontent of the peasantry in order to advance its own political position. Its politics were necessarily ethnic. Consequently, even after emancipation, the legacy of this ethnic mobilization made the Irish suspicious of nonsectarian politics, and any interreligious alliances tended to be brief and functional. Canadian federalism created a more complex situation because French Canadians were granted equal rights within the state, based on universalist principles of political participation. This provided a basis for the development of cross-cutting class cleavages within French Canada and the growth of interest-based political parties at the federal level. However, there was also a minimal recognition of the dual ethnicity of Canada's charter groups demonstrated by the protection of linguistic rights in the federal legislature and Quebec Province. This minimal recognition was undermined by the failure to acknowledge the binationality of Canada or to protect bilingualism in the other provinces. As a result of this contradiction within the confederation, politics at the federal level were not primarily ethnic, but on issues of French survival, especially conscription, schooling, and immigration, the polarization between the groups was significant. In short, the ways in which ethnic groups were incorporated into the state system conditioned the extent to which they saw their interests as primarily ethnic.

Finally, in each case, we have seen the crucial role which the minority elite played in shaping the direction of ethnic mobilization. In both cases, traditional institutions, especially the churches and related associations, served as a basis for group organization and as a link between rural and urban areas. Within these institutions, the dominant ideologies were developed and articulated. The economic concerns of the masses were incorporated into nationalist ideologies only insofar as their support was needed either to pressure the central government (as in the Home Rule movement in Ireland) or when the power of the minority elite was jeopardized by the development of new interest groups (as in the Federation of Catholic Workers in Quebec). Perhaps the most significant difference between Ireland and Canada is the extent to which the ethnic leadership emphasized the importance of cultural factors to collective interests. In both societies, the major ethnic groups differed in language, religion, and degree of urbanization. Protestant leaders used religious symbols to exacerbate ethnic antagonism; but that was not picked up by Irish nationalists. Catholic leaders downplayed the substantive cultural differences between Ulster Scots Protestants and Irish Catholics. It is true that the leaders of the Easter Rising did appeal to Gaelic traditions and to the Irish language, but there is little evidence that this appeal was more than a symbolic rallying point or that it was influential in securing support for the insurrection. Nor was the language issue a dominant one: indeed, virtually all Irish leaders of the nineteenth century were English speakers. Most important, despite the degree of difference neither Unionists nor Nationalists ever argued that Scots/Anglo Protestants or Irish/Anglo Catholics were members of separate nations. In Canada, on the other hand, cultural differences assumed a material character from the outset, and the significance of these differences was constantly underscored by the Francophone leadership. As the protector of ethnic identity, through its control over schooling, the church emphasized that French Canadian survival required protection of faith, language, and agrarian virtues. Since the economy and polity were dominated by a single language group and since social mobility within the confederacy required the ability to speak English, language struggles were a zero-sum game. Linguistic survival for the French constituted a nonnegotiable demand, an attribute which was fundamentally distinct from other cultural differences since it could not be divorced from any aspect of daily life, work, or community. The failure of the federation to recognize this dilemma preserved the sense that French and English Canadians possessed two distinct nationalities.

An adequate explanation for the different material significance of cultural attributes in the politics of the two areas requires a consideration of the extent to which cultural differences were encapsulated in the state structure *and* the extent to which the preservation of those differences reflected the political interests of the minority elite. In Ireland the effort of the Catholic leadership was to secure equal participation within the Union—hence it made sense to downplay cultural differences. They could not do this easily. The majority of the population was Catholic, and their disabilities had been rooted, at least in part, in their religious affiliations. Hence, it made sense to appeal through the institutions and ideologies of the church. But this was a pragmatic choice—not an effort to preserve a Catholic identity. In contrast, the effort of the Catholic church in Quebec was to retain its own influence over the Quebec populace—that influence was based on its control over education and politics. Hence, it made sense to link language and religion together and preserve them in segregated institutions.

To summarize, three interacting structures must be analyzed if we are to understand the relation between class and ethnic politics in industrializing states: (1) the regional concentration of industrial and capital development and the occupational distribution of ethnic groups within industry; (2) the differential incorporation of ethnic groups into the state and its institutions; (3) the extent of class differentiation within the subordinate group. Once these patterns are mapped out we can clearly delineate the interest cleavages and resource differences within and between competing ethnic groups and hence the likelihood and direction of ethnic mobilization.

101

5

Ethnic Conflict and Nationalist Movements in the Advanced Industrial States

We are British to the core. But we won't hesitate to take on
even the British if they sell our country down the river.
—Billy Hull, a Protestant ship worker
in Belfast, 1972

Vive le Quebec Libre!
—Charles de Gaulle, Montreal, 1967

The neonationalist movements among Ulster's working-class Protestants and the separatist efforts of the Irish Republican Army and
the Parti Quebecois belie any claims that increasing modernization
and secularization of the state and economy will moderate ethnic
cleavages and politics. Indeed, the slogans and cries of the last
several decades may tempt us to see ethnic nationalism as part of a
historical trajectory, the inevitable result of the long shadow of colonialism and imperalism. Or they may tempt us to see the surge
of separatism as the twentieth-century equivalent of the class struggle, with ethnicity the dominant symbol of self-determination. In
this chapter, I will argue against such simple interpretations. Certainly, patterns of colonialism shaped the stratification within and
between ethnic groups and conditioned the initial distribution of
political resources in both of these countries. Yet we have seen that
resources are not historically fixed; they can be altered by the interaction between capital, the working class of the superordinate
group, and the traditional leaders of the subordinate group. We
have seen how these shifts, shaped by capital accumulation and
state formation, set the parameters for ethnic politics during the

period of industrialization. We now turn to the advanced industrial era, when multinational corporate capitalism and welfare state systems once again challenge the traditional ethnic order. The analysis in this chapter should provide evidence that the ethnic conflicts of today are fundamentally different from the antagonisms and nationalisms of earlier periods. In Ulster, the challenge to Unionist dominance and the British connection is no longer the exclusive terrain of Catholics and Republicans. Increasingly, working-class Protestants have also rejected the authority of the British government to regulate Ulster's affairs. But their movement is not one in partnership with Catholic Republicans. Rather, the effort to maintain a Protestant state in the north, even at the cost of union with Britain, constitutes resistance to the secularization of the state and economy on the part of a militant Protestant working class. In contrast, Quebecois nationalism is a result of secularization of the state and derives from the efforts of the Francophone middle class to secure a substantial berth in the expanding state system. In both cases, the nationalist movements do represent tactical efforts on the part of a class segment to advance its own economic and political position by claiming certain ethnic rights. But they are more than this; and a comparison of these two cases should help us refine the resource mobilization model to delineate *how* the features of advanced industrial society contribute to and shape ethnic politics.

To understand their differences, I will begin each case with a review of the nature of ethnic stratification during the period of advanced industrialization, analyzing how this was altered by the development of multinational corporate capitalism and by welfare state policies. Although there is no line of demarcation for when capitalism becomes "advanced," this is not a major problem for our purposes, since we want to get a sense of change across time. For Ireland this necessitates a discussion of the structure under partition, beginning in 1922; for Quebec we will begin with the Duplessis regime during World War II. In both cases, I will trace the changing structure of the political economy through the late 1960s. I will then examine the effects of these changes on class relations within the ethnic groups and on resource competition between them. The critical developments are the emergence of Orange nationalism in response to the Catholic civil rights movement in Ulster and the emergence of the Parti Quebecois as a response to the Quiet Revolution in Quebec.

ETHNIC STRATIFICATION IN A PROTESTANT STATE: NORTHERN
IRELAND, 1921–1950

Under the Government of Ireland Act of 1921, the country was
partitioned, and the six counties of the northeast remained within
the United Kingdom, retaining representation at Westminster and a
devolved legislature at Stormont, Belfast. The act was evidence of
the success of the Orange resistance to independence. But the survival of Ulster as an integral part of Great Britain was not easily
maintained in the face of an independent Irish Free State in the
south and a one-third Catholic population in the north. Any challenge to the Unionist alliance of urban workers, industrialists, agricultural labor, landowners, and small shopkeepers would undermine the dominance of the official Unionist party and its bourgeois
(mostly local, capitalist, landed agriculture) leaders.[1] Westminster
reserved to imperial control those matters that would affect the conditions for the development of capital: issues of war and peace,
international treaties, external aid, revenue matters (raising taxes,
income levies, excess profit and corporate taxes, customs and ex-
cise duties), a preservation which would continue Northern Ireland's status as an internal colony. However, Westminster adopted
few formal controls over the internal affairs of the state.[2] The refusal, therefore, to intervene in issues of ethnic relations permitted
the continuation of patrimonial relations so long as the economic
base for these relations endured. Numerous mechanisms were
adopted to ensure the stability of the Protestant alliance in the new
state. These included some gerrymandering of electoral boundaries
to contain the power of Catholic votes, the development of an entirely Protestant police force, the passage of laws that restricted
civil liberties, and patronage in public sector jobs. And the dominance of Ulster's bourgeois elite was sustained by such mechanisms
as an additional vote, in local elections, for business premises,
which had paid a certain amount of taxes. The linchpin in the entire
system was the degree of localism in government and the existence
of a powerful Ulster bourgeoisie, which permitted Unionist Orangemen to play a leading role in sustaining patrimonial relations. In
this section I will sketch the ways in which a localist government
and economy allowed Unionist leaders to sustain an interclass alliance among Protestants. Then I will examine how fundamental
changes in the economy and the state since World War II, espe-

cially the effect of advanced capitalism on local industry and the effects of central planning and bureaucratic welfare measures on Catholic resources, eroded the Protestant interclass coalition. Finally I will analyze why these shifts precipitated the civil rights movement and the militant neonationalist mobilization by Protestant workers.

After partition, the formal organizational basis for integrating the Protestant population into the new state was the Unionist party. Although it captured two-thirds of the electoral votes in the first parliamentary election, its hegemony was not ensured. In rural areas Catholics constituted a majority of voters, and most opposed the Union. In the local elections of 1920, Nationalists won victories in Derry City, Fermanagh, and Tyrone county councils, ten urban councils, and thirteen rural councils.[3] In the next election (1925), the Unionists faced internal challenges from Labour and Independent Unionists, and their share of the votes fell to 55.0 percent (with 13.7 percent going to Protestant Labour candidates). Fearing a Catholic Nationalist bloc, the Unionist elite sought to ward off all internal conflicts and to adopt electoral mechanisms which would reduce flexibility in voting choice and ensure that the constitutional position of Ulster would be the dominant electoral issue. The reforms (single-member constituencies and plurality rule rather than proportional representation) were an effective mechanism for weakening Catholic power and internal Protestant opposition. Table 6 indicates the extent of underrepresentation of Catholics in county, urban, and rural government as a result of manipulations of electoral boundaries and of the electoral reforms.[4] As a result of these efforts, election results were virtually predetermined, guaranteeing a Unionist victory. Prior to the initial gerrymander in 1923, no candidate was unopposed, but from the inception of the new state until the late 1960s, a significant proportion of seats in general elections were unopposed, averaging 43.7 percent between 1925 and 1955.[5] In the period from 1923 to 1955, 96 percent of the rural council seats, 90 percent of county council seats, and 60 percent of urban and borough council seats were uncontested.[6] From the outset, the Unionist party was a single-claim party whose only distinctive principle was continued union with Britain.[7] For Catholics, the Nationalist party served the same function. As Richard Rose points out: "The Unionists from the very foundation of the regime did not seek to make it fully legitimate by attracting the support of Catho-

Table 6 Number of Seats per Party and Population per Seat in Several Municipal Bodies in Northern Ireland in 1950

Municipal Body	Seats per Party		Population per Seat	
	Unionist	Nationalist	Unionist	Nationalist
Derry City Council	12	15	1,541	3,665
Armagh County Council	23	50	1,638	7,098
Lurgan Borough Council	15	0	551	5,499
Omagh Urban Council	12	9	180	397
Irvington Rural Council	14	8	424	851

Source: Frank Gallagher, *The Indivisible Island: The History and Partition of Ireland* (London: Victor Gollancz, 1957), 239. Reprinted by permission.

lics. Protestant solidarity sufficed to give the Unionists a permanent hold on office and to leave the Nationalists a permanent minority, without hope of gaining power—at least by peaceful constitutional means."[8] But if Catholics were effectively subordinated in the new state, the effects within the Protestant electorate were equally important. By replacing proportional representation with a plurality system, the Unionists effectively increased the power of local capital in government and reduced the power of internal Protestant opponents. A consideration of the differences between general electoral votes and seats captured attests to this. As table 7 indicates, despite significant support for minor parties, the official Unionists were always able to capture the majority of parliamentary seats.[9]

A second mechanism for securing an interclass alliance was the shoring up of the Royal Ulster Constabulary as an entirely Protestant police force. The RUC consisted of three classes of constables: A, who were full time, uniformed, and armed; B Specials, who were part time, fully armed, and without uniforms; and C, a reserve volunteer force which included almost every Protestant male in Ulster. Licenses for firearms were restricted to the RUC. The first prime minister, Lord Craigavon, endorsed this system of arming the population, saying that "owing to the system of A, B and C Constabulary, there is no reason why every loyalist should not have arms to his hand, legally agreed to by the state."[10] The tactics of

Table 7 General Parliamentary Elections in Northern Ireland, Party by Percent Vote and Members Elected

Election	Unionists		Unofficial Unionists[a]		NILP[b]		Independent Labour[c]		Nationalist/ Republicans[d]		Liberals		Others		For Union	Against Union
	%	M.P.	%	M.P.	%	M.P.	%	M.P.	%	M.P.	%	M.P.	%	M.P.		
1921	55.9	40	—	—	—	—	0.6	—	32.3	12	—	—	0.2	—	40	12
1925	55.0	32	9.0	4	4.7	3	—	—	29.1	12	—	—	2.2	1	40	12
1929	50.6	37	14.3	3	8.0	1	0.8	—	13.0	11	6.3	—	7.0	—	41	11
1933	43.1	36	21.4	3	8.6	2	—	1	26.9	11	—	—	—	—	41	11
1938	56.5	39	29.1	3	5.7	1	1.7	—	4.9	8	—	—	2.1	—	43	9
1945	50.4	33	5.0	2	18.6	2	13.3	3	9.2	10	—	—	3.5	2	40	12
1949	62.7	37	0.6	2	7.2	—	2.1	2	27.2	9	—	—	0.2	2	31	11
1953	47.5	38	12.8	1	12.1	—	11.6	3	15.5	9	—	—	0.5	1	40	12
1958	43.6	37	9.0	—	16.0	4	12.7	2	17.5	8	—	—	1.2	1	42	10
1962	48.6	34	—	—	26.0	4	6.8	3	15.4	9	3.2	—	—	1	40	12
1965	59.1	36	—	—	20.4	2	2.4	2	8.4	9	3.9	1	5.8	2	41	11
1969	48.2	36	19.2	3	8.1	2	2.4	2	7.6	6	1.3	—	13.2	3	40	12

Adapted from: Elliott, Northern Ireland Parliamentary Election Results, 96 and 97.

[a]Includes Independent Unionists, Progressive Unionists, Protestant Unionists, and Independent O'Neill Unionists.

[b]Northern Ireland Labour party.

[c]Includes Independent Labour, Commonwealth Labour, Federation of Labour, Irish Labour, Republican Labour, and Socialist Republicans.

[d]Includes Nationalist, Republican, Sinn Fein, Fianna Fail, and Anti-Partitionists.

intimidation used by the RUC to bolster Unionist power were greatly enhanced by the Civil Authorities Act of 1922, which enabled police to search persons, premises, or vehicles without warrant, make arrests and incarcerate indefinitely anyone suspected of nationalist activities, close roads and bridges, and seize property without warning; a policy of internment of suspected terrorists was instituted. Designed to suppress Sinn Fein and IRA activities, the Civil Authorities Act was enforced against Catholics suspected of nationalist bias. All officers of the Crown were exempted from legal proceedings for acts performed in the "execution of their duty or for the defense of Northern Ireland."[11] Because the B Specials were without uniform, any armed Protestant male could be assumed to be acting under government approval. Hence the structure of the police reflected and reproduced the loyalty of Protestants to the government and assumed and, to a certain extent, assured the disloyalty of Catholics.

The decentralized structure of the state also supported a quasi-populist localism in which loyalism could be easily rewarded. Data indicate that municipal councils—even in Catholic majority areas—consistently preferred Protestant employees. For example, in 1951 only 5 percent of all nonmanual workers employed by rural councils and 11.9 percent of all manual workers were Catholic.[12] Figures of government employment by the central state also indicate the extent of discrimination in favor of Protestants. As table 8 shows, in 1927 Protestants held 91.6 percent of all civil service jobs; in 1959 this number held steady at 95.4 percent. A suppressed official report in 1973 indicated that this pattern persisted throughout the period of partition; 453 of the 477 civil servants in top grades in the early 1970s were Protestant.[13] In fact, Protestant workers did not always benefit from discriminatory patterns. For example, local governments were responsible for the allocation of public housing. Because the residents of government housing were excepted from restricted franchise, public housing was granted to Protestants whenever possible. In some cases, when this was impossible, no housing was constructed at all. For example, the Omagh Rural Council wrote to Stormont in 1935, pointing out that "in certain districts, cottages are required by Unionist workers, but we hesitate to write representations, as we know that there would be a flood from the nationalist side and our political opponents are only waiting for the opportunity to use this means to outvote us in divi-

Table 8 Civil Service Positions in Northern Ireland

Position	1927			1959		
	Total Positions	Protestant (%)	Catholic (%)	Total Positions	Protestant (%)	Catholic (%)
Permanent secretaries	5	83	17	7	100	0
Second and assistant secretaries	12	92	8	36	95	5
Principals	40	93	7	103	96	4
Deputy assistant principals	66	96	4	199	92	8
Staff officers	92	94	6	349	94	6
Total	215	91.6	8.4	694	95.4	4.6

Source: Denis P. Barritt and Charles F. Carter, *The Northern Ireland Problem: A Study in Group Relations*, 2d ed. (New York: Oxford University Press, 1972), 96. Reprinted by permission of the publisher.

sions where majorities are close."[14] Following the same logic, the Fermanagh Rural Councils built no housing between 1921 and 1945, despite the findings in a government survey that 43.7 percent of the houses needed replacement.[15] Such practices were designed to sustain the Unionist elite—not necessarily the interests of all Protestants.

The bourgeois Unionists relied heavily on the Orange Order to sustain a coherent Protestant loyalism. The order was made an integral part of the official Unionist party, nominating one-fifth of the delegates to the Ulster Unionist Council. Thus, the ordinary Orangeman felt that he had a real voice in party matters. Between 1921 and 1969, eighty-seven of the ninety-five Unionist cabinet members, every Stormont senator, and fifty-four of the fifty-six Unionists elected to Westminster were Orangemen. In nearly every case, the exceptions were women, who could not join the patriarchal Orange Order.[16] The Orange lodges played their most important role at the local level, moderating the class cleavages that could undermine Unionist solidarity in particular constituencies. Through intervention of lodge officers in local constituency associations. Protestants were able to monopolize public housing, public works, and local council employment.[17] Although it is possible to overstate the importance of the Orange Order as the *formal* organizational basis for securing the support of Protestant workers in the state, from the time of partition to World War II, it played a major informal political and ideological role in maintaining a coherent Protestant loyalty. The reinforcement of Protestant solidarity was secured through ritual marches led by government and Orange leaders, songs, and sectarian symbols. As one Orangeman put it in a letter to the Protestant *Belfast Telegraph:* "Orangemen on July 12 not only commemorate a very significant political victory, but a great deliverance from Roman slavery, in much the same way that Jews each year commemorate their deliverance from bondage in Egypt."[18] Challenges to the notion of "chosen peoplehood" and to myths about Catholics were few within the Protestant community and reinforcements many: territorial segregation (by 1951 half of Belfast's wards contained populations which were either over 90 percent Catholic or over 90 percent Protestant), separate social institutions and networks even in rural areas, and segregated schooling.[19] All these factors mitigated against interethnic contact. Small local churches, following the evangelist enthusiast tradition with its emphasis on the "open Bible" as the repository of truth and on the Pope as the antichrist, preserved myths of the Catholic threat.

If Orange loyalism was the formal ideological and informal institutional mechanism for integrating Protestants under the Unionist banner, the costs of that integration were steep. Without the patrimonial arrangment, the Unionist party would be vulnerable to Nationalist challenges and to secular class politics. The bourgeois leadership required Orangeism to maintain their power and their cliental relations within the working class. They learned well their own dependence on the working class during the labor agitation of the 1930s.

At the time of partition, we know that Ulster was the most developed region of Ireland; but its industrial base was narrow. Workers were concentrated in a few industries (shipbuilding, marine works, textiles, light engineering), and over 25 percent of the labor force was still engaged in agriculture. The dependence of industry and agriculture on British markets and its narrow economic base made Ulster very vulnerable to fluctuations in the world economy and to British regional policies. After partition, the unemployment rate in Northern Ireland ran about twice as high as the British average.[20] Not all industrialists embraced sectarian politics; to retain competitive positions, large firms would hire cheap labor—regardless of religious affiliation. When workers organized, however, rational hiring policies were quickly abandoned.[21] This was especially evident during the Great Depression. By 1932 unemployment in Northern Ireland had reached 28 percent of the wage labor populace, with nearly two-thirds of these concentrated in Belfast, where forty-five thousand workers were without jobs.[22] Workers struck throughout Belfast to pressure the state to institute public works and to protect job opportunities. These temporary and functional nonsectarian alliances did not constitute a turning by the Protestant working class to secular class politics.[23] But they shook industrialists into sectarian action. The Ulster Protestant League, an association founded by industrialists in 1931 to "safeguard the employment of Protestants,"spoke out against the strikers, claiming that "these unfortunate conditions were used as a cloak by the Communist Sinn Fein element to attempt to start a revolution in the province."[24] Privately, the government urged industrialists to discriminate against Catholics if they hoped to prevent such labor coalitions. Speaking to a group that had met to discuss the strikes, Sir

Basil Brooke, a cabinet minister, advised, ''Many in this audience employ Catholics, but I have not one about my place. Catholics are out to destroy Ulster with all their might and power. They want to nullify the Protestant vote, get all they can get out of Ulster, then see it go to hell.''[25] Even more blatantly, Sir Joseph Davison, a senator in Stormont and the Grand Master of the Orange Order, beseeched the industrialists: ''When will Protestant employers of Northern Ireland recognize their duty to their Protestant employees and employ them to the exclusion of Roman Catholics? It is time Protestant employers realized that whenever a Roman Catholic is brought into their employment, it means one less Protestant vote. It is our duty to pass the word along from this great demonstration and I suggest the slogan be 'Protestants employ Protestants.' ''[26] The government sought to splinter the movement by concentrating on Catholic workers. Troops were sent only into Catholic ghettos; food supplies were cut off from the Falls, an entirely Catholic neighborhood; and soldiers smashed the barricades constructed to protect Catholic areas.[27]

Major industrialists learned their lesson well and began to hire exclusively from the Protestant labor force. The structure of the economy during this period permitted such concessions. As Belinda Probert has pointed out, control of the important industrial enterprises ''rested firmly in the hands of Presbyterian capitalists and the predominance of 'family firms' greatly facilitated the implementation of sectarian employment practices.''[28] It is difficult to document this, since private firms have historically refused to give estimates of the religious distribution of their labor force and since the census of Northern Ireland provided no data on the relation between religion and occupation. However, recent studies of industrial segregation and inferences from unemployment data and from income and occupational figures broken down by geographical location show a persistent pattern of Protestant advantage.[29]

It would be a mistake to view discrimination and political intransigence as the only explanations of the institutionalized cleavages in Northern Ireland. Some attention must be paid to the role of the rest of Ireland and to the politics of the Catholic population.

As we noted in the last chapter, the south was divided on the issue of partition; the Free State did not dispute the boundary but concentrated its energies on ending dominion status. As Padraig O'Malley has noted, for Republicans in the south, ''the issue of sovereignty took precedence over the issue of unity."[30] Articles 2 and 3 of the 1937 Constitution of the Irish Free State explicitly rejected the border and proclaimed Dublin's authority over all thirty-two counties, which included the north. (It became political ritual for the leaders of the new state to inveigh against the border.) Irish was adopted as a compulsory language in school, and some competence was required for civil service. That the south had no deep commitment to a political solution to the conflict in the north was evident in 1948 when Ireland withdrew from the Commonwealth, despite the fact that such a withdrawal would make unification virtually impossible. Reactions to the Ireland Act of 1949 further undermined the possibility of ending partition. It guaranteed to respect the union of Ulster and Britain, so long as the Parliament of Northern Ireland affirmed the connection. To Irish Nationalists, this agreement signaled an abandonment of unification and led to a collapse of constitutional politics in both the north and south. Subsequent to its passage, the IRA stepped up a border campaign which continued until 1962. Sporadic and not supported by the Catholic populace at large, the main effect of the border campaign and of Ireland's withdrawal from the Commonwealth was "to strengthen Unionism by renewing, at a time when it might have begun to fade, the Ulster Protestant sense of being an embattled community under siege."[31] To Unionists, denunciations of the IRA by politicians in the new Republic of Ireland seemed duplicitous. Having cut off links to the Commonwealth, the new government seemed, as Padraig O'Malley put it, "to emphasize the separate identity of the Irish nation as a Catholic nation and a Gaelic nation. . . . They discounted the Irish Protestant and placed him in a political limbo outside the national consciousness."[32] In fact, Eamon de Valera, the Sinn Fein leader who was elected Taoiseach (prime minster) in 1932, referred to Ireland as a Catholic nation, further underscoring the symbolic relationship between Republicanism and Catholicism.

An additional basis for Unionist suspicion has been the role of the Catholic church, officially recognized in the Constitution of 1937 as having a "special position" in the state. It is difficult to assess the extent of the church hierarchy's influence on Irish politics. In a careful historical analysis, J. H. Whyte points out that bishops were consulted on only sixteen of the eighteen hundred statutes enacted by the Irish Dail between 1933 and 1970.[33] But

this underrepresents clerical involvement in policy making and ignores the question of authoritative influence regardless of official
consultation.[34] Governmental legislation incorporated Catholic positions on bith control, censorship, divorce, and abortion; until the
1960s, extensive literary and film censorship was unexceptional,
and Catholic schools and public schools were coterminous. There
have been numerous occasions on which the hierarchy has appealed
to its "higher authority" as moral arbiter on political issues. However insignificant these factors may be in the overall economy and
polity (and however consistent they may be with the moralism of
Stormont), fear of Catholic dominance is underscored by this clear
evidence of clerical hegemony. The extent of the fear is evident in
this statement by Brian Faulkner, former Ulster prime minister:
"The Church of Rome runs a world-wide organization—the most
political undertaking in the world. It controls newspapers, radio and
television stations and a hundred and one other avenues of propaganda. It is able to give vigorous publicity to any cause it es-
pouses."[35] The fears of northern Protestants, although quite exag-
gerated, are related to some level of reality. Despite some
secularization of Ireland in the post-Vatican period, the clergy still
exercises considerable authority. The Family Planning Act of 1979
permitted sales of contraceptive devices only to married couples
with a doctor's prescription. Intermarriage continues to be discouraged, and the Catholic partner must vow to raise any children in
the faith. The Republic is not a theocratic state; but neither is the
church simply one of a number of interest groups.

There are some parallels in church-state relations in the north. In
the period after partition, clerical influence in Nationalist electoral
politics was not unknown. Frequently during the years 1926–1937,
elite Catholics would gather and with the advice of the local priests
would select local Nationalist party candidates.[36] The church itself
has always adhered to a relatively conservative political stance
(membership in the IRA is grounds for excommunication); but individual priests have accepted the armed protection of church property by members of the IRA, tolerated the involvement of parish
members in arms procurement, and worked closely with well-
known Republican parishoners.[37] Studies indicate that clerical influence on political outlooks is minimal, but the appearance of influence is what counts in mobilizing the Protestant population.[38]
Moreover, church involvement in schooling supports ethnic antag-

onism in Ulster, where both Protestants and Catholics oppose secular education. Religious education is permitted in state-supported schools where the parents of more than ten children request such instruction. Catholics participate almost exclusively in the partially subsidized parochial school system because the bishops specifically opposed a provision which would have transferred them to state control.[39] As a result, it is estimated that 83 percent of the populace educated in Northern Ireland have never attended schools with members of the other faith.[40]

The conventional view among Protestants is that the Roman Catholic church, through its control over schools and through the local parish, dictates the politics of its adherents. Perhaps one reason that the church is seen as a monolith is that adherents to Protestantism belong to numerous denominations and sects. In 1961 over fifty-five different Protestant denominations existed in Ulster, although only five of these had a membership over 1 percent of the population. The dispersion of the population among so many denominations combines with the strong role of the Catholic church in the south to create an image of Catholic unanimity and of Protestant variety (viz., denominational liberty).

This then is an overview of the social structure of Northern Ireland between partition and World War II. The government was established in violence and maintained through a combination of coercive control, electoral manipulation, and sectarian appeal. Within this context, the stability of the government has been uneven. During severe economic crises, such as the depression of the 1930s, the uneasy alliance between the Unionist leadership and the Protestant working class was strained. On the other hand, the vehicles for integrating the Protestant population were many, owing to the small size of the state, its decentralized structure, and the dominance of local capital over the economy. Moreover, the significant social segregation muted any sense of commonality between Catholics and Protestants. Lacking opportunity for an effective voice in the state, Catholics tended to embrace Nationalist politics or not to participate in public life at all.

In short, after twenty years of partition, Northern Ireland was an "Orange state," one in which the apparatus of the state was premised upon a populist sectarianism, from which the largely bourgeois Unionist party leadership was unable to disentangle itself, even when it interfered with economic and political development. But fundamental changes in the postwar period undermined this coalition and led to the political disintegration of the state. It is to those changes and the ethnic mobilization which they precipitated that we now turn.

ADVANCED INDUSTRIALISM, ETHNIC MOBILIZATION, AND POLITICAL DISINTEGRATION IN POSTWAR ULSTER

After World War II, structural economic changes threatened the basis of the political order, revealing in the process the internal tensions within unionism. These changes were typical of the features of advanced industrial capitalist states; they included the decline of traditional industries, an increase of corporate capitalism, the expansion of multinational investment, and the growth of a welfare state. In this section, I will examine how these characteristic features altered the power resources within Northern Ireland and facilitated new forms and directions of ethnic conflict.

First, the postwar period was one of enormous economic change in Northern Ireland. The growth of multinational conglomerates, increasing automation, land consolidation, and competition with Third World manufacturers all eroded the competitive position of Ulster's traditional industries: aircraft manufacture, shipbuilding, agriculture, and textiles. In 1948, 40 percent of all employment in Ulster was in these four industries; by 1968, it had fallen to 22 percent (and by 1977 to 11 percent). Between 1949 and 1969, the number of workers fell by 50 percent in agriculture, 50 percent in linen, and 17 percent in shipbuilding. In the postwar period, Northern Ireland was more sensitive than any other United Kingdom region to cyclical variation in unemployment rates, and by 1963 real income was 25 percent below the British average; unemployment stood at 9.5 percent with no sign of falling.[41] The political pressures on the Unionist party to respond to this economic crisis threatened its coherence. Britain provided subsidies to finance industrial expansion and modernization, and Stormont utilized these in ways which reflected Unionist interests and Protestant localism.[42] By the mid-1960s, British investors were insisting that modernization, rationalization, and productive efficiency required more central planning in the allocation of factories and in economic development schemes. Local industrialists feared that such development would further undermine the independence of traditional firms and their own control over the labor market. They argued instead for changes through taxation. Neither focused on the dilemmas of labor. When the Northern Ireland Labour party captured 26 percent of urban workers' votes in 1962, it was clear that the Unionist party was in trouble.[43]

A second factor which altered the political constellation in Ulster was the postwar expansion of welfare services in Great Britain. Nationalized health care, mass education, general scholarship assistance for university students, unemployment compensation, and old age pensions were all part of Commonwealth subsidies, and their introduction provided resources to Ulster citizens that were not available in the Republic. Moreover, the distributive criteria established by Westminster required provision of social services based on standardized calculations of need. Hence, the British welfare state potentially undermined the material supports for Unionist preferential treatment of Protestants. This was not true in the application of all welfare state policies. For example, the allocation of housing under the Northern Ireland Housing Trust and Local Authority Act (which built 60 percent of the housing in postwar Ulster) was in the hands of local authorities, and they continued to locate construction in Protestant areas.[44] Nonetheless, the imposition of criteria developed by the metropolis, combined with the call for increased state control over economic development, threatened the Ulster tradition of localism.

Finally, Great Britian and Ireland, for reasons of their own economic development, began to explore the possibilities of improved trade relations. Political rapprochement required some reform of the state in Ulster. Westminster members of Parliament argued that local loyalties in Northern Ireland must give way to criteria of central planning and nondiscrimination. Under pressure from labor and Westminster, the official Unionist government in 1963 adopted a policy of modernization: planned enterprise, diversification, attraction of foreign investment, cooperation with trade unions, and negotiation with the south on issues of trade and common economic concerns. Seven "growth centers" were selected for investment of capital for industrial development. The evidence suggests that Stormont's economic development schemes did not alter the relative employment disadvantages of Catholics. In fact, a study of aggregate employment accessibility rates indicates that in the period 1959–1972 the differential between Catholic and Protestant access to jobs increased. And throughout that period, Protestant areas were favored for manufacturing growth and all sponsored development.[45] However, centralized planning and British intervention did threaten the *base* of Unionist hegemony. Foreign-owned chain stores displaced small shops; capital-intensive multinational industries slowed the growth rate in new jobs. Discrimination against Catholics was challenged, occasionally quite effectively in those arenas of the public sector which were governed by metropolitan rules of appointment and services (e.g., family allowances, medical insurance, aid for education). In border areas (those with a high proportion of Catholics), where there was some competition for jobs and housing and where unemployment rates were particularly high, erosion of local control would further undermine the position of working and lower middle class Protestants.[46] Thus any action by the Stormont government which was not overtly favorable to Protestants could be read as an assault on the loyalist covenant. As important, the evidence of support from Westminster, especially after the Labour victory in 1964, increased the resources and expectations for change among northern Irish Catholics. In 1965 the Nationalists entered Stormont as an official opposition party for the first time since the partition.

In this context, middle-class Catholics initiated a civil rights movement to reform the state. In their quiet genesis, the Campaign for Social Justice and the Campaign Democracy in Ulster were reform movements, supported by Catholic professionals and Labour M.P.'s at Westminster.[47] They sought to win changes in the system of religious patronage by documenting the extent of discrimination and pressuring Westminster for reform. The receptivity of Labour M.P.'s and the new prime minister to the campaigns raised expectations and increased resources among the small civil rights group. In 1966 a Northern Ireland Civil Rights Association was founded. Unaffiliated with existing associations, the NICRA attracted a varied backing which included the moderate Catholic reformers, Labour M.P.'s, liberal Protestants, trade union activists, and supporters of the IRA. Among the most significant early participants were student activists of the nonsectarian Queen's University at Belfast.[48] NICRA secured the support of the Labour government, and under pressure from Westminster, the Unionist government began to adopt a public appearance of nonsectarian politics.[49] Although these were mostly symbolic gestures (visits by the prime minister

118

to Catholic schools), these minor overtures were unprecedented and were read as a barometer of changing intentions.

If middle-class Catholics welcomed O'Neill's apparent willingness to build bridges, however shaky, between the two communities, Unionists did not respond with uniform enthusiasm. On the one hand, large businesses supported policies of economic development and cooperation with the south. On the other hand, small businesses and workers had little to gain from such practices. Hence when Terence O'Neill met with the Irish prime minister in an economic summit in 1965, Ian Paisley, minister of a small evangelical sect in Belfast, called on Protestants to stop the "Romeward Trend" of the Unionist party and its "furcoat brigade." "Bridges and traitors are much the same," he proclaimed; "they both go to the other side."[50] Following the economic summit, he established an Ulster Constitution Defense Committee to agitate against any political reform. Its vanguard Ulster Volunteer Force launched a terrorist campaign against the Catholic community to discourage civil rights activity, throwing petrol bombs at Catholic shops, schools, and homes and announcing a military campaign against the "IRA and all its splinter groups."[51] Denounced by official unionists as a "latter day Luther of the lumpenproletariat," the appeal of Paisley's antielitist, anti-Catholic denunciations was seriously underestimated. The UVF was banned, but the seams of the Unionist coalition had frayed beyond repair. Protestant opposition to O'Neill's reformist policies was strong among the urban youth and unemployed, to whom reform meant exclusion from jobs. Nor was there necessary support among the petty bourgeoisie, whose small businesses were endangered by monopoly capital firms. Paisleyism also appealed to Protestants in rural areas, to whom reform meant the end of preferential treatment in land sales, housing, and agricultural labor. And to fundamentalist Protestants, a small but highly committed sector of the population (about 13 percent in a 1968 study), Paisley made perfect sense, in light of O'Neill's overtures to Catholics. A public opinion poll, taken in 1966 after three Catholics were murdered by the UVF outside a Protestant pub, showed that 20 perent of Ulster's Protestants supported Paisley.[52] Peter Gibbon has analyzed the power of Paisleyism: "It has exploited the genuine social resentments of the petit-bourgeoisie and the poor against the alien landed class which has dominated Unionism for so long. Its radical rightism, initially aimed only at the Catholic minority, has now taken the demagogic form of a small men's revolt against the oligarchy. By splitting the petit-bourgeoisie and sections of the Protestant workers and peasants away from below, Paisleyism thereupon detonated a second split in the Unionist bloc, from above."[53]

Thus, the agenda for political confrontation was set; the official Unionists had a very precarious hold over the Protestant population, and the Catholic civil rights coalition was equally untenable, reflecting a variety of ideologies and interpretations. The movement itself was precipitated by a single event in County Tyrone in 1968, where a Catholic family was evicted from a council home and was replaced by the unmarried secretary of a Unionist politician. When Stormont refused to intervene, claiming that housing was the responsibility of local authorities, NICRA initiated a "squat-in" and a march to protest discrimination in housing. The march was a huge success, attracting four thousand supporters. It was also sectarian: it began in a town which was 90 percent Catholic; marchers sang Irish Republican and Catholic songs; and the formal leadership exercised quite tenuous authority.[54] Paisley responded to the march by arguing that wherever activists held a march, loyalists should hold a countermarch. In a society defined by ethnic territoriality, a march through any "Protestant" area was a sectarian challenge and spawned violent reactions on both sides, spilling over into adjacent territories.

The story of the civil rights movement is a rich and complex one, which does not need delineation here. What is important is that from the first sit-in in 1968 to the "Battle of the Bogside," after a march from Belfast to Londonderry in 1969, to the emergence of the militant Protestant Ulster Vanguard in 1970, resistance to political reform escalated in Northern Ireland. Every march by civil rights supporters precipitated counteractions by militant loyalists (many of whom were RUC men out of uniform). Nor were the secular, reformist claims of the civil rights leadership accepted as such by many of the marchers or by their opponents.[55]

Reluctant to embrace reform, yet unable to control the Protestant populace, the Unionist party began to fragment. The government adopted measures to control civil rights marchers through administrative fiats which denied the right to march, through RUC cordons to contain the marchers, and through incremental concessions. A study of support for the government in 1968 indicated the extent of political fragmentation within the Protestant populace which resulted. Although 85 percent of the Protestant respondents identified themselves as Unionist, they were quite divided over Unionist policy. About one-third of the Protestant respondents supported reform of the state; half wanted no change; and 11 percent wanted to increase the power of the Unionist party.[56] By 1969 the O'Neill government was unable to maintain order, as vigilante groups broke out in urban ghettos, protective barriers were erected on both "sides," and as the Provisional IRA and militant Protestant groups mounted neighborhood campaigns. Neither O'Neill nor his two successors were able to mediate between the contradictory demands of Catholics and Protestant loyalists. Indeed, Stormont was unable to control the RUC.

When rioting broke out in Belfast in 1969, the RUC adopted a "wink and nod" attitude toward the vigilante Protestant Shankill Defense Association, as it intimidated Catholic residents near the Shankill, burning their homes and pubs. Only the intervention of British troops ended the rioting and "for months afterwards, the private joke in the SDA was a cryptic '24 hours,' meaning that if the British Army had only delayed their arrival that long, the Catholic ghettoes would have been wiped out."[57] From the systematic accounts of these events, there is little doubt that the rioting in Belfast was planned and organized by the SDA; yet publicly the government announced that the rioting was provoked by a "republican or sinister element" and the minister of education suggested that Catholics had burned down their own homes.[58]

The intervention of the British army changed the situation drastically and unalterably. Catholics initially welcomed the troops, who protected them from SDA onslaught. And Westminster issued a series of reports that attributed the 1969 summer riots to Protestant instigators. Under pressure from Britain, the prime minister issued a communiqué promising the reforms demanded for six years by civil rights supporters. Hence, in an ironic (albeit temporary) turnabout, the British came to be seen as the protectors of Catholics and the enemies of ultraloyalists. The traditional Unionist alliance deteriorated, as the "Ultras" regularly defeated official Unionist candidates, repudiated civil rights, and elected Paisley to Westminster.

The political schisms within the loyalist population were significant, and the next four years were marked by escalating violence, controversy, and dramatic changes in the party structure as the fissures within unionism became more evident. From 1969 to 1972, new party factions emerged; and numerous militant vigilante groups, defense associations, and platoons sprang up in urban areas, each with its own self-styled leadership and its own understandings of Orange loyalism. In 1971 the most important and enduring, the Ulster Defense Association, was founded to coordinate Protestant vigilantes. In the next five years, it would claim responsibility for 400 Catholic deaths.

A similar escalation of vigilantism occurred within the Catholic community. For some, the government claims that civil rights had been accomplished and that the source of continuing conflict was IRA agitation were belied by daily experience. One-fifth of the industrial aid budget in 1970 was allocated to a single engineering firm in a Catholic Belfast neighborhood; the firm employed only five Catholics in its labor force of five hundred. Social order bills were applied almost exclusively to Catholics. Tables 9 and 10 indicate that despite official Unionist overtures, discrimination in public appointments had not ended at the state level. And the extent of unemployment and underemployment remained unchanged for Catholics in Belfast's ghetto. Although Protestant advantages were minimal, as table 11 indicates, virtually every neighborhood with a high proportion of Catholics had a much higher proportion of unemployed, a much smaller middle class and professional population and many fewer households with cars (a measure of relative affluence). For many in the Catholic ghettos, not only were civil rights reforms too little and too late, but they had lost their immediacy in the face of a need for community defense. NICRA leaders had formed defense committees in Belfast and a militant Provisional wing of the IRA emerged, rejecting political solutions and embracing a policy of community defense and guerrilla warfare. The fragile peace between the British army and the Catholic community was shattered in the spring of 1970, when troops responded to rioting in Belfast with armed cars and tear gas, failed to protect Catholic neighborhoods, and undertook a brutal house-to-house search for Republicans in the neighborhood of the Lower Falls. The tenuous ties between Catholics and the British army were finally severed when two Unionist ministers were taken on a tour of the area after the search. For many Catholics in urban Ulster only the IRA served as a source of protection and defense against the Protestant vigi-

Table 9 Membership of Some Public Boards in Northern Ireland in 1969

Board	Protestant	Catholic	Total
Electricity Board	5	0	5
Housing Trust	6	1	7
Craigavon Development Commission	8	1	9
Economic Council	16	2	18
General Health Services Board	22	2	24
Hospitals Authority	17	5	22
Pigs Marketing Board	12	1	13
Tourist Board	8	3	11
Industrial Court	21	1	22
Total	115	16	131

Source: John F. Harbinson, *The Ulster Unionist Party 1882–1973,* (Belfast: Blackstaff Press, 1973), 118.

lantes. Consequently, when a draconian Criminal Justice Bill was enacted and enforced rather arbitrarily by the army, protection shifted to the Provisional IRA, which smuggled guns from Ireland and gelegnite from Scotland and began a campaign of retaliation and selected assassination. A politics of protracted and escalating conflict ensued. Riots, rent strikes, protest marches, and demonstrations escalated throughout the fall and winter of 1971, after the Stormont government—under pressure from ultraloyalists—adopted a policy of internment and applied it exclusively to Catholics. And when British troops fired on a small group of civil rights marchers in January 1972, killing thirteen unarmed marchers, strikes broke

Table 10 Distribution of Judicial Appointments in Northern Ireland in 1969

Position	Protestant	Catholic
High Court judges	6	1
County Court judges	4	1
Resident magistrates	9	3
Commissioners for National Insurance	3	0
Clerks of the Crown and Peace	6	0
Undersheriffs	6	0
Crown solicitors	8	0
Clerks to petty sessions	26	1
Total	68	6

Source: John F. Harbinson, *Ulster Unionist Party,* 119.

Table 11 Occupation and Religion of Men of Working Age in Belfast in 1971 (In Percentages)

Neighborhood	Catholic	Unemployed	Self-employed with Staff	Managers	Foremen, Supervisors	Professionals	Households with Cars
Clifton	34.93	9.32	2.74	3.56	3.16	0.29	43.47
Court	34.15	20.27	0.5	0.37	1.17	0.06	13.13
Cromac	27.33	7.64	2.78	5.30	2.47	4.99	48.26
Dock	62.86	17.56	0.87	1.04	1.65	0.16	14.98
Duncairn	17.37	7.29	2.73	4.04	3.57	1.56	44.26
Falls	79.02	19.64	0.86	0.94	1.67	0.17	17.44
Ormeau	14.17	5.51	2.29	3.99	3.63	1.54	46.53
Pottinger	11.64	6.98	2.49	5.16	3.60	2.23	50.75
Shankill	7.84	9.43	1.38	2.36	3.32	0.74	34.76
Smithfield	74.67	16.20	0.53	0.37	0.91	0.05	8.73
St. Anne's	34.65	11.01	1.32	1.65	3.14	0.85	28.33
St. George's	2.16	10.14	0.67	0.80	1.63	0.86	18.70
Victoria	3.78	5.96	2.67	5.86	3.84	3.02	53.38
Windsor	16.16	5.57	4.74	5.26	2.72	6.57	59.91
Woodvale	15.80	12.55	1.10	1.61	2.94	0.63	30.16

Adapted from: Geoffrey Bell, *Protestants of Ulster* (London: Pluto Press, 1976), 29.

out throughout the north. Ulster was no longer governable, and in March of that year, Westminster abolished the Stormont parliament and declared direct rule.[59]

This reassertion of British power, however, was different from any other period in Ireland's history. For it was opposed, not only by members of the Catholic community (particularly in urban areas) but also by ultraloyalists, who feared potential reforms. In February 1972 Protestant extremist groups coalesced into the Ulster Vanguard, an umbrella movement which promised to form a provisional government if Westminster sought to alter the constitution. Two days after the Stormont parliament was abolished. Ulster Vanguard called for a Protestant workers' strike, and for several days, power supplies, public transport, and all major industries were shut down. The loyalist convenant had been broken.

I have focused in some detail on the chronology of events that led to direct rule in order to delineate the changing dialectic of religion and class in Ulster. With a few exceptions, most analyses of this period have tended to emphasize the relative deprivation of Catholics and the intransigence of the Unionist party as the underlying source of ethnic conflict. The foregoing analysis indicates that a more complex nexus of conflicting material interests determined Ulster's political constellation.

Throughout the postwar period, English interest in the north and south of Ireland had increased steadily.[60] The political modernization of Ulster and a rapprochement with the Republic were in the interests of British capital growth, military strategies, and global image. Reform was also in the interests of the economic and political elite of Ulster; but they were caught in the political web they had woven to ensure the stability of a Unionist state. The dependence of the ruling party on the support of a supremacist Protestant working class undermined even modest efforts at political modernization. The Unionists could not redesign the complex political machine created to maintain their political hegemony. As Michael Farrell states, "The Orange ideology was too deep rooted to be dispensed with overnight, especially at a time of change, when new industries were replacing old ones, threatening small businessmen and established skilled workers, when new blocks of flats were replacing old slums, new towns replacing old villages. Orangeism provided stability and status in a changing world and defended jobs and positions. The very suggestions of reform produced a Protestant backlash."[61] However, as we have seen, the mobilization against official Unionism was not precipitated by the economic policies but by perceived softness toward Catholics and overtures to the Republic. It was only *partially* the protection of labor market advantages and political resources which generated reactive mobilization. It was also the strongly held traditional belief that concessions to Catholics would be the first step toward union with the Republic and the beginning of a Catholic state in the north. Hence, any overtures seemed to deny the very basis of Protestant solidarity. Once the schism developed within Unionism and the Protestant working class realized the extent of its own political power (particularly under Paisley's tutelage), Unionist hegemony was challenged and the class-based ultraloyalist movement developed.

Among the Catholic population, disjunctures between classes also shaped ethnic politics. At the outset of the civil rights movement, the middle class was too small to exert significant political pressure. Only by mobilizing the masses of Catholics could they advance their platform of civil reforms. The resultant coalition of workers, students, and middle-class reformers tied the demand for universal suffrage to demands for housing and employment reform, the very issues which threatened Protestant working-class advantages. But the middle-class leadership exercised very little hegemony over the civil rights movement; without a nonsectarian political tradition, marchers used the symbols and traditions of Ireland's earlier nationalist movements, and hence the identification of civil rights and republicanism was quickly forged. Moreover, the failure of the Stormont regime to protect civil rights marchers regenerated the Irish Republican Army, and the vision of a reformed Ulster state eroded.

THE ESCALATION OF ETHNIC NATIONALISMS: NORTHERN IRELAND UNDER DIRECT RULE, 1972–1985

The declaration of direct rule in 1972 was welcomed by the general population of war-weary Ulster; but violence continued unabated in Belfast. The Provisional IRA and the Ulster Defense Association traded off in a pattern of assassination and recrimination. Youth gangs sprang up in the ghettos, terrorizing and looting. While the army sought to impose order, the government negotiated with Dublin, the Social Democratic Labour party (formerly the Nationalist party), the official Unionists, and other moderates in an effort to develop a solution agreeable to the middle classes of the various geopolitical units. The consistent failure to include Republicans and ultraloyalists in the negotiations ensured the demise of each proposal. Anti-White Paper Unionists boycotted a March 1972 referendum on the border; ultraloyalists boycotted a power-sharing assembly established in June 1972; the IRA boycotted the elections; and the Ulster Unionist Council rejected the 1972 Sunningdale Agreement, which provided for a power-sharing executive, a Council of Ireland divided equally between north and south. In 1973, when Westminster proposed constitutional reforms which would permit a coalition-based regional executive, with a power-sharing government and a Council of Ireland, the election was contested by four different groups of Unionists and an equal number of Catholic parties. The support for the right-wing Orangeist approach is evident in table 12; the official Unionists captured only 26.5 percent of the votes, and antireformist groups (the Vanguard Unionist Loyalist Coalition, the Democratic Unionist Loyalist Coalition, and the Anti–White Paper Unionists) secured 33.7 percent. Successive ini-

Table 12 Results of the 1973 Assembly Elections in Northern Ireland

Party	% Vote	Seats in Proportion to Votes	Seats Won
VULC	10.5	8.2	7
DULC	10.8	8.4	8
AWPU	12.4	9.7	10
Other Loyalist	1.6	1.2	2
Official Unionist	26.5	20.7	23
Alliance	9.2	7.2	8
NILP	2.6	2.0	1
SDLP	22.1	17.2	19
Republican clubs	1.8	1.4	0
Other Nationalist	1.4	1.1	0
Others	0.9	0.7	0

Source: Robert D. Osborne, "Voting Behavior in Northern Ireland, 1921–1977," in *Integration and Division,* edited by Frederick W. Boal and J. Neville H. Douglas (New York: Academic Press, 1982), 143. Reprinted by permission of the publisher. *Note:* VULC, Vanguard Unionist Loyalist Coalition; DULC, Democratic Unionist Loyalist Coalition; AWPU, Anti–White Paper Unionist; NILP, Northern Ireland Labour Party; SDLP, Social Democratic Labour party.

tiatives by the British government have failed to resolve the conflict: from the 1974 Ulster Workers' Council strike, which forced the end of the brief power-sharing government, onward, the "Troubles" have escalated; and relations between Catholics and Protestants have stagnated. In the last fifteen years, the conflicts have resulted in the deaths of at least 2,429 people, on both sides.[62] Why has direct rule failed to contain the conflicts in Northern Ireland?

Britain's failure in Nothern Ireland during the period of direct rule requires examination, for it is instructive about the sources and supports for the continuing ethnic strife. The first source of insolubility is the British state itself. Perhaps part of the colonial legacy has been Britain's failure to consider Northern Ireland a primary concern. No substantial efforts to develop an infrastructure for political reform have been undertaken, and no long-range strategies have been developed. Since the demise of the power-sharing executive, Northern Ireland has been ruled by a British secretary of state, a fact which erodes a sense of responsibility among the politicians in Ulster and reinforces the anticolonial sentiments of the Irish Republican Army. Moreover, the institutional British presence in Ulster is exclusively a military one. Although it has reduced its troops from thirty thousand in 1972 to seventeen thousand today, the danger of British withdrawal is evident when one examines the constituency of those troops. Today, the locally based Ulster Defence Regiment accounts for 40 percent of all troops; the UDR is almost exclusively Protestant (98 percent in 1980). And as Padraig O'Malley has pointed out: "Altogether, about 21,000 Ulster men have served in the force since 1970. Their loyalties are unmistakable. Ulster is their country. And they know the enemy."[63] When the fifteen thousand RUC men are included, the sense of Ulster as a British-sponsored Protestant garrison state is underscored among Catholics—but so is the recognition that British troop withdrawal would be dangerous indeed. Direct rule has also reinforced aspects of Ulster's nondemocratic tradition. The Diplock Courts, established to investigate terrorist activities, have undermined an independent jury system, and the various social control laws such as the Emergency Provisions and Prevention of Terrorism Acts have been extensively abused, generating distrust for the system of justice, especially among Catholics.[64]

If Great Britain has done little to solve Ulster's political stalemate, it has done even less to solve the economic crisis. We have seen that the economic problems of the 1960s helped precipitate the Troubles. In the 1970s the situation deteriorated. The "replacement industries" of the 1960s, meant to substitute for the declining traditional firms, are relocating in the south of Ireland. Between 1974 and 1984, Northern Ireland lost one-third of its industrial jobs (and about one-third of these job losses can be directly traced to the ethnic conflicts). And in the period 1976—1981, Britain invested £57 million in the Republic but only £1.3 million in Ulster.[65] At the same time, the costs of subsidization of Ulster have gone up 1500 percent since 1970 and now amount to £1,200 million a year, exclusive of the military costs. In 1979 public expenditures amounted to £1,648 per person, £400 more than in England. Yet high public expenditures have not generated new jobs. Overall unemployment stands at 20 percent, but among sixteen to eighteen year old youth, it averages 33 percent, and in the inner cities of Belfast and Londonderry, nearly half of the population is unemployed.[66] And these inner-city youths are ideal recruits for the UDA and the IRA.

The significance of the Irish Republican Army has been shaped by this political and economic context. Since 1972 popular support for the IRA has ebbed and flowed. At the outset of direct rule, there was strong local support for the Provos (members of the Provisional IRA), who constituted the major defense of the Catholic community. The significance of that support was evident soon after the imposition of direct rule, when IRA internees were granted political status, and the secretary of state for Northern Ireland agreed to hold talks with IRA leaders. Popular support declined in the period 1973—1975 when neighborhood-based IRA chapters provoked severe condemnation in urban ghettos for their "kneecappings" and other forms of violent social control over the Catholic population. The IRA reorganized in response to these criticisms. Recent studies indicate great ambivalence among Catholics about the IRA: a tendency to appreciate the protectionist role played by "our boys" in ghetto neighborhoods, but a general condemnation of terrorist tactics. Hence there was little support for and much dismay over the assassination of Lord Mountbatten in 1979; but less outcry over attacks on individual RUC men.[67] The Social Democratic Labour party has routinely and roundly condemned the Provisional IRA: but until recently voters could support both the SDLP with their ballots and the Provos with their hearts. Most IRA members are from these working-class areas and are familiar and even intimate with other residents. These residents share a general fear of and antipathy for the security forces, even if they disagree on the tactics employed. As a result, the Provos are able to evoke sympathy for their plight—especially when imprisoned. This was most evident in the hunger strike of 1982. Six years earlier, Britain had revoked the "special category" status of IRA prisoners and stated that they would now be treated as normal prisoners. This policy shift provoked outbursts in Catholic ghettos, where it is well known that these mostly young men are not normal criminals. (They have higher educational levels, lower ages and rates of recidivism, and are generally typical working-class community men.) Consequently, when prisoners in the H-blocks initiated a protest, the emotional tempers in the Catholic neighborhoods were high. Escalating from a refusal to wear prison garb (the blanket protest) to a refusal to use prison toilets or to clean the cells (the dirty protest) to a hunger strike in 1982, the IRA prisoners secured world attention. At the same time, the IRA decided to participate in electoral politics and ran hunger striker Bobby Sands for Parliament. Sands's election taught the IRA that contesting elections could be useful in mobilizing support for its goals, without jeopardizing its claim that the state itself was illegitimate. And as ten of the strikers died of starvation between May and August of 1982, the refusal of the Thatcher government to acknowledge their political status intensified support for the organization. The deaths created local heroes, martyrs who hardened anti-British sentiment in Catholic communities.

Since 1984 the IRA strategy has been to undermine popular support for direct rule in Britain through a campaign of bombs and assassinations aimed at both security forces and at high and low government officials. Its targets have ranged as high as the British prime minister and its victims have included the chairman of the Armagh district council (a Unionist with no association with provincial security), a chairman of the Ulster Young Unionist Council (a political opponent of the IRA), and ordinary British citizens, as well as members of the UDR. The IRA has abandoned its traditional policy of abstentionism (a symbolic rejection of the legitimacy of the state) to mix the bomb with the ballot. Since 1982 Sinn Fein (the political wing of the IRA) has countered the moderate Catholic SDLP by developing social services and political recruiting mechanisms in urban neighborhoods and introducing political candidates in constituencies where support is strong as symbols of IRA popularity. There is no doubt that the actions of the IRA have exacerbated sectarianism. In 1973 it was willing to embrace a policy of federalism to accommodate the concerns of Ulster's Protestants. Since 1981, when it rejected this approach as accommodationist, the IRA has made no effort to mollify Protestant concerns; indeed it reduces all loyalists to a stereotype of "neo-fascist, anti-nationalist and anti-democratic," thereby ensuring that all conflicts become a kind of zero-sum game.[69] And it hopes that this war of attrition will lead to a breakdown of British Unionist will.

There is a kind of reciprocity of nationalism between the IRA and the Protestant militants. Within the Protestant working class, anti-English sentiment has increased, as successive secretaries of state have negotiated with the Republic on policy solutions and thus failed to recognize the enduring fear of Protestants that they will become a minority in a Catholic state. Since 1975 the Ulster Defense Association has adopted a policy calling for the independence of Northern Ireland, separate from the United Kingdom and from Ireland. For a brief period in 1978–1979, the UDA eschewed sectarianism and called for a negotiated independence; but since then it has been an explicitly Protestant interest group.[70] The UDA publishes a monthly magazine, *Ulster,* which legitimates Protestant paramilitarism and violence. Ian Paisley leads a Democratic Unionist party which militantly opposes power sharing or any Irish involvement in the north. In 1981 following the second Anglo-Irish summit, he established a paramilitary group, The Third Force, which undertook mass parades, carried and displayed its arms, and sought to prepare itself to function as a bridge between the police and the army. However, there are important differences between Protestant and Catholic paramilitarism. The Catholic republican tradition is long and well romanticized; to potential allies, it is depicted as (and can be) a movement to self-determination, part of a respectable mythic tradition. Consequently, the IRA has secured significant moral (as well as financial) support, especially among some Irish Americans. In contrast, the Protestant movements are less easily identifiable and have only the symbols of the Reformation to inspire them. In a secular world, these symbols are not compelling for securing support outside Ulster. But if Protestant ultraloyalists have failed to generate much international support for their position, neither have they been as subject to media and political criticism. As Padraig O'Malley points out, "Protestant paramilitarism is fragmented. It is not always clear who carries out the 'military actions' and therefore not always clear who is to blame."[71] The IRA is an identifiable and historical organization which can be seen as behaving in a calculated and intentional program; Protestant paramilitarism can be dismissed as sporadic reactive outbursts or the work of individual psychopaths. The tendency of the British to adopt these interpretations has contributed to its failure to develop an effective political solution.

Can the Troubles in Ulster be healed by Britain or Ulster alone? Some commentators in the late 1970s argued that economic expansion in the south combined with Ulster's decline would alter the position of ultraloyalists and facilitate a Republican victory.[72] But those predictions were shortsighted. It is true that the economy of the Republic improved during the last decade. An Industrial Development Authority has provided generous incentives to capital investment, tax reliefs on profits and exports, research and development grants, etc. Relatively cheap labor and tariff-free entry for common market states produced an increase in investment in the south. Industrial output between 1959 and 1979 increased twice as fast as in the north; and while Ulster lost forty-seven thousand manufacturing jobs in this period, the Republic gained thirty thousand. However, this boom ended in 1980, as the effects of the world recession and the dependence on multinational capital hit Ireland. From then on, population growth outstripped job expansion. Economists estimate that Ireland would need to produce twenty-eight thousand new jobs a year until 1988 to bring down Ireland's 10 percent unemployment rate. Among youth the unemployment rate is even higher, up 77 percent since 1979. Given the economic stagnation in the United Kingdom, it seems unlikely that emigration will provide an economic safety valve for Ireland; and it seems clear that Ireland will not be the safety valve for Ulster. Astute analysts have suggested that reunion of the two parts of the island would be devastating for the south, requiring that it assume huge welfare burdens. Still, every Irish government has adopted public postures supporting ultimate reunification.

Since direct rule, there has been little basis for Protestants in the north to trust Irish government arguments that the border would be respected or that a devolved secular state in Ulster would be tolerated. Charles Haughey, leader of Fianna Fail and Taoiseach (prime minister) in 1979–1981 and again for six months in 1982, had been arrested for conspiracy to import weapons for the IRA in 1970. And while secretary of health in 1979, he was responsible for the enactment of the Family Planning Act, already identified as a piece of confessional legislation. During the hunger strikes, he sought to get recognition of the special category status of the strikers. In short, Haughey and Fianna Fail can be easily seen as supporters of the IRA, and Anglo-Irish summits are therefore read by Protestants as a capitulation to Republicans. Since 1981 the dominant party has been the more moderate Fine Gael, led by Garrett Fitzgerald, in coalition with minority parties like Labour. Fitzgerald has sought to secularize the Irish state, to abandon Articles 2 and 3 of the constitution because of their contribution to the Protestant siege mentality, and to support a devolved government in the north, with a future possible Irish confederation. Despite the fact that public opinion polls indicate that the electorate of the Free State is simply not interested in unification, Fitzgerald's constitutional crusade has been aborted by Irish nationalist appeals. Every effort to defuse Protestant fears was countered by Haughey as evidence that Fine Gael was less Irish and that constitutional change constituted a capitulation to an illegitimate Protestant cause.

Although neither reunification nor devolution has received broad Protestant support, the more important consequence of the debate between Fine Gael and Fianna Fail has been the certainty among Protestants that Irish nationalists will seek to impose a Catholic state in the north. No Free State government can be trusted since it can be quickly outvoted. Each is seen, therefore, to constitute a potential move toward unity. The condemnation of the IRA rings hollow for a state whose national heroes are paramilitary nationalists and whose refusal to subscribe to the European Convention on the Suppression of Terrorism is seen as a willingness to protect the IRA.[73] In short, the Republic must be held accountable for its role in exacerbating the conflict. But so too must Great Britain.

In 1973 at the failure of the Northern Ireland Convention, the Irish prime minister argued that "it is now up to the people there to reach an agreement among themselves which will allow them to live and work together in peace."[74] Since direct rule, the British Crown has failed to develop any coherent policy which would assist Ulsterites in accomplishing such an agreement. Britain dare not pull its troops out of Ulster; to do so would risk more than a bloodbath;

it would be proclaimed as a victory for the IRA, mobilize them within the rest of Ireland, and threaten England's strategic defense and trade relations with the Republic. Nonetheless, its reliance on a military solution within Northern Ireland and its failure to think about the preconditions for a democratic transition constitute a kind of moral pullout. It has made a political solution more difficult, as a generation of children grow up with minimal experience of democratic political institutions, of traditions of tolerance, or of expectations of human rights.[75] This legacy of the politics of protracted conflict is its most unsettling and underscores the importance of taking each group's concerns and fears more seriously than has been done to date. It has ensured that the old Orange slogan "No Surrender!" and the Republican cry "Ourselves Alone," which associate ethnicity and nationalism, prevail in Northern Ireland.

From Duplessisme to the Quiet Revolution: Social Structure in Postwar Quebec, 1940–1960

As we have seen in the last chapter, Quebec entered World War II in an isolationist spirit under the leadership of its nationalist premier Maurice Duplessis. His ruling Union Nationale Parti consistently adhered to the traditional ideology, which viewed French Canada as an agrarian state, industry as the terrain of non-Francophones, and labor and conflicts as disruptions of the appropriate harmony between employer and employee. The period of "duplessisme" was characterized by a paternalistic form of state administration: religiously dominated, patronage politics. But the dramatic economic changes of the postdepression and World War II era could not be easily ignored nor could they be handled through the Duplessis brand of nationalism.

Interventions into the economy and concentration of fiscal powers by the federal government begun during the Great Depression accelerated in the 1940s as a result of the close planning needed for conduct of the war. With the Liberal party at the helm, countercyclical spending policies were adopted, and welfare measures expanded federal intervention in the social realm. But few of these changes altered the situations of French Canadians to their own advantage. Despite the fact that the Liberal federal government was headed by a French Canadian, Louis Saint-Laurent, the Union Nationale resisted every effort at increased provincial-federal cooperation, refusing to participate in jointly financed hospital insurance schemes or to accept federal assistance for higher education, adopting very low levels of public expenditure, and insisting on a clear division of federal and provincial economic jurisdiction.[76]

Although the resistance of Duplessis to welfare state expansion had a detrimental effect on French Canada, it was crucial to the political power of Quebec's traditional elite. An acceptance of federalized welfare measures would undermine the close relation between church and state in Quebec. The hospital insurance system, for example, required a fiscal separation of hospitals from the religious orders which owned them. Federal bureaucratic regulations and audits would also eliminate the patronage politics and personalistic bonds in provincial government. Quebec had no effective civil service; public administration was based on political nomination, and a system of performance evaluation was nonexistent. As Dominique Clift has noted, both the administration and the distribution of social welfare reflected political patronage. "Practically all payments made out of the public treasury to hospitals, classical colleges, welfare organizations and homes for the aged and for orphans were of a discretionary nature."[77] Duplessis resisted federal economic and welfare interventions on nationalist grounds, arguing that acceptance of federal support would erode the autonomy of the province and of the French Canadians. In fact, French Canadians paid for federal welfare measures with their taxes—but received none in return. Moreover, because there was no independent civil service or training for bureaucratic administration, French Canadians were not able to benefit from the expanding federal civil service. The proportion of French Canadians in civil service jobs fell from 21.5 percent in 1918 to 12.5 percent in 1946. And those at the upper levels were few.[78] Of course, this was not exclusively the product of Union Nationale provincialism. The model on which the federal civil service was constructed was Anglo-American and assimilationist. Hence, as Norman Ward describes, French Canadian cabinet minister could find himself marooned at the head of a predominantly English Canadian organization in which English was the only departmental language and only English Canadian ideas influenced the formation of policy and the organization of the department itself."[79] But the resistance to a rationalized provincial civil service certainly contributed to the relative decline of French Canadians. The rejection of federal educational authorities and policies also sustained ethnic inequality. Duplessis gave limited fiscal support to secondary education, in the belief that elementary schooling was sufficient for a rural population; and most of the public provisions were targeted at vocational training. The French Canadians were even more underrepresented in professional and financial occupations in 1951 than they had been in 1931 (see table 13).

Despite Duplessis' attitude and policies, the percentage of the population in school between the ages of 15 and 24 increased in the postwar period. Between 1950 and 1960, the proportion of youth in secondary schools and colleges rose from 53 percent to 62 percent. Moreover, federal funds and scholarships made it possible for youth from working-class and agrarian backgrounds to continue their education.[80] Two new universities (at Quebec City and Sherbrooke) and many junior colleges (Collèges d'éducation générale et professionnelle) developed curricula with greater emphases on public and business administration and scientific training. Consequently, increasing numbers of technically and scientifically trained

Table 13 Over- and Underrepresentation in Occupational Categories in Canada by Ethnic Group

Occupational Category	French	English	Total Male Labor Force
1931			
Professional and financial	−0.8	+1.6	4.8
Clerical	−0.8	+1.5	3.8
Personal service	−0.3	−0.3	3.5
Primary and unskilled	+3.3	−4.6	17.7
Agriculture	+0.1	−3.0	34.0
1951			
Professional and financial	−1.5	+1.6	5.9
Clerical	−0.8	+1.6	5.9
Personal service	−0.2	−0.3	3.4
Primary and unskilled	+3.0	−2.2	13.3
Agriculture	−0.3	−3.5	19.4

Source: Porter, *Vertical Mosaic,* 87.

Note: The figures show the difference expressed in percentage points between the ethnic group representation in a particular occupational class and that of the total male labor force.

graduates were turned out by the provincial schools, prepared to work as accountants, technicians, and scientific researchers and at middle-management levels of industry.[81] This new class formed a significant part of the Liberal party opposition to Duplessis, sensing that his form of nationalism actually inhibited French Canadian economic development.

The Union Nationale policies did indeed have a detrimental effect on Quebec's economic development. Throughout the postwar era, the province was attractive to capital investment, given its low labor costs and extensive natural resources. Under Duplessis' laissez-faire policies and strident opposition to labor organization, the door was open to massive investments of foreign capital. In what was a typical pattern during his regime, Duplessis granted iron-mining rights to an American corporation for a royalty of one cent per ton of ore extracted. In Newfoundland, the same procedure returned a royalty of thirty-three cents a ton.[82] By 1954 foreign investors controlled three-fourths of Quebec's oil industry, one-half of the mining, and two-fifths of the manufacturing firms; over 80 percent of all foreign-controlled business was in the hands of Americans.[83] In a study of business ownership patterns in 1961, André Raynauld determined that foreign capital controlled 41.8 percent of value added in Quebec's secondary sector. Indeed, Quebec capital controlled only two industries: woodworking (83.9 percent) and leather (49.4 percent).[84] Moreover, industrial capital was concentrated in the hands of a small number of giant enterprises. In 1954 four banks controlled 77 percent of the assets held in Quebec banks, and four corporations controlled 93 percent of the steel industry, 78 percent of the mines, and 84 percent of electricity and gas.[85] In short, under Duplessis, Quebec was not exempt from the penetration and concentration of capital; it simply did not benefit from this process.

The bases for Duplessis' support were farmers (for whom he did develop some progressive policies, such as rural electrification and farm credit policies), the Catholic hierarchy, local political elites, and those involved in education. However, between 1941 and 1960, agricultural labor declined by half, and the impact of postwar industrial expansion could no longer be ignored. By 1961, 31.3 percent of Quebec's labor force was in the tertiary sector.[86] These white collar workers combined with the significant industrial labor force to oppose Duplessis. Industrial workers made the first break with the Union Nationale, when asbestos workers went on strike in 1949.[87] The success of the strike broke industrial worker loyalty to the traditional brand of ethnonationalism; for the first time, French Canadians joined with English trade unions against French Canadian bosses. The strike facilitated coordination between French Canadian trade syndicates and the internationals, which increased throughout the 1950s. In 1957 the labor syndicates in Quebec united with AFL-CIO support to demand that wages and working conditions be raised to the same levels as those in Ontario. In the same year, the syndicates supported the Canadian Labour Congress (AFL-CIO) in the Murdochville strike in the copper mines.[88] During the Duplessis regime, a growing number of Catholic clerics began to support more militant labor activism, and the traditional solidarity of church conservatism began to change. Opposition to duplessisme and support for the Liberal party were spread throughout the class structure. And with the death of Duplessis in 1959, this opposition triumphed over the Union Nationale. Under the banner "Time for a Change," the Liberal party won the 1960 provincial elections.

Jean Lesage, the new premier, implemented a program that was later called "la révolution tranquille": a program of economic modernization, secularization of social welfare, and state development. Under the slogan "maîtres chez nous," nationalists shifted from a concern with the French Canadian problem in Canada to a focus on the Quebec problem. Although French Canadians made up 28 percent of the population, only 16 percent of all Francophones lived outside Quebec Province. Among these, the number who claimed English as their first language had steadily increased from 3.5 percent in 1921 to 10 percent in 1961, and the Anglicization of the French population reached as high as 85 percent in Newfoundland (see table 14). Quebec had literally become the homeland of the Francophone Canadian. And it was a home where the French Canadian was not master.

I have already discussed the extent to which the policies of Duplessis facilitated the control of Quebec's economy by large American and Canadian firms. Within this framework of economic dependence, the French Canadians experienced continued ethnic stratification. In Montreal, during the early years of the Liberal administration, French Canadians constituted 60 percent of the work force but only 17 percent of management positions. Throughout

Table 14 Percentage of Canadians of French Origin Claiming English as Their Mother Tongue, 1961

Province	Percentage Claiming English
Newfoundland	85.0
British Columbia	65.0
Nova Scotia	57.0
Prince Edward Island	55.0
Alberta	50.0
Saskatchewan	48.0
Ontario	38.0
Manitoba	30.0
New Brunswick	12.0
Quebec	1.6

Source: Statistics Canada, *1961 Census of Canada* (Ottawa: Dominion Bureau of Statistics, 1962), tables 95 and 96.

Quebec, the 7 percent of the labor force which was Anglophone held 30 percent of all management and 80 percent of all top managerial positions.[89] Francophone income was 40 percent below the provincial average, and even when human capital factors were held constant, only half of the income differences between Quebec Anglophones and Francophones could be explained.[90]

To counter economic dependence and ethnic stratification, Lesage rejected Duplessis' weak state model and argued for a strong provincial government as the key to French Canadian survival. As he put it, "the only power at our disposal is the state of Quebec. . . . If we refuse to use our state, we would deprive ourselves of what is perhaps our only means of survival and development in North America."[91] Lesage adopted a policy of economic nationalism which had two components to it. One was direct intervention in economic development through the creation of state companies. The other consisted of fiscal strategies to modernize and support those remaining French Canadian companies. In 1962 Lesage nationalized Quebec's hydroelectric facilities, buying out its largely American and Anglo-Canadian stockholders. Numerous state enterprises followed: a state steel complex, Sidbec; a General Investment Corporation to provide financial support in association with private capital and promote the emergence of a Quebecois managerial class; Quebec Deposit and Investment Fund to invest state pension funds; and strong support for the cooperative movement. Nor was this state building limited to the economic sector. With support from Ottawa, social welfare services were secularized, hospitalization insurance and a provincial pension fund were established, a centralized department of education replaced autonomous departments of public instruction, and the responsibility for education was formally transferred from the church to the state. André Larocque has noted that the decade from 1960 to 1970 was "marked by the construction of a truly modern state. Within the general framework of British parliamentary institutions, which were more or less unquestioned, Quebec adopted its first set of modern political and administrative institutions and began to create the first truly Quebec political power."[92] In the first five years of Liberal rule, the state expanded phenomenally: new ministries, regulatory agencies, and courts increased the number of state institutions from 39 to 64 and the number of civil servants from 29,298 to 41,847.[93]

Despite this aggressive activity, it would be a mistake to characterize this period as one of fundamental change in the basic economic structure of Quebec. The Quiet Revolution did not alter the degree of external control of Quebec's economy or the province's subordinance in the wider North American economy. The sectors which were most outside state control were those in which industrial expansion and technological development generated economic growth: heavy industry, complex and expensive consumer goods, and producer goods.[94] Hence, after a decade of the Quiet Revolution, American industry controlled 80 percent of the chemical industry, 75 percent of machine production, and 66 percent of industrial machine production in Quebec.[95] And French industries still shared only a small percent of goods exported to other provinces. Indeed, some have viewed the Quiet Revolution as a kind of "French is beautiful campaign," which never challenged the basic dominance of American and Anglo-Canadian capital. Multinational corporations astutely exploited Quebec's new ethnic assertiveness. English companies tried to identify with Quebec consumers by referring to the provincial and ethnic traditions.[96]

If the Liberal policies did not seek basic restructuring of the economy, they did begin a transformation of the ethnic distribution of resources within that structure. It was essentially a bourgeois movement, seeking greater French participation in the managerial elites in business and government and economic growth within the province. In this sense, as Herbert Guindon expressed it, the "Quebec renaissance or silent revolution is a bureaucratic revolution, in which salaried white collar bureaucrats sought to challenge Anglo dominance in federal offices and private corporations."[97] It did succeed in opening opportunities to this new class. For example, Hydro-Quebec played a significant role in developing a Francophone managerial elite. By 1968 Francophones held 297 of the top managerial jobs in this second-largest North American utility. In contrast, the main private company had only a minor percentage of French Canadian managers and technicians.[98] Sidbec, the state steel complex, also promoted the development of a Francophone managerial elite: 65 percent of its managerial level employees were Francophone in 1968 and by 1975 this had been increased to 90 percent.[99] Federal-provincial relations were also altered by the Quiet Revolution. Since Quebec produced at least one-fourth of Canada's gross national product, its economic and political awakening was taken quite seriously. The economic nationalist policies of the Lesage administration were largely unopposed by Ottawa, in part because Quebec was not alone in feeling itself a satellite of United States capital nor in possessing weak indigenous secondary industries. It shared with the other provinces a dependence on foreign markets and a secondary position in research and development; and the call "maîtres chez nous" was not discordant to Canadian nationalists who felt even more fully than Quebec the impact of American culture. Consequently, the modernizing nationalism of provincial Liberals was frequently applauded on the federal level as a local version of a broad Canadian nationalism. In 1963 Ottawa established a royal Commission On Bilingualism and Biculturalism to explore the extent of inequalities between the French and the English and possible changes in the confederation which would ensure more equitable relations between these two charter groups. Federal largesse and shared-cost programs in health, education, and municipal affairs provided the funds for state expansion and the secularization of social services. Using the established "opting-out system," Quebec withdrew from twenty-nine of the forty-six federal-provincial jointly administered programs to develop its own with federal funding. This increased the independence of the Quebec state bureaucracy as well as its visibility to the provincial population.[100] The shifts in state structure did generate federal-provincial tensions, particularly when Lesage established direct relations with the governments of Western Europe in an effort to establish firms and cultural associations with these states. For the most part, however, the Quiet Revolution was supported and encouraged by the central state since it brought Quebec into closer alignment with advanced capitalism. The Quiet Revolution also precipitated a new ethnonationalist spirit, one which altered Canadian politics and Anglo-Francophone relations. It is to that nationalism that we now turn.

COMPETITION, THE NEW MIDDLE CLASS, AND THE RISE OF ETHNIC SEPARATISM

What is the nature of the Canadian confederation and what should its future be? This central question of Canadian history has been the subject of debate in Quebec politics since the Quiet Revolution. Stands on confederation have taken a particular turn in this era, as the developing state bureaucracy has displaced the church as distributor of goods and services and as the traditional nationalist ideologies of agrarian retreat have lost their material base. Like the Bleus in the nineteenth century, Liberals contended that the federal structure provided a stronger base for securing the economic interests of Quebec against encroaching United States corporate power. Although more linguistic autonomy was needed, Liberals argued that the provincial powers provided protection of French culture. Like the Rouge supporters at the time of confederation, new nationalist groups rejected Liberals and claimed that French Canadian economic and cultural interests were hampered by the federal structure. The centralized federal government, from this perspective, isolated Francophones from any effective power in Canadian affairs, in negotiating favorable trade relations, or in protecting their cultural integrity. Hence, the period of the Quiet Revolution was not as tranquil as its name implies. Ethnic activism increased in the mid-1960s as a result of demographic changes in the province, of the findings of the Royal Commission on Biculturalism and Bilingualism, and of the declining occupational opportunities for educated Francophones.

The extent to which French Canada was secularizing was evident not only in the institutional changes in the state but also in declining fertility rates. From 1964 to 1968, the French Canadian birthrate fell 25 percent, and by 1965 it was an astonishing 5 percent below the Canadian mean (in 1951 fertility rates had been 23 percent above that mean). This decline was accompanied by steady immigration into the province of "new" ethnic groups. Although in 1951 only 5.8 percent of Quebecois were of neither English nor French ethnic origin, by 1961 that percentage had increased to 8.6 percent. Of the immigrants, only 11 percent were native French speakers; 63 percent spoke neither English nor French. But those who immigrated made the choice to learn English five times as frequently as they did French. As a result, the percentage of French Quebecois declined from 82.0 percent of the province in 1951 to 80.6 percent in 1961 and 79 percent by the end of the decade.[101] In Montreal, which received 85 percent of the immigration into Quebec, the effects were felt most sharply: by the end of the 1960s, the immigrant population had increased to 19.7 percent of the metropolis. 90 percent of the immigrants' children attended English schools, signaling their intentions to assimilate into the English Canadian population.[102] Given the economic realities of North America, such decisions seemed a rational way to maximize a child's opportunities. However, it also seemed to many Quebecois to ensure the Anglicization of the largest provincial city. Indeed, some demographers predicted that by the end of the century, French Canadians would be barely a majority in this major metropolis.[103]

This threat of increased language competition was felt in conjunction with increased job competition. State expansion slowed in the mid-1960s; but the supply of educated and technically skilled Francophones increased steadily. Because there were insufficient opportunities in governmental and semigovernmental positions, these university graduates moved into the private sector, where they faced Anglophone dominance.[104] The findings of the federally supported Royal Commission on Bilingualism and Biculturalism published in the late 1960s documented and publicized the extent to which Quebec was dominated by Anglo-Canadian and American capital and the many boundaries to Francophone occupational mobility as a result of Anglophone control over upper administrative positions. It especially emphasized the psychological consequences of the ethnic occupational structure for French-speaking Canadians. To work in corporate firms not only required that they be bilingual, but also presumed a degree of assimilation to Anglo-Canadian culture and norms and hence generated a sense of ethnic alienation among aspiring French. Thus, the combination of limited occupational mobility, increased evidence of Anglicization, and the shrinking opportunities in the state sector provided a base for particularly intense discontent in this fragment of the Francophone middle class.[105]

At the outset of the Quiet Revolution, a new nationalist party, the Rassemblement pour l'Indépendance Nationale (RIN), was founded to counter Liberal federalism. RIN advocated independence from the British Crown, emphasized a policy of linguistic exclusivity rather than bilingualism in Quebec, and eschewed welfare state liberalism in favor of more social democratic policies. From RIN's perspective, Liberal policy constituted the replacement of an entrenched and arrogant economic elite by a new and younger French one. This was insufficient: greater economic autonomy and restructuring were necessary.[106] In the early years, RIN attracted little support and was mostly centered in the university communities of Montreal and Quebec, where it organized street demonstrations, marched under the slogan "Vive le Québec Libre," and debated social democratic and socialist principles of economic organization. However, its capture of 5.5 percent of the vote in the 1966 provincial elections, together with a 3 percent secured by a right-wing Ralliement National, led to the defeat of the Liberal government and the brief reascendance of the Union Nationale. This challenge to the liberals' ability to capture middle-class support, together with the media attention given to RIN (it was the RIN slogan which Charles de Gaulle shouted on his visit to Canada in 1967), underscored the political potential of antifederalist activism. And in 1968 René Levesque capitalized on that potential.

René Levesque was a leading provincial figure. A well-known television broadcaster, he had been the minister for natural resources under Lesage, had played a leading role in the nationalization of the hydroelectric industry in 1962, and had strongly advocated greater provincial autonomy and protection of the French language than Liberals had supported. In 1967 when the party rejected his proposed platform for increased provincial separation from the central state and unilingualism in provincial government, Levesque resigned and formed the Mouvement Souveraineté Association (MSA).[107] Like the RIN, the MSA was young, urban, and middle class.[108] The following year, MSA, RIN, and RN merged to form the Parti Quebecois, with twenty-five thousand members and an organization in nearly every provincial riding. The PQ was a centrist but separatist party. It advocated increased state planning of the economy but sought private and foreign investment. Its membership, as characterized by Richard Pious, were those members of the "new middle class" who were "discontented but certainly not dispossessed."[109] 37.2 percent were professionals, 22.1 percent white collar, 8.9 percent housekeepers, and only 2.7 percent unemployed: the population whose mobility was threatened by continued Anglo dominance in the private sector and declining growth in the state sector.[110] For the first time, there was a separatist party in Quebec "that united all separatists, except for a handful of the far left and the far right."[111] Its first opportunity to challenge Liberal hegemony came not on an economic issue but on the question of language rights in education.

In 1968 the school board of St. Leonard, a suburb of Montreal, passed a regulation to require immigrant children to attend French schools. Although provincial courts later struck down the legislation, the rule precipitated an electoral crisis. The Presbytery of Montreal, representing forty English churches, spoke out against the bill on economic grounds, claiming that immigrants needed to learn the dominant language of business and commerce. But their statement was not simply a rational appeal; in spirit, it recalled Lord Durham's report: they wrote, "The French Canadian system of education has not produced businessmen; the English Canadian system has done so, because it is more pragmatic. . . . Everywhere in North America, including Quebec, the English language is now an absolute necessity from the economic point of view. The English speaking people of Quebec have no alternative but to force more and more people to accept the English system and to learn English."[112] To mollify Anglophone sentiment, the provincial government introduced a bill giving each child the right to attend school in a chosen language and requiring the creation of schools in accord with those choices. Francophones opposed this freedom-of-choice plan. French high school students went on strike; demonstrations broke out throughout the province and forty thousand marched on the capital. The debate so divided the province that provincial elections were called for.

During the election campaign, the PQ proferred its platform of provincial nationalism, arguing for a form of sovereignty association which would give Quebec greater economic independence. On the language debate, it took a slightly more moderate, but still nationalist, position which would permit present immigrant students to attend school in a chosen language but would require French of all future immigrants. Claims by Liberal party spokespeople that a PQ victory would result in the loss of millions of dollars in annual revenue, that capital would desert the province, and that the standard of living would drop 35 percent played on Anglophone fears. One photograph, circulated before the election, showing eight Brink's armored trucks leaving Quebec for Ontario symbolized the fear of a capital exodus.[113] The election revealed the growth of separatist sentiment and the extent of ethnic cleavage. Although it had been in existence for only two years, the PQ captured 24 percent of the vote. Its strength was in urban areas. PQ ran second to the Liberals in every Montreal riding and secured significant support in Quebec City, the northern industrial region, and depressed areas in the south. An analysis of the electoral returns indicated that the Liberals had won twenty of their seventy-two seats only on the strength of non-French Canadian votes.[114] The 20 percent of the electorate who were Anglophones voted almost exclusively for the Liberals; and that party won largely because the antifederalist vote was divided among the three opposition parties.[115] The PQ was clearly the party of the Francophone new middle class.

But the growing ethnic antagonism was not circumscribed by electoral politics. A small neo-Maoist separatist group, Front de la Libération du Québec, emerged in the early years of the Quiet Revolution. By 1970 they had moved from ideological statements to a guerilla campaign to confront the state. In the spring of 1970, the FLQ kidnapped British Trade Commissioner James Cross and Provincial Labour Minister Pierre LaPorte. In response, Prime Minister Pierre Trudeau dispatched federal troops to Quebec and placed the entire province under martial law. And the Anglophone press associated the FLQ and the PQ, arguing that the murder of LaPorte would end the separatist movement.[116] Such hopes seemed vindicated as PQ membership fell from eighty thousand to thirty thousand in the year 1970–1971. To revitalize itself, the Parti Québecois turned to the working class to forge an alliance with labor.[117] Neither the Parti Québecois nor the Liberal party had reached out to the working class. The leadership and orientation of both were clearly bourgeois. The provincial trade unions had almost completely secularized during the Quiet Revolution, and by 1970 they were among the most militant organizations in Canada. The Liberals had not sought to diffuse working-class discontent through wage increases and consumerism, but had emphasized incorporation of the middle classes into the accrued power of industrial and middle managerial elites. Hence, rather than dissolving class consciousness, secularization of the trade unions encouraged expression of the concerns of the working class and intensified their radicalization.[118] The late 1960s were characterized by widespread strikes and demonstrations, including a major strike by Montreal police and firefighters in 1969. In the spring of 1971, the Fédération des Travailleurs du Québec joined with leaders of the Confédérations Syndicale Nationale (220,000 members) and the Corporation des Enseignants de Québec (CEQ; 70,000 members) to establish a Common Front for a socialist independent Quebec. The increasing militance of trade unionists made it clear that organized labor was a resource to be tapped. And Levesque determined to build a coalition.

The Common Front represented a huge constituency that nationalists could not afford to ignore. But the efforts of socialist labor leaders to integrate workers' concerns into the PQ platform risked alienating the middle class. The influence of radical trade unions was evident in the 1972 draft platform of the PQ but was sharply modified by the spring convention. Still, the PQ did incorporate social democratic policies into its platform in an effort to expand its constituency, including a social policy which would guarantee a national income floor and extend all forms of health care, education, and housing, and expand provincial control over financial institutions and investments. And despite ambivalence, the three major trade unions supported the PQ and increased its membership base to 62,400 by June of 1973.[119] Since unemployment fell and the Liberal party undertook a series of growth policies which attracted further investment into the province, the Liberal party handily won the election of 1973 with 54.8 percent of the popular vote. Still, PQ supporters, known as Pequistes, were a force to be reckoned with, securing 30.3 percent of the ballots. In the following two years, the difficulties of Liberal negotiating between ethnic and class concerns and federal-provincial relations thrust more and more support into the PQ camp.

The language issue did not die with the Montreal school rulings. Although the particular legislation was struck down by the courts, the debate about language continued. In 1974 the provincial legislature acted on a government-issued report by the Royal Commission on French Language and Language Rights in Quebec which recommended that French be established as the language of the province and utilized as "the language of internal communication in commerce and industry and the work milieu in general" in order "to ensure greater vertical mobility of French Canadians."[120] The commission recommendation encouraged persuasion rather than law to increase the use of French and discourage Anglicization. But the 1974 legislation responded to nationalist concerns. Bill 22, the Official Language Act, declared French the official language of the province, required its use in public administration, and encouraged its use in business and commerce. Most importantly, Bill 22 established mandatory Francophone schooling for all children from non-English-speaking backgrounds (with the exception of the indigenous populace and those with some facility in English). The education clause required that school children from non-Anglophone homes be tested for their language knowledge before entering school. Only children with a proficiency in English would be permitted to attend Anglophone schools.

The implementation of the education clause was extremely cumbersome. Siblings were often assigned to separate schools, and the non-Francophone communities mobilized in protest. Thousands of cases were appealed; many parents refused to adhere to the decision, and in the largely Italian suburb of St. Leonard, the English school admitted one thousand children who had failed the test. By 1976 Bill 22 had become the locus for ethnic conflict, but the government refused to revoke the bill; Bourassa contended conclusively, "We are against free choice in the language of teaching. Those who do not agree with us should leave."[121] That there was little fundamental disagreement by the PQ was evident in its marginally different position that present immigrants should have freedom of choice but all future immigrants should be schooled in French.

If the language crisis did not divide Francophones within Quebec, it did exacerbate ethnic conflict at both the provincial and federal levels. At the same time that Quebec was embracing a unilingual policy, the Liberal Trudeau government had passed an Official Languages Act to encourage bilingualism. Following the recommendations of the royal commission, the 1969 act required that all federal officials become bilingual by 1975 and was used to recruit Francophones into the federal civil service. By 1973 only 8 percent of the civil servants enrolled in federal language schools had completed the qualifying courses; implementation of the bill was delayed until 1978.[122] More important, the federal commitment to bilingualism was challenged in June 1976, when English-speaking airline pilots and air traffic controllers undertook a work stoppage, claiming that bilingualism in air-to-ground communication was unsafe. Trudeau's agreement to revoke French "in the air" indicated to Quebecois nationalists that only in the province would their language be protected; it reinforced commitment to the unilingual legislation there. Hence the failure of bilingualism at the federal level contributed to increased unilingual politics at the provincial level and intensified antagonism among Francophones toward the Liberal party.

But the real key to PQ success was the decline of economic growth in the 1970s. Although to the left of any other federal or provincial party, the PQ differed from the Liberals not on the fundamental structure of the economy but on the nature of economic planning. As economist Mel Watkins has pointed out, the debate between these two parties was one about different approaches to American investment. "In effect the federalists see the American relationship as being more beneficial for Quebec when Quebec is part of a broader political structure, while the separatists see greater benefits from working out a direct relationship with the U.S., not mediated through Ottawa or English Canada."[123] During the early 1970s, economic federalism seemed on the ascendant among the electorate as a whole, as unemployment fell and Liberal policies attracted further investment into the province.

However, by mid-decade the Bourassa administration faced severe economic problems. Inflation had escalated the cost of state-sponsored projects such as the Saint James Bay development schemes; some projects, such as the Olympics, were sheer losses; and the 1976 budget deficit amounted to $900 million. Moreover, labor conflict had escalated so dramatically that in 1976 Quebec accounted for 41 percent of all Canadian work stoppages. Bourassa had adopted a uniform hard-line policy against public sector strikes by teachers, nurses, and construction workers, thereby furthering the alliance between the PQ and trade unions. By the spring of 1976, research polls indicated that 56 percent of the populace were dissatisfied with the Liberals' economic policies and 41 percent considered the PQ a real alternative.[124] The Parti Quebecois victory in the election of 1976 was not, then, a victory of cultural nationalists over federalists. Both Liberals and Pequistes had supported Bill 22. Rather, it was a victory of economic provincialists who had formed an alliance with labor. And when the PQ focused solely on Bourassa's economic record, downplaying its initial commitment to separatism, it was able to secure support even among Anglophones and non-Francophone immigrants.[125] Levesque himself freely acknowledged that the victory was "not a mandate for Quebec's independence. Our commitments are clear on this point; when the time comes, it will be up to the public and to them alone, to decide the issue in a referendum."[126]

Although the success of the PQ could not be viewed as a separatist victory, it still did signal the extent to which ethnonationalism had become an integral aspect of Quebec politics. And it underscored the changes in ethnonationalisms in the postwar period. Quebec had moved from the emphasis of duplessisme on the traditional aspects of French Canadian culture (faith, farm, and family) to the modernizing nationalism of the Quiet Revolution. But it had not abandoned the cultural nationalism of the Groulx era with its emphasis on language as a definitive aspect of the ethnic group.

In the early years of the Quiet Revolution, modernizing nationalism was a movement of the new middle class against the traditional hierarchical ethos. This middle class sought more secular institutions of state and sought to overcome its subordinate status and occupational immobility by pressuring the government to incorporate the French into the expanding federal bureaucracy, to favor Francophones in business and commerce, and to nationalize industry. In short, the movement sought to provide managerial and professional jobs to the middle class. Unilingual policies are a mechanism for controlling labor market competiton between French and English speakers, providing the educated Francophones with an edge in employment. Research on the distribution of support for separatist and unilingual policies indicates that support is highest in cities where much of the populace is bilingual (indicating a higher degree of language competition). And the strongest support for the PQ has been among those with higher levels of education, who work in occupations requiring some English facility and who have more direct contact with English Canadians.[127] However, the increased articulation of middle-class interests in ethnonational terms was matched by the growing secularization and militance of trade unions. As issues of ethnic equity were raised by the middle classes, issues of economic equity were raised by trade union leaders. Thus, ethnic conflict was complicated by a growing class conflict. And the Parti Québecois sought to capitalize on class discontent by developing a political platform which responded to the economic interests of both labor and the middle-class sectors within the Francophone community.

The major legislation introduced by the PQ, Law 101, the Charter of the French Language, reveals the extent to which the PQ is essentially a culturally nationalist party, responsive to the market concerns of the middle classes. Passed in August 1977, this piece of legislation officially abolished bilingualism within the province and required that all signs on billboards and in stores be in French only. It required that business firms be certified by the newly established Office de la Langue Française as using French as the langauge of business and as undertaking affirmative actions to foster the promotion of Francophones. It limited access to English language high schools to those children certified by the government as having completed English language schooling in Quebec. This not only closed the state-supported English language schools to immigrant children but also to Anglo-Canadian children whose parents had moved from another province.

The language law provoked an antinationalist backlash at both the federal and the state level. To Pierre Trudeau, the law constituted a return to the reactionary nativism of the Groulx period. As the prime minister who had ushered in the federal $750 million bilingualism program, he argued that the language law would only further isolate Quebec. "Our Holy Mother the Church is being replaced by holy nationalism," he said in 1978.[128] Trudeau announced that he would seek to include in the amendments to the British North America Act a "Canada Clause," which would guarantee that children of Canadians have the right to English or French education in any province where numbers warrant. That Bill 101 was popular to Quebecois Francophones was evident, however, in the provincial elections of 1981; provincial Liberals supported the Canada Clause, but the Pequistes won a sweeping victory after supporting the full restrictions of Bill 101. Despite Quebecois resistance, amendments to the British North America Act were passed. And in 1984 the Supreme Court reaffirmed an earlier court decision striking down the provisions of Bill 101 restricting English language schooling.[129] If measured on the basis of provincial support for unilingualism, ethnic nationalism triumphed in Quebec against federal policies of bilingualism. But there may be greater threats to Francophone cultural integrity than English Canada. The presence of American-dominated continental culture cannot be avoided. Tourism and advertising, mass media, films, and television all pose challenges to French Canada (perhaps less than they do to Anglo-Canadian culture). Also, the success of linguistic nationalists did not necessarily bring support for the creation of an independent Quebec nation-state.

As noted above, the electoral victory was not evidence of support for state nationalism among Francophones. All public opinion polls indicated a minority of support for separatism and a concentration of that support in urban and middle-class areas. Recognizing this, Levesque adopted a gradualist policy—l'étapisme—independence by easy stages. The assumption was that the populace would support independence if the day-to-day government operations and public policies secured popularity. Rather than introduce sovereignty-association at once, Levesque proposed a referendum seeking voter support for simply negotiating with Ottawa; only later would he seek a mandate to negotiate an agreement for sovereignty. The text of the referendum question reveals how gradualist indeed was the PQ approach:

> The Government of Quebec has made public its proposal to negotiate a new agreement with the rest of Canada, based on the equality of nations; this agreement would enable Quebec to acquire the exclusive power to make its laws, levy its taxes and establish relations abroad—in other words, sovereignty—and at the same time, to maintain with Canada an economic association including a common currency; no change in political status resulting from these negotiations will be effected without approval by the people through another referendum; on these terms, do you give the Government of Quebec the mandate to negotiate the proposed agreement between Quebec and Canada? Yes. No.

In May 1980 the referendum was roundly defeated. And by 1985 polls indicated that only 20 percent of Quebecers favored any form of sovereignty.[130] Moreover, the Parti Québecois was not particularly successful on economic issues. It did make provincial income taxes more sharply progressive, eliminate sales taxes on clothing and footwear, provide income supplements for the working poor and introduce other new social welfare measures (dental care for children, property tax rebates for the elderly, free milk in schools). But it was unable to halt the postwar move of multinational headquarters to Toronto (although there is little evidence that this move was due to language policies, since large multinational and Anglo-Canadian firms were generally exempted) or to stimulate new development at a high enough rate to cope with unemployment. Because of inflation and the fact that nearly half of Quebec's labor force is in the public sector, Levesque also took a tough stand against public strikes. The provincial unemployment rate of 11 percent in 1978 did not decline during recent Pequiste years. In January 1985 it stood at 11.9 percent, compared to 8.7 percent in Ontario. As a result, the initial coalition with labor fragmented. That Quebec's economic problems eroded PQ support was evident in its declining membership from 260,000 at the last election to 113,000 at the 1985 party convention. Polls taken in early 1985 indicated that were elections to be held then, the Liberals would defeat the PQ.[131] At its party convention, the PQ agreed to eliminate a plank making independence the main campaign issue of the next election. Perhaps the Francization of business alleviated ethnic competition within the province sufficiently to erode the material base for nation-statism.

ETHNONATIONALISM IN ADVANCED INDUSTRIAL STATES: A COMPARISON

In this chapter, I have delineated the progress of two very different types of nationalist movement within advanced industrial states. In Northern Ireland, a reactionary sectarian movement on the part of the Protestant working class sought to prevent secularization of the state in order to protect what it perceived to be its political and labor market advantages. Continual civil strife and military rule have resulted. In Quebec, a mostly middle-class movement sought to secularize and nationalize the state in order to expand its market resources. Despite widespread Canadian opposition, the ethnonationalists secured their interests without great civil strife. It could be argued that these movements are so different as to be idiosyncratic. But a comparison is instructive to our efforts to draw generalizations about ethnic mobilization.

The characteristic features of advanced industrial societies (increased state interventions into the economy, multinational economic dominance and corporate expansions, a more significant secondary and tertiary sector, welfare state development) are present in both Northern Ireland and Quebec. As predicted by the resource mobilization model, such changes did erode the hegemony of traditional local elites and increase the role of the state in economic planning and the allocation of resources. As a result, ethnic antagonisms increasingly focused on control of the state apparatus. From this perspective, we would expect nationalisms to emerge out of increased competition between segments within the ethnic communities for access to political power and economic resources. As we have seen in this chapter, despite their differences, the ethnonational movements in both Northern Ireland and Quebec did emerge during periods in which ethnic competition had increased as a result of the kinds of social changes outlined above. In both cases, the movements constituted efforts to regulate or exclude potential competitors through ethnic public policy. Hence, we saw that Ulster's working-class Protestants mobilized precisely when the power of the local elites declined as a result of the deteriorating competitive position of Ulster's traditional industries, and when welfare state reforms provided greater resources to northern Irish Catholics. The modernization of the Stormont parliament would secularize the distribution of political resources even further; consequently, Catholic efforts to normalize politics (through electoral participation and support for one man–one vote legislation) threatened the very base of incremental Protestant advantages. Similarly, the penetration of multinational capital into postwar Quebec and the expansion of the federal bureaucracy both threatened the position of the traditional clerical and political elite. Mobility within these expanding state and economic sectors, however, required facility in English and conformity to Anglo-Canadian culture. Quebec's Quiet Revolutionaries mobilized, initially, for bilingual legislation; nationalists adopted unilingual policies only as evidence on assimilation trends in the province indicated that there would be greater language competition in the private and public sectors, and as the supply of jobs for well-educated Francophones was saturated. In short, both bilingual and unilingual legislation provided resources for reshifting the competition between Anglophones and Francophones. Similarly, separatists nationalized particular industries and mobilized for state sovereignty in order to counter the English-dominated economy and to break down the cultural division of labor.

A comparison of these two cases is also instructive for underscoring the extent to which physical space shapes ethnic boundaries. In both cases, ethnic identities and conflicts have been most intense in urban areas, where groups come into more frequent contact and competition. In Northern Ireland, the conflicts have been sharpest in Belfast and Londonderry. In part, the urban competition is territorial: outbursts are strongly related to ''invasions'' of clearly defined communal boundaries by members of other groups. In Quebec, support for separatists is strongest in Montreal and Quebec City, where there is a more significant English presence and more direct evidence of linguistic competition. Hence, both cases provide strong support for our resource competition model of ethnic conflict. However, as in the earlier periods, our analysis allows us to refine the model considerably to take into account the important role of class and state structure in shaping ethnic relations.

In both Northern Ireland and Quebec, ethnic mobilization was the outcome of a class struggle within the ethnic communities as well as of resource competition between the ethnically defined groups. As we have seen, the coherence of Ulster's state rested on two bases: the consistent exclusion of Catholics from the political resources *and* an interclass coalition of the Protestant bourgeoisie and working class through the institutions of the Unionist party and the Orange Order. So long as those bases were unaltered, the stability of the government and the integration of the Protestant population under the dominance of capital was ensured. Once the Unionist leadership agreed to make minor concessions to Catholics, they called into question the tenets of the entire state system and revealed the inherently unstable bases of Ulster unionism. Orange nationalism is a call to return to the Anglo-Protestant Ascendancy on which Unionist loyalism claimed to be predicated. But it is also a rejection of the class hegemony of the traditional Unionist elite. In Quebec, the contours of class have also shaped the patterns of nationalism. As we have seen, historically the dominance of the Catholic church and a traditional elite retarded the political and economic development of the Quebecois through appeals to a special ethnic and agrarian nationalism. However, the fundamental social changes of the postwar period (urbanization, educational development, trade union organization, and state expansion) altered the material base which supported class dominance and legitimated national ideology. Increased industrialization and declining primary sectors belied the myth of an agrarian French Canada; hence, industrial labor activists eschewed nationalism and formed alliances with federal and international trade unions. During the later period of state expansion in the 1960s, the base for traditional patronage and localistic power disappeared. It was the new middle class, in the burgeoning state and administrative bureaucracies, which sought increased Francophone control of the provincial treasury and industry. The Quiet Revolution and early separatist movement were largely the domain of the middle class. Few attempts were made to address the problems of rural or urban workers. The class bias of this movement has been evident both in the grievances articulated and in the policies adopted. But this new nationalist class has not simply replaced the traditional elites. It does not exercise the same dominance over the population as the traditional elite did. Class conflicts are much more endemic to modern Quebec and cut across nationalist lines. Hence, in neither case can it be argued that the mobilized ethnic groups are unified in their position, nor that they constitute an "ethnic class." Rather, the ways in which ethnicity has been politicized are the product of the interaction between class conflicts within the ethnic communities and resource competition between the ethnic communities.

However, the two cases differ in several important ways. Perhaps most fundamental is the cultural divide between the competing ethnic groups. In Northern Ireland, as we have seen, the segregation of communities and of communal institutions reinforces ethnic antagonisms, but substantive cultural differences between the groups are actually minimal. Religion is a *symbol* of differences, and many stereotypes about religious belief are attached to each group. But the conflict itself is not a religious one. In Quebec, however, language differences not only reinforce ethnic cohesiveness, they also create material problems for the organization of the economy and the maintenance of the polity. Efforts to change a cultural division of labor automatically introduced competition and conflict over the language of labor and management. Similarly the efforts of Francophones to move into managerial positions in industry and federal bureaucracies required a shift in the language of work. Consequently, Anglophones resist not only economic displacement but the linguistic closure which that displacement involves. In this sense, language constitutes a zero-sum competition; and it has a multiplier effect, increasing the costs of other forms of competition. As Stanley Lieberson has pointed out, "The optimal linguistic conditions for the speakers of each tongue are incompatible, since the gains that one language makes are to the detriment of the other. . . . The role of language in the maintenance of ethnic boundaries is too important from the perspective of the groups seeking to maintain their boundaries for such loss to be readily accepted."[132]

Given this, however, we might expect more intense conflict in Quebec than in Northern Ireland. How then do we explain the different intensities and forms which the ethnic mobilization has taken in the two situations? First, both situations must be understood in terms of their linkages to contiguous territories, for these shape their political economies and the resources within which each group competes. Both situations are in fact structured by a tripartite geo-unit relation: in Ulster, ethnic relations are conditioned by connections to Ireland and England (and their interaction with each other); in Quebec, ethnic relations are informed by connections to Canada and the United States (and their relations to one another). For Catholics and Protestants in Ireland, we have seen that this triangular relationship has only exacerbated ethnic antagonisms. Politicians in the Republic of Ireland have capitalized on the romantic symbols of their "revolutionary" past to affirm a commitment to reunification. They have thus made martyrs and heroes of the Irish Republican Army, at the same time that they have condemned it. Together with a reluctance to fully secularize the state and the involvement of leading government figures with the IRA, this has ensured that Protestants distrust the participation of the Republic in negotiations about the Troubles. Similarly, Britain has never seriously pursued a political solution to the Northern Ireland situation; prior to direct rule, it treated Ulster as a virtually autonomous region, paying no attention to its violations of universalist liberal principles. Since intervention, Westminster has relied largely on military control of the province. Hence, it has never fostered nor provided incentives for the development of a democratic infrastructure. The Quebec situation stands in dramatic contrast to this. Whereas Ireland never sought to forge economic and political relations with the north, the Canadian federal government has aligned itself with Quebec in efforts to resist American economic and cultural hegemony. This creates a shared context within which political debate is developed. There is little doubt that the federal government is interested in Quebec's economic development and has tolerated a range of autonomous actions and experimented with different political solutions to foster that.

Clearly related to the divisions of power geographically is the significance of differences in state structure. In Ulster, since partition, the state was organized to maximize ethnic exclusion. Not only were communal identities structured into the state system but the entire discriminatory state administration was legitimated on the basis of the assumed political beliefs of the Catholic population. And when the legitimacy of that state system was challenged, there was no historical base on which to trust that it could be reformed. The only "normal politics" in Ulster have always been communal and discriminatory. In Canada, on the other hand, a liberal pluralist structure existed at the provincial level, thereby encouraging the development of crosscutting cleavages in political party formations. And because provincial parties are connected to federal parties, these cleavages tend to reach beyond the province and to moderate the ethnic identifications even more. Also, the very fact that French Canadians could secure political power within Quebec and could use the provincial-federal structure to advance their own interests provided a routinized framework for negotiating conflicts. It has also created a more variegated political constellation. Conflicts over the nature and desirability of federalism split the populace in Quebec and in the other provinces as well. Hence, one party advocates bilingualism and biculturalism and a strong federal administration; the other emphasizes unilingualism, separatism, and a strong provincial administration.

An additional factor differentiating the two cases is the extent of external support for the competing ethnic groups. As I have pointed out, northern Irish Catholics have been able to secure extensive political and monetary support from the south and from American sympathizers. This has expanded the resources of the IRA, further isolated Protestants, and cemented the recalcitrance of loyalists. In Quebec, with the exception of political rhetoric and a few symbolic trade agreements, there has been little external support for nationalists. As during the colonial period, metropolitan France has treated Quebec as a provincial backwater and invested little there. One might have seen a quite different outcome if the French or French Americans had demonstrated even some of the uncritical enthusiasm, money, or arms that have been directed to Ulster's Republicans. The weak historical links with the metropole make such a comparison merely speculative.

The differences between these two cases clearly indicate that ethnic nationalism does not necessarily lead to particular political ideologies or ethnic and class formulations. It is a flexible ideology that can be adopted by members of both dominant and subordinate ethnic groups to protect or advance their material interests. What connects Ulster and Quebec is that ethnic nationalism in each case represents the response of sections of one ethnic group to the real or perceived threat of political domination by the other. What differentiates them is equally significant for it points to the importance of a liberal pluralist political system in moderating ethnic alliances. Were culture to have significance, in and of itself, we would have expected a much more intense and conflictual separatism in Quebec than in Ulster. Instead, we find a state system which can accommodate itself to a unilingual movement within one area, thereby absorbing significant linguistic and cultural differences while deflecting nationalist tendencies.

6

Ethnic Conflicts and Nationalisms in the First World: Some Conclusions

There is no lack of theories, interpretations, hypotheses, and of "newly trained people with novel means and novel results." The academic penchant to quantify, to isolate a single factor as primarily causative, is obsessional as though the delineation of a clear cut cause and effect relationship would open the way to a miracle solution.

—Padraig O'Malley

There is a middle channel between the academic "penchant to quantify, to isolate a single factor as causative" and O'Malley's social scientific agnosticism. Social theory need not obscure the world; it can provide frameworks within which we can more clearly view social relations. If we are to look only at the complexities and nuanced history of a particular experience or group expression, then we cannot see the difference between the typical and the idiosyncratic. We must risk some abstraction, even myopia, in the search for explanations which can move beyond the particular. Without that abstraction, it is difficult to see how proposals can be suggested or evaluated. We must also undertake some quantitative analyses if we are to evaluate the relative contribution of varying factors to an event. On the other hand, reliance on abstract theorizing or on quantitative measurement can dim our perceptions of what is truly interesting about group behaviors or the intricacies of an individual case. In this book I have tried to steer that middle channel, to dive beneath the theoretical surface into the complexities of the ethnic history of each case but to continually resurface to look for the logic to separatist politics in both. In this closing chapter, I will underscore the major findings about that logic, point out areas that need deeper exploration, and identify some questions that remain unanswered.

A RECONSIDERATION OF THEORIES OF ETHNIC MOVEMENTS

In this book, we have seen the wide range of tactics and ideologies adopted by the competing ethnic groups: the reactionary nativism of the ultramontane Quebecois clergy, the universalist republicanism of the United Irishmen, the cultural nationalism but economic federalism of the Quiet Revolution, and the ethnoseparatisms of the Provisional IRA and Ulster Defense Association. How adequately do the theories examined explicate this range of political actions? In a sense, O'Malley is right. No single explanation can account for such a wide historical sweep and range of behaviors. But some accounts are more credible than others; and our analysis does underscore the basic shortcomings in each major theory. It is worth reviewing their explanatory value by reconsidering particular manifestations of ethnic conflict and separatist activity.

According to the modernization approaches, one would expect ethnonationalist activity to be strongest among those who are not fully assimilated into the universalist norms and behavioral patterns of the advanced industrial world. It derives from a kind of culture lag, in which groups adhere to the old ways for security, as the world around them is transformed. There is little support for this thesis in either case; in both Ireland and Canada, the support for ethnonationalist claims is strongest among those engaged in work in the secondary and tertiary sectors, and among those who are long-resident in urban areas. According to plural society theorists, ethnonationalist activity is best explained by the legacy of high degrees of political domination and social segregation; from this perspective it is an effort on the part of the subordinate group to break down the colonial state legacies and to assert its own value in the modern state system. In Ulster it is true that state structures and separate social institutions reinforce the salience of ethnic attachments in daily life. And the ethnonationalism of both the UDA and the Provisional IRA is an effort to reconstruct the traditional state in its own interests. But the plural society model cannot adequately account for the emergence of strong ethnonationalist claims in Que-

161

bec precisely when the institutional supports for cultural segregation and Anglo dominance were breaking down.

Similarly, neo-Marxist theories provide only partial explanations. The uneven development model is an essential starting point for understanding the material bases for divergent interests and the class relations which retarded the development of secular nationalisms in both Ireland and Canada. It is especially useful in explaining the role of patrimonial elites in deflecting class alliances, as was the case in Unionist Ulster and in provincial Quebec under Duplessis. But this model is incapable of spelling out the conditions under which patrimonialism breaks down, assuming as it does that the collapse is simply the product of economic crisis at the center. This may very well be the case in Northern Ireland, where the working class has been abandoned by Britain's Tories, for it no longer has the strategic or economic importance it once possessed. It is not so applicable to Quebec, where the decline of the traditional elites and the Quiet Revolution were strongly supported by the political and economic "center."

Moreover, the uneven development model fails to explore the *process* of building a patrimonial relationship and hence tends to attribute too much power to the center or to the metropolitan elite. In the cases under consideration, split labor market theory has been quite useful in countering this tendency to overestimate the power of economic elites in shaping ethnic relations. We have seen throughout Irish history that the Protestant laboring classes played a major role in creating the contours of ethnic and class relations; their conditional loyalty was evident both during colonialism and during the Union (in the rural outbursts against renting land to Catholic tenant farmers, in the smashing of Catholic looms, in the exclusion of Catholics from the shipyards). They set limits on the dominance of capital and in so doing reproduced a class structure based on an ethnic division of labor. However, we have also seen that the split labor market model is limited to certain times and places, that frequently it was capital which sought to "play the Orange hand," in order to break down possible interethnic labor alliances. The current troubles in Ulster are not rooted in the displacement of the Protestant labor force as a result of a corporate search for cheap labor. Rather, it is the political privileges which are challenged. This ethnic "class fraction" has organized against a secularizing state bureaucracy, which would erode the basis of differential advantages, not all of which are economic. There is more evidence of a split labor market pattern of ethnic antagonism in Quebec, insofar as Francophones have used their greater political clout to eliminate the economic advantages of Anglo workers and to restrict language competition by imposing unilingual policies. It is interesting to note that this has resulted in much less overt antagonism and conflict than the less competitive situations in Northern Ireland. In short, both split labor market and uneven development models are useful in elucidating *aspects* of the ethnic conflicts in the two cases, but neither considers sufficiently the *range* of competitive situations nor the role of institutions and ideologies in reinforcing ethnic political identity.

Like these other neo-Marxist approaches, the internal colonial model is useful in understanding aspects of ethnic struggle, but it too has limitations as an explanation of the patterning of recent ethnic conflicts. Its claim that ethnic separatism is most likely to arise when the metropole seeks to integrate a less developed hinterland, with a cultural division of labor, into its sphere may apply to late eighteenth-century Ireland. Language and religious differences, combined with the ethnic division of labor, certainly prevented a nationalist movement along any but ethnic lines. However, unless we assume a historical trajectory, this model cannot explain the recent antagonisms and separatist tendencies. It is true that Protestant militants have resisted further integration into the metropole because this would break down the ethnic division of labor, but the model predicts that resistance will be fiercest in the areas which are least economically developed. And, as we have seen, this is not the case in Ulster, where resistance is strongest in urban industrial ghettos. Similarly, the internal colonial model rightly predicts a reaction against integration into the Anglo-Canadian economy on the part of some Francophone Quebecois. The PQ emerged, in part, to counter the centralizing trends of the federalists. But, again, the resistance came not from the rural underdeveloped hinterland but from the most advanced, industrial, and educated middle classes.

RESOURCE COMPETITION, DEVELOPMENT, AND ETHNIC POLITICS

The cases of historical and modern Ulster and Quebec provide more consistent support for resource mobilization predictions about the conditions for ethnically circumscribed competition and conflict.

They also illustrate the important mediating role of cultural attitudes and beliefs, apart from concrete resource competition. In the early chapters of this book, I argued that ethnicity is not simply a subjective characteristic which can be "manipulated to organize groups for political ends in the competitive scramble for resources," but neither is it a primordial attachment that persists regardless of the broader environment in which groups live.[1] Ethnicity is a social creation and so we must look first at the social conditions which give rise to and maintain a sense of commonality. Among these conditions are shared cultural attributes (language, religion, custom, dress). But cultural commonality is not sufficient for the emergence of an ethnic identity. There must also be a sense of difference from others and an interest in maintaining that difference. Hence, ethnic boundaries are most likely to be constructed when there is competition for some scarce resources, when leaders within one or both of those groups persuade others that those resources are best secured through ethnic organization and solidarity, and when ethnic organizations and institutions provide a material basis for cultural identification. Because ethnic collectivities are produced by a combination of subjective affiliation, shared characteristics, and objective interest, their boundaries and significance will shift with political and economic developments that alter any of these. This argument is demonstrably supported by the analysis of both Ireland and Canada.

Prior to colonization, the indigenous population of Ireland had a common language and religion, but the decentralized tribal economy and political structure mitigated against a notion of "peoplehood." Ethnic boundaries did not develop until long after conquest and colonization had begun. Despite ethnocentric claims on the part of the metropole, the early English settlers did not resist absorption into the indigenous culture. It was only with the extended efforts at colonization and resistance by indigenes that distinctions between the populations were considered significant and ethnic boundaries were constructed. Not until the fourteenth century was miscegenation forbidden; but then, the use of Irish language, costumes, music, poetry, surnames, and laws was gradually banned until by the second half of the seventeenth century, everything Irish had been outlawed. For political reasons, cultural attributes were used to distribute resources; and conversion to Protestantism and acquisition of English became the criteria for participation in the state and for economic security. Even then the indigenous population did not see itself as *Irish* or *Gaelic* and did not express an identity that was more than localistic until well into the nineteenth century. Political elites sought to construct an Irish identity in order to secure support for *their* particular interests. For the United Irishmen, the building of a sense of cultural commonality was crucial to the case for independence from the Crown. For the movements for Catholic emancipation and Home Rule, it was essential in securing mass support for their case in order to apply pressure to Westminster. Similarly, the distinctive Ulster ethnic identity was not the simple product of shared customs and cultural attributes among Protestants as separate from Ulster Catholics. Rather, the idea of the "Orangeman" was carefully constructed by political elites in order to secure their class interests. And as we have seen, the Protestant supporters of the early Unionist party saw themselves as Irishmen as well as Orangemen—there was not a necessary separation of the two. In a sense, the Ulsterman is a relatively new construct, adopted in an effort to legitimate the partition of Ireland and to claim a political identity separate from the Catholic claims on Irishness.

In Canada, a sense of peoplehood also had to be built. The habitants of New France did share a common religion and language and in time a set of customs and styles which clearly differentiated them from the nonsettler French and the Anglo settlers in North America. Their relative isolation from a market economy further distinguished them. There is little evidence of a sense of a collective French Canadian identity among the habitants, however, until this population was legally demarcated from the English. The powers granted to the Catholic church under the Quebec Act imputed a political significance to cultural identity and supplied an institutional basis for its maintenance. If these attributes had not been retained in political institutions, the boundaries between the French and English might have been much fuzzier (as they were later for French Canadians outside Quebec Province). It seems clear then, as Weber contended, that cultural attributes facilitate construction of political communities; but they do not automatically produce them. Indeed, it is often "the political community, even when formed in a highly artificial way, which gives rise to beliefs in ethnic identity, which survive even its downfall."[2] In both Quebec and Northern Ireland, the provincial governmental elites sought to create and preserve ethnic boundaries to advance their own interests—but the case of Ulster makes clear that these boundaries could not be abandoned even with the demise of the state.

The mere existence of ethnic interests and their exploitation by competing elites do not give rise to ethnic politics. Individuals must be *persuaded* to see their interests as primarily ethnic. In the previous chapters, we have seen situations in which class alliances have been forged across ethnic lines: the United Irishmen, the strikes of James Connolly and Big Jim Larkin, industrial mobilization in Ulster during the Great Depression, Canada's federal and provincial Liberal and Conservative parties, and the postwar labor alliances between Quebec syndicates and international unions. To understand why social grievances are seen as ethnic and by whom, and why other forms of politics are abandoned, we must analyze the interaction between class and ethnic structures during particular periods. It is from this perspective that we examined the origins of ethnic inequalities in the colonial era and the impact of capital and state development on those inequalities.

Regional economic and political structures constitute the deepest soil in which ethnic relations are embedded. As we have seen, the interests and actions of colonial core states, their patterns of trade and economic specializations, and their investments in the colonies or exploitation of them shaped the resources of the ethnic groups in Canada and in Ireland. In both cases, metropolitan actions produced uneven regional development. And because the territories were ethnically distinct, they also fostered a cultural division of labor. This is not simply the automatic by-product of economic development. Elites within the core state may introduce cultural divisions of labor in order to protect their own political interests; elites within the periphery may collaborate in order to preserve a political or economic niche for themselves; or members of one class segment may successfully mobilize to protect a labor market advantage. In any case, we have seen that the existence of an ethnic division of labor does not necessarily foster conflicts between the unequal groups. More direct competition is needed.

Because of the different patterns of colonialism, capital development, and state formation, the forms of competition and conflicts differed quite dramatically in Ireland and Canada. Irish peasants consistently resisted plantation schemes and attacked the Protestant settlers who had displaced them from the land. But the locus of

ethnic conflict was land. And, as predicted by the resource competition model, those conflicts were narrowly focused and localized. The suppression of the church and the elimination of an indigenous middle class left the Irish peasant with no institutional
mechanisms for political organization and no effective leadership
for the articulation of broadly shared interests. In contrast, at the
time of the Canadian conquest, there was no competition between
habitants and the English for land or labor. The exodus of the Francophone commercial bourgeoisie left the region with an economically undifferentiated population. French Canadians lived an isolated rural existence, participating in very minimal ways in a
market economy. Hence, there was little mobilization along ethnic
lines *except* by the church hierarchy, which feared losing institutional control in the rangs. Even the industrialization of Quebec did
not introduce ethnic competition, since the province was largely
Francophone, the labor force was unskilled, and the French lacked
the capital and skills for industrial management and economic
growth. Here again, it was the small middle-class elite, especially
politicians, who were in direct ethnic competition with Anglophones.

As we have seen, patterns of economic and political development
can sharply alter the distribution of resources and accentuate ethnic
competition. Factors generally associated with modernization—urbanization, industrialization, expansion of the tertiary and state sectors—all increased intergroup contact and competition. Thus ethnic
conflicts were frequent in industrial Ireland, precipitated by challenges to the split labor market, by claims that political reforms
(Catholic emancipation, Home Rule) would erode the advantages
of Protestant labor, and by ritual marches through (symbolic invasions of) communally defined neighborhoods. In contrast, ethnic
competition in the labor market was less pronounced in Quebec
until the postwar period, because its development was retarded by
the policies of the provincial government. The major ethnic outbursts in the industrial period occurred in opposition to proposed
conscription into the English-dominated army. Resisting service in
a unilingual armed services can be seen as opposition to an expanding state system which gave little recognition to Francophone linguistic rights. Only with the secularization of Quebec's provincial
government and increased education was there frequent labor mar-

ket competition between skilled Francophones and their Anglophone counterparts. It was then that a broader ethnic politics was adopted.

Groups can choose *not* to mobilize along ethnic lines. The comparison of Quebec and Ulster points to the significance of state structures in shaping those choices. Working-class Protestants and Catholics have a history of brief functional labor alliances; but persistent tolerance for ethnic discrimination by Stormont and Westminster ensured that these were temporary. The special privileges granted to the Catholic church in the Republic also undercut the potential for secular politics. Together, these actions have retarded the development of a political party system in which questions of class could be addressed across confessional lines. In contrast, the pluralist democracy in Canada encouraged the development of crosscutting cleavages within the ethnic groups, especially of class and province-federal allegiances.

Finally, even if members of a group do choose ethnic over other allegiances, this does not tell us the conditions under which their politics will be nationalist or separatist.

I argued in chapter 2 that ethnic nationalist claims will increase to the extent that the principles of ethnic group grievances and rights have been broadly disseminated. This requires mechanisms of communication and intellectuals who will espouse the principles of self-determination. This is likely to increase with development, as the result of the technologies of communication and what Walker Connor has called the contagion effect of successful independence movements. Both Catholics in Ulster and French Canadian students drew on the rhetoric of the American civil rights movement to make their claims. The Provos, the UDA, and the PQ have drawn parallels to anticolonial and anti-imperial movements elsewhere. But the logic of the ethnic nationalist is to call upon the special history and culture of the group which distinguishes it from others. Consequently, previous ethnic movements play a special role in shaping the ideology and direction of present ethnic tactics. One of the reasons for the power of the IRA is its ability to draw on a rich mythology and long history of Irish resistance to British rule; and there is potency for the UDA in the symbols and traditions of a loyalist covenant. Although the PQ may eschew the traditional clerical dominance, it draws on the romantic vision of a special civilizing mission of the Quebecois in its opposition to English Canada.

Conclusion

If our consideration of the patterning of ethnic and class relations in Northern Ireland and Quebec has pointed out the limitations of our current conceptual paradigms, it has also underscored their utility. This analysis points us in the direction of a more unitary approach, one which is grounded in appreciation for the complex interactions of ethnic and class structures and processes. It prepares us to develop more explicit statements about which factors influence ethnic identities and to create testable propositions and measures that can calculate their relative contributions. If we are sensitive to the richness of history, we can avoid the indictment of social scientists as abstract quantifiers. What this analysis does not help us do, however, is to evaluate the principle of nationalism. Ethnic nationalism depends on the principle of self-determination for its justification. But from there, it swims in many ideological currents, confounding attempts to create a singular explanation of its genesis, development, and persistence. This principle of group rights to self-determination presents difficult problems for the analyst who is concerned about fairness and the meaning of ethnicity in the modern world. Can we legitimate the distribution of goods and resources on the basis of ethnicity? Is the nation-state a legitimate goal for justice?

Some critics have argued that the invocation of a principle of ethnic self-determination constitutes a reactionary impulse, which automatically denies universalist principles of equality and impersonal justice. At its most extreme, such an invocation tends toward racism and the fascist romanticization of "the people," a convergence of particularism and exclusionary mysticism.[3] From this perspective, efforts to maximize equality would minimize the validity and salience of ethnicity. The ethnic group is bounded by a particularistic attachment to a communal identity. Universalistic humanism knows no such boundaries.

Yet for others, the call to universalism is seen as a smokescreen for continued inequality and for forced assimilation into the culture of a dominant group. It ignores that the historical distribution of social resources along ethnic lines has significantly affected the relative positions of ethnic groups in contemporary societies. The "individualist" and "universalist" ethos may simply reflect and reinforce this inequality. Moreover, the support which states that espouse a universalist culture have given to "herrenvolk" democracies like South Africa and Northern Ireland makes many subordinate ethnic groups suspicious of universalist claims. To dismiss the call to ethnic self-determination as a "reactionary impulse" is to trivialize this complex reality.

This then is the paradox of ethnicity in the modern world: the contradiction between enduring group inequalities and principles of individualism. And this, I would argue, is a major problem for scholars of ethnic relations: to attempt to grapple with the paradox and to initiate a serious dialogue about the principled bases for ethnic group rights.

Notes

CHAPTER 1

1. See Glazer, "Universalization of Ethnicity," 8–17 Crawford Young, "Temple of Ethnicity," 652–62.

2. See Daniel Bell, "Ethnicity and Social Change," 141–76.

3. In this sense, the framework is a disciplined set of questions that should be useful in developing hypotheses. The notion of a theory sketch rests on Carl Hempel's concept of an explanation sketch in historical analysis, which consists of "a more or less vague indication of the laws and initial conditions considered as relevant and which needs 'filling out' in order to turn it into a full-fledged explanation" ("Function of General Laws in History," 465).

4. Schermerhorn, *Comparative Ethnic Relations, 12.*

5. See Anthony Smith, *Ethnic Revival.*

6. Shils, "Color and the Afro-Asian Intellectual," 4. See also Isaacs, *Idols of the Tribe.*

7. Weber, *Economy and Society,* 389.

8. Barth, "Introduction," in *Ethnic Groups and Boundaries,* 9–38; Patterson, *Ethnic Chauvinism.*

9. Van den Berghe, *Race and Racism,* 6.

10. Kohn, *Idea of Nationalism,* 16.

11. Silvert, *Expectant Peoples,* 46.

12. Hah and Martin, "Synthesis of Conflict and Integration Theories," 362.

13. Coleman, *Nigeria,* 421–22.

14. Ibid., 420–24.
15. See Smelser, *Essays in Sociological Explanation*, 125–46; Eisenstadt, *Modernization;* Apter, "Political Religion in the New Nations," 57–104; idem, "Ideology and Discontent," 15–46.
16. Deutsch, *Nationalism and Its Alternatives;* idem, "Nation Building and National Development," 1–16; Connor, "Self-Determination," 55–59.
17. See Gellner, *Thought and Change;* and Mayo, *Roots of Identity;* for a summary see Anthony Smith, *Ethnic Revival*, 50–56.
18. Coleman, *Nigeria*, 88–89. For similar interpretations see Kautsky, *Political Change in Underdeveloped Countries;* Emerson, *From Empire to Nation.* These works focus much more on the conflictual aspects of development and the roots of nationalism in colonial exploitation and discrimination than do modernization theories. Therefore, they do not strictly belong within that school. But modernization theorists almost alone have pointed out the important role of a self-interested intellectual elite.
19. Connor, "Nation-Building or Nation-Destroying?" 332. Also see Glazer, "Universalization of Ethnicity."
20. Connor, "Nation-Building or Nation-Destroying?" 341.
21. See Hah and Martin, "Synthesis of Conflict and Integration Theories," for a good review of these critiques.
22. M. G. Smith and Kuper, *Pluralism in Africa;* Despres, *Nationalism in Guyana.*
23. William J. Wilson, *Power, Racism and Privilege*, 49. Also see van den Berghe, *Race and Racism;* Schermerhorn, *Comparative Ethnic Relations;* Katznelson, *Black Men–White Cities*, 17–28.
24. Wilson, *Power, Racism and Privilege*, 50–55.
25. International Communist and Working Class Movement, *Revolutionary Movement of Our Time and Nationalism*, 45–48.
26. Ibid., 54.
27. Lenin, *Nationalism and Imperialism*, 46–47.
28. Marx, *Capital*, pt. 3, "The Law of the Tendency of the Rate of Profit to Fall," 241–66.
29. Lenin, *Right of the Nations to Self-Determination;* Fieldhouse, *Theory of Capitalist Imperialism.*
30. This ambivalence is most marked in the famous Bauer Luxemburg debate about eastern European cultural autonomy movements. For a good discussion of Marx's views on nationality and the later debate see Davis, *Nationalism and Socialism;* and Herod, *Nation in the History of Marxian Thought.*
31. The ideological ambivalence of Marxists on the question of nationality that emerged in the Bauer Luxemburg debate still persists. Perhaps the lack of clarity on the "proper stance" is clearest in the People's Re-

public of China, where policies have wavered between a tolerance of ethnic differences and an assimilationist approach. Here, as Cynthia Enloe argues, is the "core of the Marxist ideological dilemma in multi-ethnic states: all peoples are essentially members of socioeconomic classes, but imposing class consciousness on a group whose traditions obscure class divisions leads to oppression from above. How can Marxism-Leninism-Maoism be true to both class analysis and to anti-imperialism?" (*Ethnic Conflict and Political Development*, 52). For a good explication of the orthodox Marxist perspective see Edelstein, "Pluralist and Marxist Perspectives," 45–57. For a brilliant review of the problem of nationalism in Communist states, see Connor, *National Question in Marxist Leninist Theory and Strategy*.

32. Wallerstein, *Modern World System;* Strauss, *Irish Nationalism and British Democracy;* Boal and Douglas, *Integration and Division*.

33. Hechter, *Internal Colonialism;* see Stone, "Internal Colonialism in Comparative Perspective," 255–59; MacDonald, "Colonialism in Ireland." For a parallel argument, applied to the United States, see Blauner, "Internal Colonialism and Ghetto Revolt," 395–408.

34. Hechter and Levi, "Comparative Analysis of Ethnoregional Movements," 260–74. Also see Gellner, *Thought and Change;* Gourevitch, "Reemergence of 'peripheral nationalisms,' " 303–22.

35. Hechter, *Internal Colonialism,* 265; see also Stinchcombe, "Sociology of Ethnic and National Loyalties," 557–622.

36. Olzak, "Contemporary Ethnic Mobilization," 360.

37. Nairn, *Break Up of Britain,* 42. This argument draws not only from world systems theory but also from neo-Marxist analyses of state development, especially the work of Anderson, *Lineages of the Absolutist State*.

38. Bonacich, "Theory of Ethnic Antagonism," 547–59; and idem, "Past, Present and Future of Split Labor Market Theory," 17–64.

39. Ryerson, "Quebec," 224.

40. Anthony Smith, "Theory of Ethnic Separatism," 22.

41. Crawford Young, "Temple of Ethnicity," 656.

CHAPTER 2

1. Lieberson, "Stratification and Ethnic Groups," 173.

2. That interpretation also leads too easily to the conception of a "sedimentary" society, with groups layered into permanent social positions. As Lloyd Fallers has pointed out, the stratigraphic image "oversimplifies, by attempting to capture with a single graphic image, the multiple bases of differentiation and inequality which exist within Western societies" (*Inequality,* 29).

3. Noel, "Theory of the Origins of Ethnic Stratification," 106–27.

4. Ibid., 112.

5. Ibid., 114.

6. The following discussion draws on Schermerhorn, *Comparative Ethnic Relations*, 92–103.

7. Lieberson, "Stratification and Ethnic Groups," 904; Schermerhorn, *Comparative Ethnic Relations*, 148–506.

8. Schermerhorn, *Comparative Ethnic Relations*, 101.

9. Anthony Smith, *Ethnic Revival*, 74–79.

10. See Bonacich and Modell, *Economic Basis of Ethnic Solidarity*, for an interesting discussion of the ways in which patterns of ethnic identity and stratification are shaped by conditions of migration and labor competition.

11. Castles and Kosack, *Immigrant Workers in Western Europe*. See as well Schmitter, "Immigrants and Associations," 179–92.

12. This shares the assumptions of rational choice theory, but I think the supposition is implicit in all interest-group interpretations of race and ethnic relations. Banton, *Racial and Ethnic Competition*, 100–139. For this approach applied more generally, see Olsen, *Logic of Collective Action*.

13. Daniel Bell, "Ethnicity and Social Change," 165.

14. Patterson, *Ethnic Chauvinism*, 37–50.

15. Kahler, *Decolonization in Britain and France*, 40.

16. Quoted in Falardeau, "Importance of the Church in French Canada," 417.

17. I have considerably condensed the complexities of the motif of resistance within accommodation. For excellent discussions see Blassingame, *Slave Community;* Genovese, *Roll, Jordon, Roll;* William Julius Wilson, *Declining Significance of Race*.

18. Linton, "Nativistic Movements," 249.

19. Foster, *Class Struggle in the Industrial Revolution;* Lodhi and Tilly, "Urbanization, Crime and Collective Violence," 296–318.

20. Nagel and Olzak, "Ethnic Mobilization in New and Old States," 127–43.

21. Ibid., 132.

22. Ibid; and William Julius Wilson, *Power, Racism and Privilege,* 140–51; Shorter and Tilly, *Strikes in France,* 287–95; Lincoln, "Community Structure and Industrial Conflict," 199–220; Morris, "Black Southern Student Sit-in Movement," 744–67.

23. See Sklar, *Corporate Power in an African State*.

24. Nagel and Olzak, "Ethnic Mobilization in New and Old States," 130–139; also see Banton, *Racial and Ethnic Competition;* Enloe, *Ethnic Conflict and Political Development;* Fox, Aull, and Cimino, "Ethnic Nationalism and the Welfare State," 198–245; Olzak, "Contemporary Ethnic Mobilization"; Rothschild, *Ethnopolitics*.

25. Lieberson, *Language and Ethnic Relations in Canada,* 9; Zolberg, "The Spectre of Communalism," 25.

26. Olzak, "Contemporary Ethnic Mobilization," 365.

27. Anthony Smith, *Ethnic Revival,* 35.

28. Johnson, "Theoretical Model of Economic Nationalism," 14–15.

29. Coleman, *Nigeria,* 126–29; McCulley, *English Education and the Origins of Indian Nationalism;* Anthony Smith, "Theory of Ethnic Separatism," 28–33.

30. See Ronen, *Quest for Self-Determination,* 1–70, for a fuller discussion. Ronen argues that despite the range of such visions since the time of the French Revolution, the major ideologies have conceived of the state as the obstacle to the realization of these aspirations. The ideologies include the Enlightenment ideal of the rationally constructed democratic community, the European nationalist ideal of the Volk free from alien rule, Marxist visions of class emancipation, anticolonial independence movements, Pan-Africanism, and current ethnic resurgence movements. The major political ideological competitors to nationalism in the modern world may be the Enlightenment ideal of the rationally constructed democratic community and the Marxist vision of class emancipation and statelessness.

CHAPTER 3

1. Each religious abbey coincided with a territorial kingdom with its own priests and bishops. Marriage and divorce remained secular affairs, and hereditary succession through married priests was customary. For a discussion of the social organization of this population and its cultural characteristics, see Fields, *Society under Siege;* Frederick Engels, "History of Ireland," in Marx and Engels, *Ireland and the Irish Question,* 171–209; MacEoin, *Northern Ireland.*

2. Ellis, *History of the Irish Working Class,* 29.

3. The following account of colonization up to the time of James I is drawn from a number of sources. I have relied most heavily on Beckett, *Making of Modern Ireland;* Inglis, *Story of Ireland;* Moody and Martin, *Course of Irish History;* Quinn, *Elizabethans and the Irish.*

4. Canny, "Ideology of English Colonization," 575–98 (quotes from page 588), cited in Frederickson, *White Supremacy,* 16.

5. Rose, *Governing without Consensus,* 80.

6. Quinn, *Elizabethans and the Irish,* 131–41.

7. Buchanan, "Planter and the Gael," 49–73.

8. The following discussion draws on a number of sources: Beckett, *Making of Modern Ireland;* Cullen, *Formation of the Irish Economy;* idem, *Economic History of Ireland;* de Paor, *Divided Ulster;* Gibbon, *Origins of Ulster Unionism;* Moody and Martin, *Course of Irish History;* Robinson,

"Plantation and Colonization," 19–47; Rose, *Governing without Consensus*.

9. Robinson, "Plantation and Colonization," 43.

10. Rose, *Governing without Consensus,* 79. Rose points out that the colonial plantations in Ireland were fundamentally different from those in America, although the grand design of the architect, James I, was the same. "Because settlement proceeded by the grant of specific estates to undertakers, rather than by a gradual movement of settlers from east to west as in America, the native Catholic Irish, while subject to loss of title to land, were not systematically forced out of the country. In America, settlers achieved a final solution of the Indian problem by force, and Protestant Ulstermen who migrated there were pre-eminent in the vigour with which they pursued wars of elimination against Indians" (ibid., 79).

11. Miller, *Queen's Rebels,* 16.

12. Engels, "History of Ireland," 266–67; Rose, *Governing without Consensus,* 79; Kee, *Green Flag,* 19–42.

13. Miller, *Queen's Rebels,* 23.

14. The following discussion draws from Kee, *Green Flag;* Carty, *Ireland from the Flight of the Earls to Grattan's Parliament;* Lecky, *History of Ireland,* 37–115; Pim, *Conditions and Prospects of Ireland.*

15. Kee, *Green Flag,* 21. In 1853 Marx described the situation which had developed historically and still existed. In the *New York Daily Tribune,* he wrote that "a tenant having incorporated his capital in one form or another in the land, and having thus effected an improvement of the soil . . . in steps the landlord with demands for increased rent. If the tenant concede, he has to pay the interest for his own money to the landlord. If he resist, he will be very unceremoniously ejected and supplanted by a new tenant, the latter being enabled to pay a higher rent by the very expenses incurred by his predecessors. . . . In this easy way, a class of absentee landlords has been enabled to pocket not merely the labour, but also the capital of whole generations, each generation of Irish tenants sinking a grade lower in the social scale" (Marx and Engels, *Ireland and the Irish Question,* 60–61).

16. Inglis, *Story of Ireland,* 62–65; Kee, *Green Flag,* 19–22.

17. For evidence on the nonsectarian nature of these rebellions, see Connolly, *Labour in Irish History.* Connolly cites a typical outbreak in 1762 in which rewards were offered for the capture of five Whiteboy leaders (a group similar to the Oakboys) in Cork. The Protestant landlords offered three hundred pounds for the chief and fifty pounds for each of his men. Catholic landlords offered two hundred pounds for the chief and forty pounds for each of the men. For a discussion of the distinction between primitive rebellions and political movements, see Tilly, "Collective Violence in European Perspective," 4–45.

18. Cullen, *An Economic History of Ireland,* 16–36.
19. Inglis, *Story of Ireland,* 177.
20. Strauss, *Irish Nationalism and British Democracy,* 25.
21. Arthur Young, *Tour of Ireland* 2:30.
22. Gibbon, *Origins of Ulster Unionism,* 1–30.
23. Ibid., 33.
24. Ibid., 34–45.
25. Strauss, *Irish Nationalism and British Democracy,* 23.
26. Ellis, *History of the Irish Working Class,* 64–68; (quote is from p. 66).
27. Gallagher, *Indivisible Island,* 43.
28. Ellis, *History of the Irish Working Class;* Kee, *Green Flag;* de Paor, *Divided Ulster;* Edwards, *Sins of Our Fathers.*
29. Wade, *French Canadians* 1:1–44; and McRae, "Structure of Canadian History," 220–24. There was a very early phase of commercial activity carried out by French Huguenots, but their efforts were undermined by the policies of Colbert and Louis XIV discouraging commercial competition.
30. Frederickson, *White Supremacy,* 14–17.
31. Wagley and Harris, *Minorities in the New World,* 178.
32. Wade, *French Canadians* 1:14.
33. Corbett, *Quebec Confronts Canada,* 14.
34. The following discussion is based on Wade, *French Canadians* 1:1–44; McRae, "Structure of Canadian History," 219–74; Guindon, "Social Evolution of Quebec Reconsidered," 533–51; Falardeau, "Seventeenth Century Parish in French Canada"; Garigue, "Change and Continuity in French Canada," 123–27.
35. The earliest settlers were clerics, who performed diplomatic functions for the colonial government or acted as financial agents for the fur traders. For many, the religious mission was ancillary to these more secular roles and conversion of native Americans considered an adjunct to negotiation of trade relations. Frère Gabriel Sagard wrote in his memoirs in 1632: "I had hoped to promote a peace between the Hurons and the Iroquois so that Christianity could be spread among them and to open the roads to trade with many nations which were not yet accessible; but, some members of the Company advised me that it was not expedient, since if the Hurons were at peace with the Iroquois, the same Iroquois would lead the Hurons to trade with the Dutch and divert them from Canada" (Wade, *French Canadians* 1:12).
36. Falardeau, "Seventeenth Century Parish in French Canada," 21.
37. As Kenneth McRae points out: "The essence of Canadian feudalism lay in its mildness, its relaxation, its absence of systematic harshness or oppression. The proof of this lies in the almost incredible survival of seig-

norial tenure long after the end of the French regime. . . . Feudal dues and obligations were not terminated until 1854, and even at this date, the rights of the seigneurs were merely converted into fixed annual rentals which the habitant could pay off in a lump sum. . . . Only in 1935 did the Quebec legislature incorporate a syndicate to buy out the remaining rights of the seigneurs'' ("Structure of Canadian History," 224–25).

38. Falardeau, "Seventeenth Century Parish in French Canada," 346.

39. Wade, *French Canadians* 1:48.

40. Corbett, *Quebec Confronts Canada,* 15; Brunet, "Conquête anglaise," 12–22.

41. Rioux, *Quebec in Question,* 34.

42. Garigue, "Change and Continuity in French Canada," 131.

43. Ibid.

44. Sweeney, "Sketch of the Economic History of English Quebec," 73–75.

45. Ossenburg, "Conquest Revisited," 211.

46. Quoted in Rioux, *Quebec in Question,* 45.

47. Ibid., 36.

48. Dumont and Rocher, "Introduction to the Sociology of French Canada," 190.

49. Cited in Sweeney, "Sketch of the Economic History of English Quebec, " 77.

50. Ibid., 78–79.

51. Wade, *French Canadians,* vol. 1.

52. Sweeney, "Sketch of the Economic History of English Quebec," 78.

53. Although referred to as "radicals" in much of the historical literature, the Parti Patriote more closely resembled a petty bourgeois nationalist organization. It was informed by the liberal values of the American regime, and its leaders were mostly middle class (although Papineau was a seigneur). On the basic conservatism of the Patriotes see Wade, *French Canadians* 1:280–83; Rioux, *Quebec in Question,* 47–50.

54. Wade, *French Canadians* 1:283.

55. Ibid., 284.

56. Dubuc, "Crisis of Canadian and Quebecois Society," 3.

57. Cited in Legendre, "French Canada in Crisis," 7.

58. Ibid.

CHAPTER 4

1. Also see Weber, *Economy and Society* 2:927–36; and Parsons, "Theory of Social Stratification," 86–139.

2. Blumer, "Industrialization and Race Relations," 220–240.

3. Strauss, *Irish Nationalism and British Democracy*, 75. In Cork, weavers and combers who had numbered 6,000 in 1800 were only 488 in 1834; in Kilkenny, the 56 blanket manufacturers with 3,000 workers had been reduced to 40 industries and 925 workers after twenty years of the Union. See Marx and Engels, *Ireland and the Irish Question*, 131–32.

4. Kennedy, *The Irish*, 33.

5. Pomfret, *Struggle for Land In Ireland*, 7–8; Strauss, *Irish Nationalism and British Democracy*, 134–37; Marx and Engels, *Ireland and the Irish Question*, 121–38; O'Tuathaigh, *Ireland before the Famine*.

6. Thomas Wilson, *Ulster under Home Rule*, i–xviii.

7. Despite its less fertile soil, an acre of crop land in prefamine Ulster yielded an average value of £6 3*s*., whereas the yield in the south was only £5 18*s*. (Pomfret, *Struggle for Land in Ireland*, 54–56).

8. Of 825,000 tenant farms in 1841, less than 7 percent were over thirty acres; the vast majority of holdings were occupied by tenants who held less than five acres; and of these, 30 percent held only one acre. The tenants on all holdings were required to furnish their own buildings and were responsible for all improvements on the land. Moreover, the majority lived on annual unwritten leases, so that landlords were free to withdraw land from tillage whenever it was profitable to do so. The figures on grain are from Strauss, *Irish Nationalism and British Democracy*, 134. The population figures are from Strauss, *Irish Nationalism and British Democracy*, 80, and Marx, *Capital*, vol. 3, pt. 3, p. 136.

9. In 1845, the first year of the famine, Ireland exported more wheat, barley, and flour to England than in the three prevoius years. It shipped 30,000 oxen, 330,000 sheep, 200,000 pigs, and 3,250 quarters of wheat (Connolly, *Labour in Irish History*, 106).

10. It is true that the repeal of the Corn Laws was intended to permit the free movement of grain, but as a grain-exporting country, these free trade measures merely brought Ireland into competition with Continental trade, lowering agricultural prices even further (ibid., 107–10).

11. The common policy according to one commissioner of the Poor Relief Acts was that it was "desirable to allow things to take their normal course . . . to go to their natural termination" (Kee, *Green Flag*, 140–76; quote is from p. 176).

12. Between 1861 and 1886, the acreage under cultivation for cereals and green crops decreased by nearly 600,000, and the number of livestock increased by nearly a million, causing Marx to declare that "1,032,694 Irishmen have been displaced by about one million cattle, pigs and sheep." It is true that money wages increased by about 20 percent after the famine, but they did not keep up with the cost of living. Rents were raised by 20 percent, the price of potatoes rose nearly 200 percent, and the cost of living increased 100 percent between 1846 and 1866. See Marx, *Capital*, vol. 3,

pt. 3, pp. 121–22 and 138. The figures on the shift from crops to grazing are from Coyne, *Ireland,* 301.

13. During the famine period of 1849–1855, 26 percent of the 1.3 million emigrants were evicted persons; during the other significant famine period, 1876–1882, only 15 percent of the 527 thousand emigrees had been evicted (Kennedy, *The Irish,* 31). The Irish who emigrated to England and Scotland played a significant role in industrial relations in those countries, which in turn affected the development of England's Irish policy. By 1826 the *Edinburg* estimated that Irish labor constituted nearly one-third of the wage workers in western Scotland and England, where they played a significant role in the Chartist and trade union movements. See E. P. Thompson, *English Working Class,* 429–44 passim.

14. Gearard O'Tuathaigh writes, ''After 1800, official policy regarding the Irish economy was decided by an assembly only a sixth of whose membership was Irish, an assembly in which Ireland's needs were seldom the main and never the sole consideration in the process through which decisions on economic policy were reached'' (*Ireland before the Famine,* 40). For a discussion of these points see Lyons, *Ireland since the Famine,* 40–45; Lee, ''Capital in the Irish Economy,'' 53–63.

15. Lysaght, ''Making of Northern Ireland.''

16. O'Tuathaigh, *Ireland before the Famine,* 39.

17. Small farms decreased from 100,000 in 1841 to 30,000 in 1851 (Budge and O'Leary, *Belfast,* 28 and 30).

18. Gallagher, *Indivisible Island,* 45.

19. Edwards, *Sins of Our Fathers,* 75.

20. Gallagher, *Indivisible Island,* 47.

21. O'Tuathaigh, *Ireland before the Famine,* 63–64.

22. In 1829 O'Connell accepted a bill for partial emancipation which allowed Catholics to serve in municipal offices but limited the franchise to £10 freeholders, thereby disenfranchising the 40*s,* freeholders who had been free to vote since 1793. Under the terms of the Great Reform Bill of 1832, restrictions on the franchise were retained in Ireland. As a result of the reform in England and Wales 4 percent of the male population could vote; in Ireland only 0.8 percent of the male populace was enfranchised. Whereas England had one M.P. for every 27,800 residents, Ireland had one for every 74,000 (Strauss, *Irish Nationalism and British Democracy,* 110).

23. O'Tuathaigh cites a number of Irish poems with strong millennial streaks. One written by Pastorini in 1771 prophesied the extinction of Protestantism by 1825 (*Ireland before the Famine,* 67).

24. Ibid., 77; also see Conor Cruise O'Brien, ''Ireland: The Shirt of Nessus,'' 30–32.

25. Gibbon, *Origins of Ulster Unionism,* 64. For a more detailed dis-

cussion of the schism and appeal to the rural proletariat, see Gibbon, *Origins of Ulster Unionism*, 44–66.

26. Miller, *Queen's Rebels*, 56.

27. Ibid, 57.

28. Ibid., 56–78.

29. Lyons, *Ireland since the Famine*, 111–28.

30. Conor Cruise O'Brien, "Ireland: The Shirt of Nessus," 31.

31. Edwards, *Sins of Our Fathers*, 129. Gaelic was a dying language. By 1825, 75 percent of the population was bilingual and only 5 percent spoke no English.

32. Moody, *Ulster since 1900*, 97.

33. Gibbon, *Origins of Ulster Unionism*, 95–97; Fitzgibbon, *Red Hand*, 245; Beckett and Glassock, *Belfast*.

34. Gibbon, *Origins of Ulster Unionism*, 69–77.

35. Ibid., 80.

36. Budge and O'Leary, *Belfast*, 89–90. To the extent that parliamentary elections with Home Rule candidates were presented as a threat to Protestant workers, we can find support for an economic interpretation of these conflicts. But that movement was not effectively mounted until the 1870s.

37. Strauss, *Irish Nationalism and British Democracy*, 172.

38. Mansergh, *Irish Question*, 230–35.

39. Between 1903 and 1909 more than half of the land in Ireland was transferred to peasant ownership, increasing from 3 percent of all farmers in 1870 to 29 percent in 1891 to 64 percent in 1926. But Catholics maintained an income level which was consistently one-third that of Protestants. According to Emmet Larkin's estimates, Catholic per capita income in 1801 was £13; a century later it was virtually identical, 12.4 for Catholics, 35.6 for Protestants ("Economic Growth," 882).

40. Conor Cruise O'Brien, "Ireland: The Shirt of Nessus," 32.

41. See Miller, *Queen's Rebels*.

42. Edwards, *Sins of Our Fathers*, 85. It should be pointed out that the efforts of Tories to play the Orange hand were rooted in their exploitation of the Home Rule conflict in order to counter Liberal power. The Liberal party was so depleted by 1910 that it needed the eighty Irish Nationalists at Westminster to maintain a parliamentary majority.

43. Edwards, *Sins of Our Fathers*; Gallagher, *Indivisible Island*; de Paor, *Divided Ulster*.

44. Gibbon, *Origins of Ulster Unionism*, 136–37.

45. The Conservative party supported Ulster Unionists less out of a commitment to Ulster than as an effort to destroy Liberals. But they did so vociferously. Sir Henry Wilson, the director of military operations in Britain, encouraged English officers to resign their commissions rather than

undertake any action to defeat the Ulster Volunteer Force. See Stewart, *Ulster Crisis,* 161–75.

46. Dangerfield, *Strange Death of Liberal England.*

47. Gibbon, *Origins of Ulster Unionism,* 136, claims that the Ulster Unionist Convention in 1892 signaled the birth of an Ulster national identity. But at that convention, the pavilion was decorated with a huge banner with "Erin Go Bragh" emblazoned across the front. For evidence on the sense of shared nationality, see Miller, *Queen's Rebels,* 18–20.

48. The church hierarchy opposed nationalist activities almost uniformly, denouncing the Sinn Feiners and forbidding clerical participation in the land League.

49. The church played a neutral role in these elections, likely having been promised by Sinn Fein substantial clerical power in an independent republic. See Miller, *Church, State and Nation in Ireland.*

50. For a discussion of this period see de Paor, *Divided Ulster,* 80–93.

51. Jackson, "Language Question in Quebec," 372.

52. Wade, *French Canadians* 1:324–27. The debate between them prefigured the current struggle between federalists and provincialists (see chapter 5).

53. Scott, "Areas of Conflict," 84.

54. Tetley, "The English and Language Legislation," 381–84.

55. The antagonism which assimilationist policies engendered was underscored in 1885. A group of native Americans and French Catholic migrants who had rebelled against federal encroachment on territorial lands secured broad Quebec support when their leader, Louis Riel, was hung after a trial riddled with judicial error. Hundreds of meetings were held throughout Quebec to protest the execution, and a popular protest song, the "Riel Marseillaise," called for the day when "we'll be the conquerors."

56. Sweeney, "Sketch of the Economic History of English Quebec," 83–84.

57. Siegfried, *Race Question in Canada.*

58. Guindon, "Social Evolution of Quebec Reconsidered," 19.

59. Wade, *French Canadians* 1:289.

60. Ibid., 290.

61. Ibid., 360; Falardeau, "Importance of the Church in French Canada," 349–52.

62. Cohen, *Quebec Votes,* 27.

63. Wade, *French Canadians* 2:669.

64. Hughes, "Industry and the Rural System in Quebec," 80.

65. Porter, *Canadian Social Structure,* table C4.

66. Legendre, "French Canada in Crisis," 8.

67. The remainder were from western and eastern Europe. See U.S. Immigration Commission, *Immigration Situation in Canada*, 14–20.

68. Cohen, *Quebec Votes*, 31.

69. Wade, *French Canadians* 2:669.

70. Cited in Cohen, *Quebec Votes*, 36.

71. Hughes, "Industry and the Rural System in Quebec," 84.

72. Clark, "French Speaking Population."

73. Everett Hughes, *The Sociological Eye*, 248–49.

74. Ibid., 245.

75. For explicit data see Porter, *Vertical Mosaic*, 87.

76. Banff Conference Papers, *Problems of Canadian Unity*, 55.

77. Brunet, "Continentalism and Quebec Nationalism," 511–27.

78. Taylor, "French Canadians as Industrial Entrepreneurs," 45.

79. Wade, *French Canadian Outlook*, 62.

80. Legendre, *French Canada in Crisis*, 9.

81. Wade, *French Canadians* 1:338.

82. Sheilagh Hodgins Milner and Henry Milner, *Decolonization of Quebec*, 119–20.

83. See Henry Milner, "The Anglophone Left in Quebec," 401–3; McRae, "Structure of Canadian History," 338.

84. Milner and Milner, *Decolonization of Quebec*, 121.

85. Ibid., 115–17.

86. Wade, *French Canadians* 2:879. The basic focus of the nationalist movements was on the survival of the French language, history, and religion and on the dangers of English imperialism, industrialization, and urbanization. Little attention was paid to the problems of wage labor. Gerard Fortin analyzed *L'action française* for the period 1917–1953 and determined that it was only in the last decade that the magazine addressed the problems of the working class (see "An Analysis of the Ideology of a French Canadian Nationalist Magazine" [M.A. thesis, Cornell University, 1956]; cited in Rioux, *Quebec in Question*, 64–65).

87. Milner and Milner, *Decolonization of Quebec*, 130.

88. Ibid., 130–31. For a review of the extent of anti-Semitism in Quebec see Rome, "Jews in Anglophone Quebec," 161–75.

89. Wade, *French Canadians* 2:940–2.

90. Ibid., 950.

91. Ibid., 968.

92. Falardeau, "Changing Structure of Contemporary Canada," 115.

93. Weber, *Economy and Society* 2:936–37.

94. Falardeau, "Les Canadiens francais et leur ideologie," *Canadian Dualism: Essays on Relations between French and English Canadians*, ed. Mason Wade.

CHAPTER 5

1. Mansergh, *Government of Northern Ireland;* John F. Harbinson, *Ulster Unionist Party.*

2. From 1921 until the recent conflicts, the House Speaker at Westminster regularly ruled against any discussion of the political affairs of Ulster. See Calvert, *Constitutional Law in Northern Ireland,* 96–110.

3. Farrell, *Northern Ireland,* 25.

4. Unionists adopted other explicitly discriminatory techniques to discourage Catholic voting, e.g., placing polling booths at a great distance from minority settlement. For a discussion of gerrymandering, see Northern Friends Peace Board, *Orange and Green;* Gallagher, *Indivisible Ireland,* 217–22.

5. See Elliot, *Northern Ireland Parliamentary Election Results,* 98.

6. Farrell, *Northern Ireland,* 85.

7. Rose, *Governing without Consensus,* 223.

8. Ibid., 93.

9. Also see John F. Harbinson, *Ulster Unionist Party,* 1–20.

10. Boulton, *The UVF,* 62.

11. Ibid., 21–37.

12. See Francis W. O'Brien, *Divided Ireland,* 43; Barritt and Carter, *Northern Ireland Problem,* 96.

13. David Donneson, "Civil Servants and Religion in Stormont," *New Society,* 5 July 1973. Not all Unionist leaders were receptive to sectarian strategies. An element of the party was loyal to Britain but was also concerned that receptivity to Protestant working-class demands would short-circuit capital growth. This segment was well received in the Ministry of Finance and in the civil service, although clearly they did not temper sectarian employment patterns. See Bew, Gibbon, and Patterson, *The State in Northern Ireland,* 75–101.

14. *London Sunday Times* Insight Team, *Northern Ireland,* 36.

15. Ibid.

16. John F. Harbison, *Ulster Unionist Party,* 18–25; For evidence of the bourgeois makeup of the Unionist leadership, see Farrell, *Northern Ireland,*69.

17. There are numerous data to support this assertion. See Barritt and Carter, *Northern Ireland Problem;* Geoffrey Bell, *Protestants of Ulster;* Probert, *Beyond Orange and Green.*

18. Rose, *Governing without Consensus,* 258.

19. For data on the extent of segregation, see Barritt and Carter, *Northern Ireland* Problem; Harris, *Prejudice and Tolerance in Ulster;* Burton, *Politics of Legitimacy,* 37–129; Robert Harbison, *No Surrender;* Holland, *Too Long a Sacrifice;* Jones, "Distribution and Segregation of Roman Catholics," 167–89.

20. Probert, *Beyond Orange and Green*, 51–67.

21. Such a response had occurred at the formation of the Ulster state, during a nonsectarian strike by engineering and textile workers. Then, a total of ten thousand Catholic men and one thousand women were fired from their Belfast jobs at the Clark and Co. shipyard, the four major engineering works, and a number of linen mills. The expulsion of Catholic workers "put a premium on loyalty and cemented the Orange alliance, since 'disloyal' Protestants were likely to be the next to go" (Farrell, *Northern Ireland*, 29).

22. Ibid., 124.

23. Wright, "Protestant Ideology and Politics," 213–80.

24. Farrell, *Northern Ireland*, 131.

25. Mansergh, *Government of Northern Ireland*, 240.

26. Farrell, *Northern Ireland*, 137.

27. Ibid., 124.

28. Probert, *Beyond Orange and Green*, 53.

29. See Aunger, "Religious and Occupational Class," 1–17; Barritt and Carter, *Northern Ireland Problem*, 93–108; Geoffrey Bell, *Protestants of Ulster*, 20–29; Probert, *Beyond Orange and Green*, 5–53.

30. O'Malley, *Uncivil Wars*, 62.

31. De Paor, *Divided Ulster*, 128.

32. O'Malley, *Uncivil Wars*, 71.

33. Whyte, *Church and State in Modern Ireland*.

34. O'Malley points out that this can also be read as a reflection of Ireland's sensitivity to clerical positions; the church does not *need* to intervene (*Uncivil Wars*, 61–69).

35. Quoted in Edwards, *Sins of Our Fathers*, 72.

36. McCracken, "Political Scene in Northern Ireland," 353–66.

37. Individual priests however were not openly involved in the civil rights movement, and the hierarchy expressed serious concern about the socialist tendencies of civil rights leaders. Indeed, some Catholic leaders argued that the church undermined efforts to mobilize the Catholic community. See, for example, Devlin, *Price of My Soul*, 61–71.

38. Richard Rose's surveys of the relation between religious involvement and political attitudes showed a very weak correlation among Catholics. There was a stronger correlation among Protestants. Rose, *Governing without Consensus*, 264–65.

39. Edwards, *Sins of Our Fathers*, 228; Barritt and Carter, *Northern Ireland Problem*, 77–92.

40. Rose, *Governing without Consensus*, 336. There is little evidence that segregation itself plays a direct role in the development of sectarian attitudes. Rose found minimal differences in the political attitudes of children educated in mixed as opposed to segregated schools. However, to-

gether with the patterns of segregated housing and employment, separate schooling does reinforce the sense of cultural alienation and antagonism between the two religious groups.

41. Farrell, *Northern Ireland*, 227; Probert, *Beyond Orange and Green*, 51–67.

42. Between 1945 and 1965 the only town with a Catholic majority that received any allocation was Londonderry; and despite the fact that its population was three times as large as the other communities, it received the smallest amount of government-subsidized factory space. See Probert, *Beyond Orange and Green*, 83.

43. Bew, Gibbon, and Patterson, *The State in Northern Ireland*, 136–57.

44. Of the 1,589 houses built between 1945 and 1967, only 35 percent were allocated to Catholics (who constituted 56.4 percent of the populace). Local municipalities would reduce their public-housing programs rather than move Catholics into Protestant wards. Geoffrey Bell, *Protestants of Ulster*, 26–27; *London Sunday Times* Insight Team, *Northern Ireland*, 36.

45. Six of the seven growth areas were located within a thirty-mile radius of Belfast; whereas Derry the second-largest city, with a 20 percent unemployment rate, was excluded from the growth sites and rejected as the location of the New University College, in favor of the Protestant town of Coleraine (Farrell, *Northern Ireland*, 239–42). Recent studies indicate that investment patterns could be justified by rational economic criteria; but in Ulster such a rationalization had great political import. See Hoare, "Problem Region," 195–224.

46. Gibbon, "Dialectic of Religion and Class,"20–41; Bew, Gibbon, and Patterson, *The State in Northern Ireland*, 163–75; Daugherty, "Geography of Unemployment," 225–47.

47. The civil rights movement was initially dominated by the middle class, which had grown in the postwar period to about 12 percent of the Catholic populace. See Aunger, "Religious and Occupational Class," 1–17.

48. This group represented the first generation to attend the university under the postwar educational reforms. They came largely from middle-class and petty bourgeois families; but separation from their religious backgrounds, combined with the character of university life, provided an opportunity for independent thinking. For a discussion of the early civil rights movement and its relation to metropolitan politics, see Bew, Gibbon, and Patterson, *The State in Northern Ireland*, 103–70.

49. O'Neill did not, in fact, adopt nonsectarian policies. Only 2 of the 102 members of statutory committees and 7 of 49 appointees to public boards in 1966–1967 were Catholic. See Rose, *Governing without Consensus*, 100; Farrell, *Northern Ireland*, 242.

50. Rose, *Governing without Consensus,* 101.
51. Boulton, *The UVF,* 44.
52. Ibid., 60.
53. Gibbon, "The Dialectic of Religion and Class in Ulster," 36.
54. See Devlin, *Price of My Soul,* 91–96, for a description of the events.
55. For detailed accounts of the civil rights movement, see Bew, Gibbon, and Patterson, *The State in Northern Ireland,* 170–94; Boulton, *The UVF;* Cameron Report, *On Disturbances in Northern Ireland;* Devlin, *Price of My Soul,* 122–203; Farrell, *Northern Ireland,* 249–84; Hastings, *Ulster 1969.*
56. It is difficult to ascertain the extent to which these different attitudes are correlated with class positions or economic interests. Analysis of these data by John Thompson compared regression models which took religiosity (support for a series of evangelical fundamentalist-attitude measures), class, and economic nonclass factors (employment sector location, family income, education, unemployment, home ownership, residence, region) into account to explain the likelihood of support for reform of the Unionist party. His findings indicate that the economic factors, covering a range of competitive situations, were not as strong a predictor as religiosity in explaining opposition to reform. This is not to deny the importance of economic competition in understanding the difficulties that the Unionist party faced, but to emphasize that where "religious values are rooted in relatively autonomous social institutions, they are likely to have a substantial political impact independent of economic factors" and that religious conviction is not a "cover" for class or other economic interests (John L. Thompson, "Plural Society Approach," 127–52).
57. Boulton, *The UVF,* 122.
58. Ibid., 108–22. The Scarman Tribunal on these disturbances emphasized the arbitrary pattern of violence; but a careful review of the evidence presented before the tribunal does not support its conclusions, as was later evident in Westminster's own investigations, the Hunt and Cameron commissions.
59. The accounts of this period are extensive. Among the most comprehensive are Boserup, "Contradictions and Struggles," 157–92; Boulton, *The UVF;* Boyd, *Holy War in Belfast;* Burton, *Politics of Legitimacy,* 68–128; Dillon and Lehane, *Political Murder;* Fisk, *Point of No Return;* Miller, *Queen's Rebels;* Nelson, *Ulster's Uncertain Defenders;* Rose, *Northern Ireland; Sunday Times* Insight Team, *Ulster.*
60. By 1971, 60 percent of the profits of southern firms, 55 percent of imports, and 60 percent of exports were tied to British firms. In 1974, 45 percent of all northern firms employing over 250 workers were controlled by British capital. See Farrell, *Northern Ireland,* 326–28.

61. Ibid., 329.

62. *Detroit Free Press*, 1 March 1985,p. 10A.

63. O'Malley, *Uncivil Wars*, 216–17.

64. See Hadden, Boyle, and Hillyard, *Ten Years On.*

65. O'Malley, *Uncivil Wars*, 245.

66. Ibid., 89 and 246.

67. For an excellent discussion of this ambivalent relationship see Burton, *Politics of Legitimacy*, 68–128.

68. For an unusually critical statement, see Jack Beatty, "The Troubles Today," *The New Republic*, 15 November 1980, pp. 16–21.

69. O'Malley, *Uncivil War*, 258–313.

70. Protestant fears of future minority status even within Ulster may escalate. Demographers estimate that as a result of high Catholic fertility rates and Protestant emigration, Catholics may constitute a majority in Ulster by 2025 (they now count for approximately 40 percent of the population). Ibid., 324–25.

71. Ibid., 355.

72. Bernard D. Nossiter, "Economics May Solve the Problem of Ireland," *Washington Post,* 1 July 1979.

73. See O'Malley, *Uncivil Wars*, 77, for data on lack of concern in the south; see pp. 61–97 and 363–66 for an analysis of the role of Ulster in Republican politics.

74. Farrell, *Northern Ireland*, 320.

75. See Frazier, *Children in Conflict.*

76. Clift, *Quebec Nationalism in Crisis*, 1–17; Wagley and Harris, *Minorities in the New World*, 196.

77. Clift, *Quebec Nationalism in Crisis*, 15.

78. Chavalier and Taylor, "Dynamics of Adaptation in the Federal Services," 4. Also see Posgate and McRoberts, *Quebec.*

79. Ward, *Government of Canada*, 4.

80. Of the population in school, 36 percent came from semiprofessional, small business, and white collar families, 31 percent from working-class families, and 11 percent from farms. Brazeau, "Quebec's Emerging Middle Class," 31.

81. Wade, *French Canadians* 2:1118.

82. Rioux, *Quebec in Question*, 73.

83. Brunet, "Continentalism and Quebec Nationalism," 511.

84. Raynauld, "Business Ownership in Quebec."

85. Confédération des syndicates nationaux, "It's Up to Us," 6.

86. Brazeau, "Quebec's Emerging Middle Class," 32.

87. The Labor Relations Board took away the certification of the union and used provincial police as strikebreakers. Indeed, the measures to suppress the strike were so severe that Catholic clergy intervened in the ne-

gotiations on behalf of the workers. Jean Charles Falardeau called this strike the "significant rite of passage of the Catholic syndicates to adulthood and to maturity" *(Essais sur le Quebec contemporain,* 116). Also see Richard Ossenburg, "Social pluralism in Quebec."

88. Jamieson, "Labour Unity in Quebec," 290–308.

89. Milner and Milner, *Decolonization of Quebec,* 87–89.

90. Raynauld, "Quebec Economy," 146–48.

91. Quoted in Fournier, "Parti Québecois and the Quebec Economic Situation," 17.

92. Larocque, "Political Institutions and Quebec Society," 73–78 (quoted material, p. 75).

93. Legendre, "French Canada in Crisis," 10.

94. Milner and Milner, *Decolonization of Quebec,* 35.

95. Canadian Department of Industry Trade and Commerce, *Foreign Direct Investment in Canada,* 1–40.

96. Pepsi Cola even sought to capitalize on the Quiet Revolution by "substituting for its English advertisement 'Come alive, you're in the Pepsi generation,' the phrase, 'Oui, ça bouge, en notre génération Pepsi.' Ça bouge, meaning that things are moving, was a phrase identified with the Quiet Revolution" (Elkin, "Mass Media, Advertising and the Quiet Revolution," 187).

97. For a discussion see Guindon, "Social Unrest," 150–62 (quoted material p. 156). Also see Charles Taylor, "Nationalism and the Political Intelligentsia," 167–68.

98. Fournier, "Parti Québecois and the Quebec Economic Situation," 17.

99. Ibid., 16.

100. Legendre, "French Canada in Crisis," 10; Leland, "Federal Option," 177.

101. Ares, *Les positions,* 34–35.

102. Rioux, *Quebec in Question,* 119–20.

103. It is not simply rational economics that explains the high degree of Anglo assimilation in Quebec. Traditional French Canadian insularity and ethnocentrism may have contributed as well. See Fortin, "Le Québec," 7–13.

104. Legendre, "French Canada in Crisis," 10.

105. Laferriere, "Nationalisme Québecois," 477–97.

106. McWhinney, "French Language," 488. On the history of separatism in the 1960s, see Hagy, "Quebec Separatists," 229–35; Pious, "Canada and the Crisis of Quebec," 53–64; Rioux, *Quebec in Question,* chap. 10.

107. For a discussion of the Levesque/Liberal schism, see Saywell, *Rise of the Parti Quebecois,* 9–21.

108. Of the 10,073 supporters, 49.5 percent were under thirty; 24 percent were students, 21 percent professionals, 19 percent white collar workers, 17 percent blue collar, 5 percent housekeepers, and 4 percent farmers. Hagy, "Quebec Separatists," 235.

109. Pious, "Canada and the Crisis of Quebec," 58.

110. Ibid., 59. For an explicit outline of the PQ policies, see Levesque, *Option for Quebec.*

111. Hagy, "Quebec Separatists," 235.

112. Rioux, *Quebec in Question,* 155.

113. Saywell, *Rise of the Parti Québecois,* 46.

114. Breton, "Sociopolitical Dynamics of the October Events," 228–29.

115. Saywell, *Rise of the Parti Québecois,* 44.

116. Although publicly denounced by Quebecois labor activists and nationalists, public opinion polls indicated that the majority of the population supported federal intervention. See Bourne and Eisenbert, *The Law and The Police,* 240.

117. Saywell, *Rise of the Parti Québecois,* 52.

118. Ibid., 60–77.

119. Ibid., 79.

120. Quoted in McWhinney, "French Language," 491.

121. Quoted in Saywell, *Rise of the Parti Québecois,* 139.

122. In 1968 only 15 percent of the 650 senior federal officers were Francophones. For a discussion of ethnic differentiation in the federal bureaucracy see Coutier, "Senior Public Service Officials," 398–407.

123. Watkins, "North American Triangle," 14.

124. Saywell, *Rise of the Parti Québecois,* 123–24.

125. A midcampaign phone poll indicated that 31 percent of non-Francophone immigrants and 11 percent of Anglophones planned to vote for the PQ, a relatively high proportion considering their nearly uniform opposition to independence. See Stern, "Quebec's Non-Francophones," 18.

126. Quoted in Saywell, *Rise of the Parti Québecois,* 172–73.

127. Olzak, "Ethnic Mobilization in Quebec," 253–75; Laferriere, "Nationalisme québecois"; Ornstein, Stevenson, and Williams, "Public Opinion and the Canadian Political Crisis," 158–207; Hamilton and Pinard, "Basis of Parti Québecois Support," 3–26.

128. Quoted in *Time Magazine,* 13 February 1978, p. 38.

129. *Globe and Mail,* 27 July 1984, pp. 1–2 and 6.

130. *New York Times,* 27 January 1985, p. E5.

131. Ibid.

132. Lieberson, *Language and Ethnic Relations in Canada,* 10.

CHAPTER 6

1. Van den Berghe, *Race and Racism*, 6.
2. Max Weber, "Race Relations," in *Weber: Selections in Translation*, 364.
3. Patterson, *Ethnic Chauvinism*, 230–90.

Bibliography

Anderson, Perry, *Lineages of the Absolutist State*. London: New Left Books, 1975.

Apter, David. "Ideology and Discontent." In *Ideology and Discontent*, edited by David Apter, 15–46. New York: Free Press, 1963.

———. "Political Religion in the New Nations." In *Old Societies and New States*, edited by Clifford Geertz, 57–104. New York: Free Press, 1963.

Ares, Richard. *Les positions—ethniques, linguistiques et religieuses—des canadiens français à la suite du recensement de 1971*. Montreal: Editions Bellarmin, 1975.

Aunger, Edmund A. "Religious and Occupational Class in Northern Ireland."*The Economic and Social Review* 7, no. 1 (1975): 1–17.

Banff Conference Papers. *National Conference on the Problems of Canadian Unity*. Banff, Alberta: Banff Center for Continuing Education, 1964.

Banton, Michael. *Racial and Ethnic Competition*. Cambridge: Cambridge University Press, 1983.

Barritt, Denis P., and Charles F. Carter. *The Northern Ireland Problem: A Study in Group Relations*. 2d ed, New York: Oxford University Press, 1972.

Barth, Fredrik, ed. *Ethnic Groups and Boundaries*, Boston: Little, Brown and Co., 1967.

Beckett, J. C. *The Making of Modern Ireland, 1603–1923*. London: Faber and Faber, 1981.

Beckett, J. C., and R. G. Glassock. *Belfast: The Origin and Growth of an Industrial City*.London: BBC Publications, 1967.

Bell, Daniel, "Ethnicity and Social Change." In *Ethnicity: Theory and Experience,* edited by Nathan Glazer and Daniel P. Moynihan, 141–76. Cambridge: Harvard University Press, 1975.

Bell, Geoffrey. *The Protestants of Ulster*. London: Pluto Press, 1976.

Bew, Peter, Peter Gibbon, and H. Patterson. *The State in Northern Ireland, 1921–1972*. Manchester: Manchester University Press, 1979.

Blassingame, John W. *The Slave Community: Plantation Life and the Antebellum South*. New York: Oxford University Press, 1972.

Blauner, Robert. "Internal Colonialism and Ghetto Revolt." *Social Problems* 16 (Spring 1968): 395–408.

Blumer, Herbert. "Industrialization and Race Relations." In *Industrialization and Race Relations,* edited by Guy Hunter, 220–40. London: Oxford University Press, 1965.

Boal, Frederick W., and J. Neville H. Douglas, eds. *Integration and Division: Geographical Perspectives on the Northern Ireland Problem.* New York: Academic Press, 1982.

Bonacich, Edna. "A Theory of Ethnic Antagonism: The Split Labor Market." *American Sociological Review* 37, no. 5 (October 1972): 547–59.

————. "The Past, Present and Future of Split Labor Market Theory." In *Research in Race and Ethnic Relations* edited by Cheryl Leggon and Cora Marrett, 17–64. Greenwich, Conn.: JAI Press, 1979.

Bonacich, Edna, and John Modell. *The Economic Basis of Ethnic Solidarity: Small Business in the Japanese American Community*. Berkeley: University of California Press, 1980.

Boserup, Anders. "Contradictions and Struggles in Northern Ireland." *Socialist Register* 9 (1972): 157–92.

Boulton, David. *The UVF, 1966–1973: An Anatomy of Loyalist Rebellion.* Dublin: Torc Books, 1973.

Bourne, Paula, and John Eisenbert. *The Law and the Police*. Toronto: General Publishing Co., 1971.

Boyd, Andrew. *Holy War in Belfast*. Tralee: Avon, 1969.

Brazeau, Jacques. "Quebec's Emerging Middle Class." *Canadian Business* 36 no. 3 (March 1963): 30–40.

Breton, Raymond. "The Sociopolitical Dynamics of the October Events." In *Quebec Society and Politics,* 213–38. *See* Dale C. Thomson 1973.

Brunet, Michel. "La conquête anglaise et la déchéance de la bourgeoisie canadienne, 1760–1793." *Amérique Française* 12 (June 1955): 13–22.

————. "Continentalism and Quebec Nationalism: A Double Challenge to Canada." *Queen's Quarterly* 76, no. 3 (Autumn 1969): 511–27.

Buchanan, Ronald H. "The Planter and the Gael." In *integration and Division,* 49–73. *See* Boal and Douglas 1982.

Bibliography

Budge, Ian, and Cornelius O'Leary. *Belfast: Approach to Crisis; A Study of Belfast Politics, 1613–1970*. New York: Macmillan Co., 1973.

Burton, Frank. *The Politics of Legitimacy: Struggles in a Belfast Community*. London: Routledge and Kegan Paul, 1978.

Caldwell, Gary, and Eric Waddell, eds. *The English of Quebec: From Majority to Minority Status*. Quebec: Institut québecois de recherche sur la culture, 1982.

Calvert, Henry. *Constitutional Law in Northern Ireland*. London: Stevens, 1968.

Cameron Report. *On Disturbances in Northern Ireland*. Belfast: Her Majesty's Stationery Office, 1969.

Canny, Nicolas P. "The Ideology of English Colonization: From Ireland to America." *William and Mary Quarterly* 30, no. 4 (October 1973): 575–98.

Carty, James. *Ireland from the Flight of the Earls to Grattan's Parliament* Dublin: C. J. Fallon, 1951.

Castles, Stephen, and Godula Kosack. *Immigrant Workers in Western Europe*. Oxford: Oxford University Press, 1973.

Chavalier, Michel, and James R. Taylor. "Dynamics of Adaptation in the Federal Services." In *Studies of the Royal Commission on Bilingualism and Biculturalism*. Ottawa: Information Canada, 1971.

Clark, Samuel Delbert. "The Position of the French Speaking Population in the Northern Industrial Community." In *Canadian Society: Pluralism, Change and Conflict*, edited by Richard J. Ossenberg 62–85. Scarborough: Prentice-Hall of Canada, 1971.

Clift, Dominique. *Quebec Nationalism in Crisis*. Kingston and Montreal: McGill-Queens University Press, 1982.

Cohen, Ronald I. *Quebec Votes: The How and Why of Quebec Voting in Every Federal Election since Confederation*. Montreal: Sage, 1965.

Coleman, James. *Nigeria: Background to Nationalism*. Berkeley: University of California Press, 1963.

Confederation des syndicates nationaux. "It's Up to Us." In *Quebec: Only the Beginning*, edited by Daniel Drache, 1–10. Toronto: New Press, 1972.

Connolly, James. *Labour in Irish History*. New York: Connolly Press, 1919.

Connor, Walker. *The National Question in Marxist Leninist Theory and Strategy*. Princeton: Princeton University Press, 1984.

———. "Nation Building or Nation Destroying?" *World Politics* 24 (April 1975): 319–55.

———. "Self-Determination: The New Phase." *World Politics* 20 (October 1967): 55–59.

Corbett, Edward M. *Quebec Confronts Canada.* Baltimore: Johns Hopkins University Press, 1958.

Coutier, Sylvian. "Senior Public Service Officials in a Bicultural Society." *Canadian Public Administration* 11 (Summer 1968): 398–407.

Coyne, William P. *Ireland: Industrial and Agricultural.* Dublin: Browne and Nolan, 1902.

Cullen, L. M. *An Economic History of Ireland since 1660.* London: B. T. Batsford, 1972.

———. ed. *The Formation of the Irish Economy.* Cork: Mercier Press, 1968.

Dangerfield, George. *The Strange Death of Liberal England.* New York: Putnam, 1961.

Daugherty, Paul. "The Geography of Unemployment." In *Integration and Division,* 225–47. *See* Boal and Douglas 1982.

Davis, H. B. *Nationalism and Socialism: Marxist and Labor Theories of Nationalism to 1917.* New York: Monthly Review Press, 1967.

De Paor, Liam. *Divided Ulster.* Harmondsworth: Penguin, 1970.

Despres, Leo. *Nationalism in Guyana.* Berkeley: University of California Press, 1968.

Deutsch, Karl W. *Nationalism and Its Alternatives.* New York: Knopf 1969.

———. "Nation Building and National Development: Some Issues for Political Research." In *Nation Building,* edited by Karl W. Deutsch and William Foltz, 1–16. New York: Atherton Press, 1963.

Devlin, Bernadette. *The Price of My Soul.* New York: Alfred A. Knopf, 1969.

Dillon, Martin, and Denis Lehane. *Political Murder in Northern Ireland.* Harmondsworth: Penguin, 1973.

Dubuc, Alfred. "The Historical Foundations of the Crisis of Canadian and Quebecois Society." In *Quebec and the Parti Quebecois,* edited by Marlene Dixon and Susanne Jonas, 1–14. San Francisco: Synthesis Publications, 1978.

Dumont, Fernand, and Guy Rocher. "An Introduction to the Sociology of French Canada," In *French Canadian Society,* 1:194–97. *See* Rioux and Martin 1964.

Edelstein, Joel. "Pluralist and Marxist Perspectives on Ethnicity and Nation Building." In *Ethnicity and Nation Building: Comparative, International and Historical Perspectives,* edited by Wendell Bell and Walter E. Freeman, 45–57. Beverly Hills: Sage, 1974.

Edwards, Owen Dudley. *The Sins of Our Fathers.* Dublin: Gill and Macmillan, 1970.

Eisenstadt, S. N. *Modernization: Protest and Change.* Englewood Cliffs, N.J.: Prentice-Hall, 1966.

Bibliography

Elkin, Frederick. "Mass Media, Advertising and the Quiet Revolution." In *Canadian Society: Pluralism, Change and Continuity,* edited by Richard J. Ossenberg, 184–205. Scarborough: Prentice-Hall of Canada, 1971.

Elliott, Sydney. *Northern Ireland Parliamentary Election Results, 1921–1972.* Chichester: Political Reference Publications, 1973.

Ellis, P. Berresford. *A History of the Irish Working Class.* London: Victor Gollancz, 1972.

Emerson Rupert. *From Empire to Nation: The Rise to Self-Assertion of Asian and African Peoples.* Cambridge: Harvard University Press, 1960.

Enloe, Cynthia. *Ethnic Conflict and Political Development.* Boston: Little, Brown and Co., 1973.

Falardeau, Jean Charles. *Essais sur le Québec contemporain.* Quebec: Les Presses de l'Université Laval, 1961.

———. "Les Canadiens français et leur idéologie." In *Canadian Dualism: Essays on Relations between French and English Canadians,* 20–38. *See* Wade 1960.

———. "The Changing Structure of Contemporary Canada." In *French Canadian Society* 1:19–32. *See* Rioux and Martin 1964.

———. "The Role and Importance of the Church in French Canada." In *French Canadian Society* 1:34–57. *See* Rioux and Martin 1964.

———. "The Seventeenth Century Parish in French Canada." In *French Canadian Society* 1:76–85. *See* Rioux and Martin 1964.

Fallers, Lloyd. *Inequality: Social Stratification Revisited.* Chicago: University of Chicago Press, 1973.

Farrell, Michael. *Northern Ireland: The Orange State.* London: Pluto Press, 1976.

Fieldhouse, D. K., ed. *The Theory of Capitalist Imperialism.* New York: Barnes and Noble, 1967.

Fields, Rona. *Society under Siege.* Philadelphia: Temple University Press, 1976.

Fisk, Robert. *The Point of No Return.* London: Times Books, 1975.

Fitzgibbon, Constantine. *The Red Hand: The Ulster Colony.* New York: Doubleday, 1971.

Fortin, Gerald. "Le Quebec: une société globale à la recherche d'elle-même." *Recherches Sociographiques* 8, no. 1 (1967): 7–13.

Foster, John. *Class Struggle in the Industrial Revolution.* New York: St. Martins Press, 1974.

Fournier, Pierre. "The Parti Quebecois and the Quebec Economic Situation." In *Quebec and the Parti Quebecois,* edited by Marlene Dixon and Susanne Jonas, 15–24. San Francisco: Institute for the Study of Labor and Economic Crisis, 1978.

Fox, Richard, Charlotte F. Aull, and Louis Cimino. "Ethnic Nationalism and the Welfare State." In *Ethnic Change,* edited by Charles F. Keyes, 198–245. (Seattle: University of Washington Press, 1981.

Frazier, Morris. *Children in Conflict: Growing Up in Northern Ireland.* New York: Basic Books, 1977.

Frederickson, George M. *White Supremacy: A Comparative Study in American and South African History.* New York: Oxford University Press, 1981.

Gallagher, Frank. *The Indivisible Island: The History of the Partition of Ireland.* London: Victor Gollancz, 1957.

Garigue, Philippe. "Change and Continuity in French Canada," In *French Canadian Society.* 1:123–37. *See* Rioux and Martin, 1964.

Gellner, Ernest. *Thought and Change.* Chicago: University of Chicago Press, 1969.

Genovese, Eugene. *Roll, Jordan, Roll: The World the Slaves Made.* New York: Pantheon, 1974.

Gibbon, Peter, "The Dialectic of Religion and Class in Ulster." *New Left Review* 55 (May–June 1969): 20–41.

———. *The Origins of Ulster Unionism.* Manchester: Manchester University Press, 1975.

Glazer, Nathan. "The Universalization of Ethnicity." *Encounter* 44, no 2. (February 1975): 8–17.

Gourevitch, P. A. "The Reemergence of 'Peripheral Nationalisms': Some Comparative Speculations on the Spatial Distribution of Political Leaders and Economic Growth." *Comparative Studies in Society and History* 21, no. 3 (July 1979): 303–22.

Guindon, Herbert. "The Social Evolution of Quebec Reconsidered." *Canadian Journal of Economics and Political Science* 26 (November 1960): 533–551.

———. "Social Unrest, Social Class, and Quebec's Bureaucratic Revolution." *Queen's Quarterly* 71, no. 2 (Summer 1964): 150–62.

Hadden, Tom, Kevin Boyle, and Paddy Hillyard. *Ten Years On: The Emergency Powers Act.* New York: Cobden Trust, 1981.

Hagy, James W. "The Quebec Separatists: The First Twelve Years." *Queen's Quarterly* 76 (Summer 1969): 229–35.

Hah, Chong-Do, and Jeffrey Martin. "Toward a Synthesis of Conflict and Integration Theories of Nationalism." *World Politics* 27 (April 1975): 361–86.

Hamilton, Richard, and Maurice Pinard. "The Basis of Parti Québecois Support in Recent Quebec Elections." *Canadian Journal of Political Science* 9, no. 1 (December 1976): 3–26.

Harbinson, John F. *The Ulster Unionist Party, 1882–1973.* Belfast: Blackstaff Press, 1973.

Harbison, Robert. *No Surrender.* London: Times Books, 1968.

Bibliography

Harris, Rosemary. *Prejudice and Tolerance in Ulster*. Manchester: Manchester University Press, 1972.

Hastings, Max. *Ulster 1969*. London: Victor Gollancz, 1970.

Hechter, Michael. *Internal Colonialism: The Celtic Fringe in British National Development*. Berkeley: University of California Press, 1975.

Hechter, Michael, and Margaret Levi. "The Comparative Analysis of Ethno-regional Movements." *Ethnic and Racial Studies* 2, no. 3 (July 1979): 260–74.

Hempel, Carl. "The Function of General Laws in History." In *Readings in Philosophical Analysis*, edited by Herbert Feigl and Wilfred Sellars. 321–344. New York: Appleton-Century-Crofts, 1949.

Herod, Charles. *The Nation in the History of Marxian Thought*. The Hague: Martinus Nijhoff, 1976.

Hoare, Anthony G. "Problem Region and Regional Problem." In *Integration and Division*, 195–224. *See* Boal and Douglas 1982.

Holland, Jack. *Too Long a Sacrifice*. New York: Dodd Mead, 1981.

Hughes, Everett. "Industry and the Rural System in Quebec." In *French Canadian Society*. Vol. 1. 76–85 *See* Rioux and Martin 1964.

————. *The Sociological Eye: Selected Papers on Institutions and Race*. Chicago: Aldine-Atherton, 1971.

Information Canada. *Foreign Direct Investment in Canada*. Ottawa, 1972.

Inglis, Brian. *The Story of Ireland*. London: Faber and Faber, 1956.

International Communist and Working Class Movement. *The Revolutionary Movement of Our Time and Nationalism*, translated by Vic Schneierson. Moscow: Progress Publishers, 1975.

Isaacs, Harold. *Idols of the Tribe: Group Identity and Political Change*. New York: Harper and Row, 1975.

Jackson, John D. "The Language Question in Quebec: On Collective and Individual Rights." In *The English of Quebec*, 363–78. *See* Caldwell and Waddell 1982.

Jamieson, Stuart. "Labour Unity in Quebec." In *Canadian Dualism*, 363–78. *See* Wade 1960.

Johnson, Harry G. "A Theoretical Model of Economic Nationalism in New and Developing States." In *Economic Nationalism in Old and New States*, edited by Harry G. Nationalism, 1–16. Chicago: University of Chicago Press, 1967.

Jones, Emrys. "The Distribution and Segregation of Roman Catholics in Belfast." *Sociological Review* 4 (1956): 167–89.

Kahler, Miles. *Decolonization in Britain and France*. Princeton: Princeton University Press, 1984.

Katznelson, Ira. *Black Men–White Cities: Race, Politics and Migration in the United States, 1900–1930, and Great Britain, 1938–1968*. New York: Oxford University Press, 1973.

Kautsky, John H. *Political Change in Underdeveloped Countries: Nationalism and Communism*. New York: John Wiley, 1962.

Kee, Richard. *The Green Flag: The Turbulent History of the Irish Nationalist Movement*, New York: Delacorte, 1972.

Kennedy, Robert E., Jr. *The Irish Emigration, Marriage and Fertility*. Berkeley: University of California Press, 1973.

Kohn, Hans. *The Idea of Nationalism: A Study in Its Origin and Background*. New York: Macmillan Co., 1944.

Laferriere, Michel. "Nationalisme québecois et conflits de classes." *Mondes en Développement* 27 (1979): 477–97.

Larkin, Emmet. "Economic Growth, Capital Investment and the Roman Catholic Church in 19th Century Ireland." *American Historical Review* 72 (April 1967): 852–84.

Larocque, Andre. "Political Institutions and Quebec Society." In *Quebec Society and Politics*, 73–78. *See* Dale C. Thompson 1973.

Lecky, W. E. H. *A History of Ireland in the Eighteenth Century*. Chicago: University of Chicago Press, 1975.

Lee, Joseph S. "Capital in the Irish Economy." In *Formation of the Irish Economy*, 53–63. *See* Cullen 1968.

Legendre, Camille. "French Canada in Crisis: A New Society in the Making." *Minority Rights Group*, Report no. 44 (1980): 4–19.

Leland, Gillis. "The Federal Option." In *Quebec Society and Politics*, 173–78. *See* Dale C. Thomson 1973.

Lenin, V. I. *The Right of the Nations to Self-Determination*. New York: International Publishers, 1968. (Originally published 1914.)

Levesque, Rene. *An Option for Quebec*. Montreal: McClelland and Stewart, 1968.

Lieberson, Stanley. *Language and Ethnic Relations in Canada*. New York: John Wiley and Sons, 1970.

Lieberson, Stanley. "Stratification and Ethnic Groups." In *Social Stratification: Research and Theory for the 1970's*, edited by Edward O. Laumann, 172–81. Columbus: Bobbs-Merrill, 1970.

Lincoln, J. R. "Community Structure and Industrial Conflict." *American Sociological Review* 43 (1978): 199–220.

Linton, Ralph. "Nativistic Movements." *American Anthropologist* 45 (April/June 1943): 230–40.

Lodhi, A. Q., and Charles Tilly. "Urbanization, Crime and Collective Violence in 19th Century France." *American Journal of Sociology* 79, no. 2 (September 1973): 296–318.

London Sunday Times Insight Team. *Northern Ireland: A Report on the Conflict*. New York: Vintage, 1972.

———. *Ulster*. London: Deutsch, 1972.

Lyons, F. S. L. *Ireland since the Famine*. (London: Weidenfeld and Nicholson, 1972).

Lysaght, D. R. O'Connor. *The Making of Northern Ireland*. Dublin: Citizen's Committee, 1969.

McCracken, J. L. "Political Scene in Northern Ireland, 1926–37." *Economic and Social Review* 6, no. 3 (April 1975): 353–66.

McCulley, B. T. *English Education and the Origins of Indian Nationalism* Gloucester, Mass.: Smith, 1966.

MacDonald, Michael. "Colonialism in Ireland." Paper presented at Comparative and International Studies seminar, University of California at Santa Cruz, March 1982.

MacEoin, Gary. *Northern Ireland: Captive of History*. New York: Holt, Rinehart and Winston, 1974.

McRae, Kenneth, "The Structure of Canadian History." In *The Founding of the New Societies*, edited by Louis Hartz, 219–74. New York: Harcourt Brace and World, 1967.

McWhinney, Edward. "The French Language and the Constitutional Status of French Canadians." In *Case Studies on Human Rights and Fundamental Freedoms: A World Survey*, 3:483–98. The Hague: Martinus Nijhoff, 1976.

Mansergh, Nicholas S. *The Government of Northern Ireland*, London: Allen and Unwin 1936.

———. *The Irish Question, 1840–1921*. London: George Allen and Unwin, 1965.

Marx, Karl. *Capital*, vol. 3, edited by Friedrich Engels. New York: International Publishers, 1967.

Marx, Karl, and Friedrich Engels. *Ireland and the Irish Question: A Collection of Writings*, edited by R. Dixon. New York: International Publishers, 1972.

Mayo, Patricia. *The Roots of Identity*. London: Allen Lane, 1974.

Miller, David W. *Church, State and Nation in Ireland*. Pittsburgh: University of Pittsburgh, Press, 1973.

———. *Queen's Rebels: Ulster Loyalism in Historical Perspective*. Dublin: Gill and Macmillan, 1978.

Milner, Henry. "The Anglophone Left in Quebec and National Self-Determination." In *The English of Quebec*, 399–414. *See* Caldwell and Waddell 1982.

Milner, Sheilagh Hodgins, and Henry Milner. *The Decolonization of Quebec*. Toronto: McClelland and Stewart, 1973.

Moody, T. W. *Ulster since 1900: A Social Survey*, London: BBC, 1957.

Moody, T. W., and F. X. Martin, eds. *The Course of Irish History*, Cork: Mercier Press, 1967.

Morris, Aldon. "Black Southern Student Sit-in Movement." *American Sociological Review* 46 (1981): 744–67.

Nagel, Joane, and Susan Olzak. "Ethnic Mobilization in New and Old States: An Extension of the Competition Model." *Social Problems* 30, no. 2 (December 1982): 127–43.

Nairn, Tom. *The Break Up of Britain: Crisis and Neo Nationalism.* London: New Left Books, 1977.

Nelson, Sarah. *Ulster's Uncertain Defenders: Loyalists and the Northern Ireland Conflict.* Belfast: Appletree Press, 1984.

Noel, Donald. "A Theory of the Origins of Ethnic Stratification." In *The Origins of American Slavery and Racism,* edited by Donald L. Noel, 106–28. Columbus: Charles E. Merrill, 1972.

Northern Friends Peace Board. *Orange and Green.* Belfast: Northern Friends, 1969.

O'Brien, Conor Cruise. "Ireland: The Shirt of Nessus." *New York Review of Books* 29, no. 7 (29 April 1982): 30–32.

O'Brien, Francis W. *Divided Ireland: The Roots of the Conflict.* Rockford, Ill.: Rockford College Press, 1972.

Olsen, Mancur. *The Logic of Collective Action: Public Goods and the Theory of Groups,* Cambridge: Harvard University Press, 1965.

Olzak, Susan. "Contemporary Ethnic Mobilization." *Annual Review of Sociology* 9 (1983): 355–74.

———. "Ethnic Mobilization in Quebec." *Ethnic and Racial Studies* 5, no. 3 (July 1982): 253–75.

O'Malley, Padraig. *Uncivil Wars.* Boston: Houghton Mifflin, 1984.

Ornstein, Michael D., H. Michael Stevenson, and A. Paul M. Williams. "Public Opinion and the Canadian Political Crisis." *Canadian Review of Sociology and Anthropology* 15 (May 1978):158–207.

Ossenberg, Richard J. "The Conquest Revisited: Another Look at Canadian Dualism." *Canadian Review of Sociology and Anthropology* 4, no. 4 (November 1967): 201–49.

———. "Social Pluralism in Quebec: Continuity, Change and Conflict." In *Canadian Society; Pluralism, Change and Conflict* edited by Richard J. Ossenberg, 103–25. Scarborough: Prentice-Hall of Canada, 1971.

O'Tuathaigh, Gearard. *Ireland before the Famine, 1798–1848.* Dublin: Gill and Macmillan, 1972.

Parsons, Talcott. "A Revised Analytic Approach to the Theory of Social Stratification." In Talcott Parsons, *Essays in Sociological Theory,* rev. ed., 386–439. New York: Free Press, 1954.

Patterson, Orlando. *Ethnic Chauvinism: The Reactionary Impulse.* Cambridge: Harvard University Press, 1978.

Pim, Jonathon. *The Conditions and Prospects of Ireland.* Dublin: Hodges and Smith, 1848.

Pious, Richard, "Canada and the Crisis of Quebec," *Journal of International Affairs*, 27 no. 1 (April 1973): 53–64;

Pomfret, John E. *The Struggle for Land in Ireland, 1800–1923*. Princeton: Princeton University Press, 1930.

Porter, John. *Canadian Social Structure: A Statistical Profile*. Toronto: McClelland and Stewart, 1967.

————. *The Vertical Mosaic*. Toronto: University of Toronto, Press 1967.

Posgate, Dale, and Kenneth McRoberts. *Quebec: Social Change and Political Crisis*. Toronto: McClelland and Stewart, 1976.

Probert, Belinda. *Beyond Orange and Green: The Political Economy of the Northern Ireland Crisis*. London: Zed Press, 1978.

Quinn, David Beers. *The Elizabethans and the Irish*. Ithaca: Cornell University Press, 1966.

Raynauld, André, "Business Ownership in Quebec." Paper presented to the Royal Commission on Bilingualism and Biculturalism, May 1967.

————. "The Quebec Economy: A General Assessment." In *Quebec Society and Politics*, 146–48. *See* Dale C. Thompson 1973.

Rioux, Marcel. *Quebec in Question*. Toronto: James, Lewis and Samuel, 1971.

Rioux, Marcel, and Yves Martin, eds. *French Canadian Society*, vol. 1. Toronto: McClelland and Stewart, 1964.

Robinson, Philip. "Plantation and Colonization: The Historical Background." In *Integration and Division*, 19–47. *See* Boal and Douglas 1982.

Rome, David. "Jews in Anglophone Quebec." In *The English of Quebec*, 161–75. *See* Caldwell and Waddell 1982.

Ronen, Dov. *The Quest for Self-Determination*. New Haven: Yale University Press, 1980.

Rose, Richard. *Governing without Consensus: An Irish Perspective*. Boston: Beacon Press, 1971.

————. *Northern Ireland: A Time of Choice*. London: Macmillan and Co., 1976.

Rothschild, Joseph. *Ethnopolitics: A Conceptual Framework*. New York: Columbia University Press, 1981.

Ryerson, Stanley. "Quebec: Concepts of Class and Nation." In *Capitalism and the National Question in Canada*, edited by Gary Teeple, 220–40. Toronto: University of Toronto Press, 1972.

Saywell, John. *The Rise of the Parti Québecois, 1967–1976*.Toronto: University of Toronto Press, 1977.

Schermerhorn, Richard A. *Comparative Ethnic Relations: A Framework for Theory and Research*. New York: Random House, 1970.

Schmitter, Barbara. "Immigrants and Associations: Their Role in the Socio-Political Process of Immigrant Worker Integration in West Germany and Switzerland.'' *International Migration Review* 14, no. 2 (Summer 1980): 179–92.

Scott, Frank R. "Areas of Conflict in the Field of Public Law and Policy." In *Canadian Dualism. See* Wade 1960.

Shils, Edward. "Color, the Universal Intellectual Community, and the Afro-Asian Intellectual." In *Color and Race,* edited by John Hope Franklin, 1–17. Boston: Beacon Press, 1968.

Shorter, N., and Charles Tilly. *Strikes in France.* New York: Cambridge University Press, 1974.

Siegfried, André. *The Race Question in Canada.* Toronto: McClelland and Stewart, 1966.

Silvert, K. H. *Expectant Peoples: Nationalism and Development,* New York: Vintage, 1963.

Sklar, Richard. *Corporate Power in an African State.* Berkeley: University of California Press, 1975.

Smelser, Neil J. *Essays in Sociological Explanation.* Englewood Cliffs, N.J.: Prentice-Hall, 1968.

Smith, Anthony. *The Ethnic Revival in the Modern World.* Cambridge: Cambridge University Press, 1981.

———. "Towards a Theory of Ethnic Separatism." *Ethnic and Racial Studies* 2, no. 1 (January 1979): 28–33.

Smith, M. G., and Leo Kuper, eds. *Pluralism in Africa.* Berkeley: University of California Press, 1969.

Stern, Michael. "Quebec's Non-Francophones; November 12 and After." *Canadian Forum,* no. 688 (February 1977): 18.

Stewart, A. T. Q. *The Ulster Crisis.* London: Faber and Faber, 1967.

Stinchcombe, Arthur. "The Sociology of Ethnic and National Loyalties. In *Handbook of Political Science.* Vol. 3. Edited by Frank Greenstein and N. Polsby, 557–622. Reading, Pa.: Addison Wesley, 1975.

Stone, John. "Internal Colonialism in Comparative Perspective." *Ethnic and Racial Studies* 2, no. 3 (July 1979): 255–59.

Strauss, Eric. *Irish Nationalism and British Democracy.* New York: Columbia University Press, 1951.

Sunday Times. See *London Sunday Times* Insight Team.

Sweeney, Robert. "A Brief Sketch of the Economic History of English Quebec." In *The English of Quebec,* 73–90. *See* Caldwell and Waddell 1982.

Taylor, Charles. "Nationalism and the Political Intelligentsia." *Queen's Quarterly* 72, no. 1 (Spring 1965): 167–68.

Taylor, Norman W. "French Canadians as Industrial Entrepreneurs." *Journal of Political Economy* 68, no. 1 (February 1960): 37–52.

Tetley, William. "The English and Language Legislation." In *The English of Quebec,* 381–84. *See* Caldwell and Waddell 1982.

Bibliography

Thomson, Dale C., ed. *Quebec Society and Politics: A View from the Inside*. Toronto: McClelland and Stewart, 1973.

Thompson, E. P. *The Making of the English Working Class*. New York: Vintage Books, 1963.

Thompson, John L. "The Plural Society Approach to Class and Ethnic Political Mobilization." *Ethnic and Racial Studies* 6, no. 2 (April 1983): 127–52.

Tilly, Charles. "Collective Violence in European Perspective." In *Violence in America*, edited by Hugh Davis Graham and Ted Robert Gurr, 83–118. Beverly Hills: Sage, 1979.

U.S. Immigration Commission. *The Immigration Situation in Canada*. Washington, D.C.: U. S. Government Printing Office, 1910.

Van den Berghe, Pierre. *Race and Racism: A Comparative Perspective*. 2d ed. New York: Wiley, 1978.

Wade, Mason. *The French Canadian Outlook*. Montreal: University of Montreal Press, 1947.

————. *The French Canadians*. 2 vols. Toronto: University of Toronto Press, 1968.

————. ed. *Canadian Dualism: Essays on Relations between French and English Canadians*. Toronto: Univerity of Toronto Press, 1960.

Wagley, Charles, and Marvin Harris. *Minorities in the New World*. New York: Columbia University Press, 1958.

Wallerstein, Immanual. *The Modern World System*. New York: Academic Press. 1974.

Ward, Norman. *The Government of Canada*. 4th ed. Toronto: Dawson McGregor, 1963.

Watkins, Mel. "The North American Triangle." *Canadian Forum* 65, no. 668 (February 1977): 14–17.

Weber, Max. *Economy and Society*. 2 vols. Edited by Guenther Roth and Claus Wittich. New York: Bedminster, 1968.

————. *Weber: Selections in Translation*. Edited by W. C. Runciman. Cambridge: Cambridge University Press, 1978.

Whyte, J. H. *Church and State in Modern Ireland*. Dublin: Gill and Macmillan, 1972.

Wilson, Thomas. *Ulster under Home Rule, a Study of The Political and Economic Problems of Northern Ireland*. London: Oxford University Press, 1970.

Wilson, William Julius. *The Declining Significance of Race: Blacks and Changing American Institutions*. Chicago: University of Chicago Press, 1978.

————. *Power, Racism and Privilege*. New York: Macmillan 1973.

Wright, Frank. "Protestant Ideology and Politics in Ulster." *Archives of European Sociology* 14 (1973): 213–80.

Bibliography

Young, Arthur. *A Tour of Ireland*. Vol. 2. London, 1780.

Young, Crawford. "The Temple of Ethnicity." *World Politics* 35, no. 4 (July 1983): 652–62.

Zolberg, Aristide. "The Spectre of Communalism." Paper presented at Auberge Hindfield Conference on le nationalisme québecois vis-á-vis Les Etats-Unis, May 1974.

INDEX

Adrian I, 35
advanced industrialism, 102–59;
  characteristics of, 116, 154; effect on
  Northern Ireland economy, 116–17;
  and ethnic nationalisms, 153–59; in
  Republic of Ireland, 132
Alberta, 82, 86, 139
American War of Independence, 44,
  51–52
Anglican Church, 35, 45, 69–70. See
  also Protestant
Anglo-Normans, 34–35
annexation, 21–23, 50–52
anti-Catholicism, 38–39
anti-Semitism, 92–94
Apprentice Boys, 39
Apter, David, 172n
Ares, Richard, 189n, 193n
assimilation: Canadian policies of, 56,
  81–86, 96; and ethnic conflict, 182n;
  in French Canada, 96–97, 143; in
  Irish Pale, 35
Aunger, Edward, 185n, 186n

Banff Conference, 183n
Banton, Michael, 174n
Barritt, Denis P., 184n, 185n

Barth, Fredrik, 171n
Beatty, Jack, 188n
Beckett, J. C., 175n, 181n
Belfast, 41, 104; industrial growth, 62–
  63, 65–66, 76; population changes,
  71–73; riots in, 74, 112, 121–25;
  segregation in, 72, 124
Bell, Daniel, 171n, 174n
Bell, Geoffrey, 184n, 185n, 186n
Bew, Peter, 184n, 186n
bilingualism: Canadian policies, 81–83,
  148–49; decline in Canada, 138;
  migration and, 85–86; Quebec
  policies, 145, 151–52
Bill 22 (Official Language Act), 148–
  49
Bill 101 (Charter of the French
  Language), 151–52
Blassingame, John, 174n
Blauner, Robert, 173n
Bloc Populaire, 94
Blumer, Herbert, 178n
Boal, Frederick W., 173n
Bonacich, Edna, 15, 173n, 174n
Boserup, Anders, 187n
Boulton, David, 184n, 187n
Bourassa, Henri, 86–87, 148–50

207

Index

Cromwell, Oliver, 38–39
Cross, James, 146
Cullen, L. M., 175n, 177n

Dangerfield, George, 182n
Daugherty, Paul, 186n, 187n
Davis, H. B., 172n
Davison, Sir Joseph, 112
Davitt, Michael, 75
Defenders, Catholic, 43, 45, 47
de Gaulle, General Charles, 102, 144
de Paor, Liam, 175n, 177n, 181n,
    182n, 185n
Derry. See Londonderry
Despres, Leo, 172n
Deutsch, Karl, 172n
development: and ethnic mobilization,
    26–28; impact on elites, 27–28;
    modernization theory of, 6–8. See
    also uneven development
Devlin, Bernadette, 185n, 187n
Dillon, Martin, 187n
Diplock Courts, 128
direct rule, 128–34
discrimination: extent of reform, 122–
    23; in local government of Northern
    Ireland, 108–9; and state structure in
    Northern Ireland, 105–9, 186n
Dubuc, Alfred, 56, 178n
Duplessis, Maurice, 61, 93–94, 103.
    See also duplessisme.
duplessisme: characteristics of, 134;
    decline of, 137–39; and education,
    136–37; and welfare state, 135–37.
    See also Duplessis, Maurice; Union
    Nationale
Dumont, Fernand, 178n
Durham, Lord, 53, 55–57, 145
Durkheim, Emil, 6

Easter Rising, 78, 80, 100
Edelstein, Joel, 173n
education, 83–84, 95, 115, 145
Edwards, Owen Dudley, 71–72, 177n,
    180n, 181n, 185n
Eisenbert, John, 190n
Eisenstadt, S. N. 172n
elites, minority: in colonial Ireland, 58,

67–68; in colonial Quebec, 53, 56–
59; and ethnic movements, 14–15,
27–31, 99–100; welfare state and,
135–40, 142–44. See also class;
patrimonial relations
Elizabeth I, 35
Elkin, Frederick, 189n
Elliot, Sydney, 84n
Ellis, P. Berresford, 175n, 177n
Engels, Frederick, 175n, 176n, 179n
Enloe, Cynthia, 173n
ethnic conflict. See conflict, ethnic
ethnicity: defined, 3; distinguished from
    nation, 5; theories of, 3–4
ethnic nationalism. See nationalism,
    ethnic
ethnic stratification. See stratification,
    ethnic
ethnocentrism, 19, 21; in colonial
    Ireland, 36; in colonial Quebec, 55–
    57

Falardeau, Jean Charles, 49, 50, 96,
    174n, 177n, 182n, 183n
Fallers, Lloyd, 173n
famine. See Great Famine
Farrell, Michael, 125, 184n, 185n,
    186n, 187n, 188n
Faulkner, Brian, 114
federalism (Canadian): and
    bilingualism, 83, 148–49; and the
    Quiet Revolution, 138–41; and
    religion, 82–83
feudalism, 11–12; and Canadian social
    structure, 49–50, 177n; and Irish
    social structure, 34–37
Fianna Fail, 132–33
Fields, Rona, 175n
Fine Gael, 133
Fisk, Robert, 187n
Fitzgerald, Garrett, 133
Fitzgibbon, Constantine, 181n
Fortin, Gerald, 189n
Foster, John, 174n
Fournier, Pierre, 189n
France: and United Irishmen, 44–45;
    colonial enterprise in Canada, 48–50
Frazier, Morris, 189n

Index

Index